RUSSIA ABROAD

RUSSIA ABROAD

A Cultural History
of the Russian Emigration,
1919–1939

MARC RAEFF

New York   Oxford
OXFORD UNIVERSITY PRESS
1990

Oxford University Press

Oxford   New York   Toronto
Delhi   Bombay   Calcutta   Madras   Karachi
Petaling Jaya   Singapore   Hong Kong   Tokyo
Nairobi   Dar es Salaam   Cape Town
Melbourne   Auckland

and associated companies in
Berlin   Ibadan

Copyright © 1990 by Oxford University Press, Inc.

Published by Oxford University Press, Inc.,
200 Madison Avenue, New York, New York 10016

Library of Congress Cataloging-in-Publication Data
Raeff, Marc.
Russia abroad: a cultural history of the Russian emigration,
1919–1939/Marc Raeff.
p.   cm. Includes index.
ISBN 0-19-505683-3 (alk. paper)
1. Russians—Foreign countries.   2. Russians—Intellectual life.
3. Soviet Union—History—Revolution, 1917–1921—Refugees.
4. Refugees, Political—Soviet Union.   I. Title.
DK35.5.R34   1990
305.8'917104'09042—dc20   89-34887   CIP

2 4 6 8 9 7 5 3 1
Printed in the United States of America

*To my Mother and the memory of my Father
in bittersweet remembrance of our
residence in Russia Abroad*

Preface

Between 1919 and 1939 one could meet émigré Russians practically everywhere in the world, but most frequently in France, Germany, Czechoslovakia, the Baltic states, the Balkans, and China. In their own minds, and in fact, they were the other Russia—Russia Abroad, in contrast to the one under the Soviet system. The history of this exile society, beyond the borders of its homeland, has not been written. Yet its activities, especially its contributions to the contemporary cultural scene, are increasingly attracting the attention of scholars and critics, both in the Soviet Union and in the West. So far, however, most studies have dealt with isolated individual personalities, groups, or events detached from the overall picture and history of Russia Abroad. The aim of this book is to provide a backdrop to and framework for the activities and accomplishments of individual émigré personalities and institutions. The book is intended to help put the "Great Russian Emigration" of the 1920s and 1930s into proper historical perspective by relating it to Russia's past and present, as well as to the foreign world in whose midst the émigrés lived.

The sources for the literature about Russia Abroad are too extensive and scattered for a single individual to cover fully and thoroughly. I have, therefore, chosen to sketch those facets which, to my mind at least, are most essential for a proper understanding of the cultural life of Russia Abroad. The examples and references are primarily illustrative and can, of course, be multiplied almost indefinitely. My purpose is to describe those aspects of émigré cultural life that defined the attitudes, ideals, and intentions of those exiles who preserved and carried on their country's traditions and creativity in foreign lands. Thus the book consists of separate essaylike chapters, each illuminating one significant "region" of Russia Abroad, but in such a manner as to afford a glimpse of the whole "country," even though it makes no pretense at giving a full description. I make no claim of covering every émigré activity or institution; nor should the reader expect to find mention of all personalities that may have had an impact on their respective field of endeavor. Those who are mentioned were either truly outstanding or simply happen to be better documented—the presence or absence of mention of any one person or institution does not imply a value judgment on the author's part as to their historical importance.

In some sense I have been gathering the material for this book all my conscious life—I wish neither to hide nor to deny its autobiographical aspect. Naturally, the many individuals on whose biographies and memories I have drawn, more or less consciously, cannot be listed here. The final stage of planned research, however, was much facilitated by grants and fellowships from the National Endowment for the Humanities and the John Simon Guggenheim Foundation for which I express my deep appreciation; Columbia University complemented these awards with leaves of absence. The Hoover Institution generously covered my expenses for the period of my work in its rich archives. I am most grateful to the officers of the Hoover Institution and to the friendly and efficient staff of its library and archives for their help and cooperation in every respect. The Curator of the Bakhmeteff Archive for the History and Cultures of Russia and Eastern Europe at Columbia University has been of great help, and so have the staffs of all the libraries where I worked—principally the Library of Congress, the Widener Library at Harvard, Columbia University Library, and Preussischer Kulturbesitz Berlin.

The New York Public Library has always been most hospitable to all who have mined its extraordinary resources. Indeed, Edward Kasinec, the Director of its Slavonic Division, is truly the scholar's librarian: he took a very personal interest in my work, suggesting and seeking out many rare materials, and he guided me on the path of bibliographic accuracy and comprehensiveness. His help has been invaluable, and I am most grateful to him. Madame T. A. Ossorguine in Paris shared her vast knowledge of "Russian Paris" and called my attention to several unpublished dissertations and works in progress. I am very grateful to all; any errors and deficiencies are strictly my own.

I have summarized some of my observations in several contributions to collective volumes, but in very different form and context; none is reproduced here. Translations are my own. Russian names and words have been translated according to the Widener Library practice, with slight modifications.

Tenafly, N.J.   M. R.
July 1989

Contents

RUSSIA ABROAD

Tu proverai si come sa di sale
    lo pane altrui, e come è duro calle
lo scendere e 'l salir per l'altrui scale
                    Dante, *Paradiso,* Canto XVII, 57–60

You will taste the salt bitterness of another's bread
And learn how hard it is wearing down
The steps of a staircase not your own.
                    Translated by Paul Montazzoli

1

Introduction: The Uprooted

The revolution and the civil war split Russia in two—literally and figuratively: one lost the very name of Russia and became first the RSFSR and then the USSR; the other, defeated by Lenin's government, rejecting and escaping the newly created RSFSR, constituted itself into a Russia beyond the borders, Russia Abroad. Thus a Russian society found itself in exile and proceeded to organize itself in the expectation that its existence "beyond the borders" of the homeland would be only temporary. How a Russia Abroad came about, in what manner and with what means the *society in exile* carried on a culturally creative life in its new "country," is the subject of this book. In other words, it is the history of the cultural life of a "society" exiled from its homeland in another "country" without physical or legal boundaries.

First, we must explain the meaning of the key terms in the preceding paragraph in the context of our account. Indeed, on the face of it, the terms do not automatically convey the reality of a Russia Abroad, for they do not have the scientific or scholarly precision of the vocabulary used by sociologists or anthropologists.

Exile implies forced departure from one's homeland for fear of political or religious persecution. An exile is often simply a refugee if departure took place under abnormal circumstances or a direct threat of violence. For example, immediately following World War I, Europe saw many refugees: people displaced by military action, threatened by ethnic massacre, deprived of their homes and livelihood as a consequence of territorial adjustments ordered by the peace treaties, and finally those compelled to flee for political reasons. To deal with such people in an orderly and helpful manner, the League of Nations and international organizations such as the Red Cross set up special programs and institutions for refugee affairs.[1] Implicit in the term *refugee*—and in the way refugees were dealt with—was the assumption that the refugees would return to their homelands once the unusual conditions had ended and life returned to normal patterns. Alternatively, though less

3

desirable but likely, the refugees would find a permanent home and become integrated, that is, accepted and absorbed, in the country of asylum. In our case, all the Russians who escaped the victorious Red Army, who chose not to live under the Bolshevik regime, or who were expelled by the Soviet authorities, were also originally refugees. As such they claimed and received the help of the various humanitarian programs established to cope with the refugee problem during and in the aftermath of the First World War.

But contrary to the expectations of the international refugee organizations, most Russians neither returned to their homeland nor integrated into the societies that had given them refuge. True, to a large extent the host countries did not facilitate their assimilation. But even more important, the Russians continued to consider themselves exiles, retaining the hope that their residence beyond Russian borders would be temporary, and that their return would soon be possible with the collapse, deemed imminent, of the Soviet government. Most Russian refugees saw themselves as recapitulating the pattern set by the political émigrés of the nineteenth and early twentieth centuries who had gone abroad better to pursue their fight against the tsarist regime. For did not most of those who were abroad at the time of the revolution return to resume their normal political life at home? Exile and emigration were viewed as a temporary condition, a stage beyond the mere survival of the refugee.

At first the exiles organized their lives to be ready to return and to reintegrate into the political, social, and cultural activities of their homeland the moment Russia would be freed from the tyrannical Bolshevik regime. In a most literal sense they did not "unpack" their suitcases; they sat on their trunks. Quite naturally, too, they did not think of melding into the host societies, even when assimilation might have been relatively easy, as for example in the Kingdom of Serbs, Croats, and Slovenes (the future Yugoslavia), in contrast to the unreceptive attitudes of Germany and France. For this reason, too, they wanted their children (whether born in Russia or abroad) to remain Russians, and they feared their "denationalization" most. Of course, in the long run, such exclusiveness could not be maintained, and for reasons and under circumstances described later, some degree of integration did occur. Yet, characteristically, most émigré children grew up bicultural, with a dual national identity—Russian as well as that of the land of their asylum.

In these circumstances, exile or emigration also entailed a sense of mission, beyond the mundane task of mere physical survival. The mission was to preserve the values and traditions of Russian culture and to continue its creative efforts for the benefit and ongoing spiritual progress of the homeland—whether one was fated to return or to die in exile. For this reason, the Russian émigrés in the 1920s and 1930s should not be compared to immigrants whose aim in leaving their homes is primarily to create a better life in a new environment, regardless of their motives for leaving the homeland in the first place. The national quota system and the stringent immigration policies adopted by the United States in 1920 were not the only factors in keeping out most Russian "refugees," nor did the high cost of transportation alone prevent their mass resettlement in South America. Most decisive was their desire to stay as close to Russia as possible, and even more significant was their adamant refusal to become assimilated—their refusal to become "regular immigrants" like those who had come to the New World (and Australia) in the decades before the First World War. This is the explanation for the absence of a genuine "province" of Russia Abroad in the Americas, although a few individuals did settle there. This was not quite the case, however, in the late 1930s for the sizable groups from Manchuria and China who settled in the San Francisco area, and for an increasing stream of individuals escaping the clouds of war that were gathering over Europe.

I have spoken of a *society* in exile. What made the Russian emigration of the 1920s and 1930s into a society and not merely a group of people who had exiled themselves for political reasons? Two factors contributed to the way that the émigré Russians constituted themselves into a genuine, albeit not perfectly complete, society. First of all, most social classes of prerevolutionary Russia were represented abroad, although not quite in the same proportions.[2] In the emigration, we find not only the former ruling elites—the government and the court—and members of the intellectual or professional leadership, but also petite bourgeoisie, artisans, craftspeople, workers, and employees, as well as a fair number of peasants, especially if we consider the Cossacks to be basically peasants. Nor was the Russian emigration homogeneous in its religious, ethnic, educational, and economic makeup: the major religions of the Russian Empire were represented and continued their faiths and the most numerous ethnic minorities also had representatives in exile. Although the average level of education of the Russians in emigration was higher than at home, there still was a very wide spread, even including some illiterates. The original economic condition of those who chose, or were forced into, exile was as diverse as that of the population in the Empire.

In the second place, and much more telling than their cross-representation according to sociological, economic, or cultural criteria, was the fact that the émigrés were committed to carrying on a meaningful *Russian* life. They were determined to act, work, and create as part and parcel of *Russia*, even in a foreign environment. They needed "producers" and "consumers" of cultural "goods" and values maintained in exile. Russia Abroad was a society by virtue of its firm intention to go on living as "Russia," to be the truest and culturally most creative of the two Russias that political circumstances had brought into being. Though it was a somewhat distorted society in strictly sociological terms—including its demographic makeup, as we shall see—the émigrés did think of themselves as a "country" or society. They strove to act creatively as if the emigration represented Russia in the fullest cultural and philosophical sense.

The Russian emigration was the direct consequence of the defeat of the White Armies in 1920–1921 and the final establishment of the boundaries of the Russian Soviet Federated Socialist Republic (RSFSR) by the Treaty of Riga in 1921. But in its fullest sense, Russia Abroad came into being as a result of a process lasting several years. As long as the borders of the RSFSR (since December 1922 the Union of Soviet Socialist Republics, USSR) remained somewhat open and fluid—as they were until the mid-1920s and the onset of collectivization and the First Five Year Plan—Russia Abroad did not attain its definitive form either. For this reason our starting date of 1919 is somewhat arbitrary and marks merely the beginning of that process. But even after its structure was more or less solidly in place, in about 1928, Russia Abroad did not remain unchanged. True, its membership ceased being replenished by more refugees from Russia, although there were individuals who escaped from prisons or detention camps, as well as some defectors or the so-called nonreturners (those on assignment abroad who refused to return to the Soviet Union) and their families. External political events, however, did make for some further changes. Several "provinces" of Russia Abroad dwindled or disappeared altogether as a consequence of political developments in host countries. The nationalist policies of Poland, Rumania, and to a lesser extent Latvia, forced many exiles to move again, and an active Russian cultural life came virtually to a standstill in those countries. Exiles in Kharbin in the Far East were decimated and forced into mere vegetative survival by Japan's invasion of China and the creation of the Empire of Manchukuo. Finally, Hitler's takeover in Germany and eventually his occupation of Czechoslovakia sapped the creative potential of the Russian émigré centers there, and snuffed out their literary, scholarly, and cultural vitality.

The final blow to Russia Abroad was dealt by the outbreak of World War II in 1939, and more specifically by the German invasion and defeat of France in May–June 1940. Under military and Nazi occupation there was no place for a creatively free Russian emigration, not to speak of the material hardships that constrained all existence in Hitler-dominated Europe. Individual Russian émigrés, of course, survived the war; many gallantly fought for the country that had given them asylum. But the Russian emigration could not survive as a "society in exile" with a vital life of its own.

In 1945 two significant events occurred which shape our story. First, the young generation of émigrés who had participated in the war against Germany, and their children, became fully integrated into the societies where they had settled.[3] While retaining their Russian language and culture, many behaved as regular citizens of their host countries after the war ended in Europe. Some took advantage of their dual cultural background to further the study of Russian history and literature, however, as we shall see in greater detail in another chapter. Second, a new wave of Russian refugees—the so-called Displaced Persons (DPs), began to arrive. Some of them were émigrés who had lived in the Balkans or Central Europe and had to flee once more at the advance of the Red Army. But most were former German prisoners of war, deportees from the Soviet Union (*Ostarbeiter*), or people who had decided, for whatever reason, to use the opportunity offered by the German occupation and retreat to escape Stalin's regime. Unlike their predecessors of 1920–1921 (with the partial exception of those who had lived in Russia Abroad before World War II), these new refugees were not eager to reconstitute a Russia Abroad. They only yearned to find peace, security, and a stable livelihood, far from Soviet Russia's grasp. Most went on to become immigrants in the United States, Canada, Latin America, or Australia. Whether the so-called third wave of Russian emigration since the 1970s will establish another Russia Abroad remains to be seen, although most indications are to the contrary. For all these reasons, we can consider the years between 1919 and 1939 as the life span of Russia Abroad, a *society* in exile.

The preceding observations suggest that Russia Abroad was geographically neither homogeneous nor a self-contained unit. Its members were dispersed in many countries and continents. Centers formed wherever a significant number of scholarly and artistically productive émigrés found more or less stable circumstances where they could engage in creative work. Transcending physical distances and the barriers of national frontiers, the Russian exiles retained close contact among themselves, strengthening their cultural identity and unity as Russia Abroad. We shall see in subsequent chapters by what means and at what cost they achieved this cohesiveness.

Naturally, some cities were more significant than others, and not only because of the numbers of émigrés, though a critical mass was a prerequisite. Such places arose around energetic and creative individuals who continued to contribute to Russian culture, and who worked in media amenable to dissemination. Berlin, Paris, Prague, Kharbin, and—to a lesser extent and for a shorter period—Belgrade, Riga, and Sofia were lively nuclei of Russia Abroad. Such centers became possible because there was a "hinterland" of Russians ready and willing to "consume" the cultural products of their fellow exiles. The Baltic states, Poland, and Romania had a large number of Russian residents but they did not have the benefits that large, energetic urban centers could offer. This was also the case in Yugoslavia, Greece, the agricultural settlements of Bulgaria and Czechoslovakia, and the small communities of Russians working in the provinces of France, Belgium, and Germany. Almost everywhere, Russian émigrés were eager to read, hear, and see what was produced by their compatriots in the diaspora. Russia Abroad retained a pattern that had prevailed before 1917 in Russia. Before the revolution, the two capitals and a very few other cities (Kiev and Odessa, for example) generated all the culture that the vast expanses of Russia's provinces then enjoyed.

The preceding pages have dwelled on the cultural life and creativity of the "Russia beyond the borders." And the following chapters will focus on this aspect of émigré existence. What, then, will be excluded from our story and why?

Since the Russian diaspora arose from the political changes in the homeland after a long war, a radical political revolution, and a bloody civil war, it could be expected that political concerns, interests, and prejudices would be at the center of attention of the émigré community of Russia Abroad. But this was true only in a broad sense. One political notion shared by practically all émigrés who gave a moment's thought to politics was an absolute rejection of the Bolshevik regime. But even this statement should be qualified, for as time went on, some émigrés came to reconcile themselves to the existence of that regime as a fact, and even saw some positive aspects (for example, the great Russian nationalism promoted by Stalin). This "gut reaction" against the new Russia, however, established only the outward boundaries of émigré political attitudes. The overwhelming majority was so preoccupied by the struggle for life in complex circumstances that they could ill afford the "luxury" of direct and serious involvement in the politics of the emigration. Their strong anti-Bolshevik emotions were often tempered by a nostalgic nationalism, which they displayed, if at all, on a few set occasions. Aside from this, they evinced little interest in political programs and viewed political parties with suspicion. They were even less concerned with or informed about the political life of the countries of asylum, except when it affected their legal or economic status directly.

As a consequence, only a minority of intellectuals and some former army officers were concerned with politics. As we shall see, Russia Abroad contained the full gamut of political sentiment and affiliation of pre-October 1917 Russia. Although most émigrés were monarchist in a vague, sentimental way, monarchist parties and groups were far from commanding the allegiance of a majority of the denizens of Russia Abroad. Moreover, the monarchists themselves were split in several ways—from radical reactionaries to moderate liberal constitutionalists. The situation was further complicated by disagreements over the "rightful" pretender to the Russian throne. On the opposite extreme of the political spectrum were the anarchists, Mensheviks, and Socialist Revolutionaries, who were in turn split into left and right factions, as were the liberal "bourgeois" constitutionalists, the Kadets. As is usually the case in émigré political milieus, constant and acrimonious infighting bedeviled all groups, factions, and parties, for they never had to face any practical problem that they could help solve together. The arguments turned on two major issues. How had the Bolsheviks captured and retained power and whose fault was it? The second problem involved the future of the Bolshevik system. Indeed, any plan to defeat or replace that system hinged on the émigrés' responses to the first set of questions. Moreover, in the "vacuum" of émigré existence personal issues or likes and dislikes often loom larger than tactics and programs.

In the first years of emigration, exiled political leaders still might have hoped to influence the Russian policies of the governments of the countries to which they had fled. But these hopes waned rapidly as it became clear that there would be no further armed intervention, and as more and more states recognized the Soviet government as the de facto, or even de jure, legitimate authority in Russia. On occasion, émigrés were involved in international political skullduggery or shady activities (e.g., illegal border crossing or the murder of Soviet diplomatic agents) directed against the Soviet Union. But

they all ended lamentably in discomfiture. The most notorious of such instances was the so-called Trust, in which the Soviet intelligence and police
apparatus tricked several right-wing émigré organizations and diplomats of the
Baltic states, Poland, and Romania.[4] Instances of Soviet infiltration into émigré
organizations—for example, the Rossiiskii obshchevoennyi soiuz (ROVS),
the main veterans' organization, and the Menshevik party—which resulted in
the abductions of General E. K. Miller, General A. P. Kutepov, and the son
of the Menshevik leader, threw émigré milieus into disarray and showed the
futility of their political activities.[5]

In short, émigré politics consisted of unending squabbles stemming from
inadequate information, helplessness, and nostalgic or angry recollections of
the past. Unceasing personal feuds led to fragmentation of the original organizations. In the final analysis, without direct and effective contact with sympathizers in the home country—as had been enjoyed by the political émigrés
in the nineteenth and early twentieth centuries—political life in exile is nothing but shadowboxing. In the case of Russia Abroad, the possibility of contacts with Soviet Russia became, by the early 1930s, impossible thanks to the
ruthless and efficient way in which the Soviet police imposed domestic control
and sealed off the borders with the outside world. Such efficiency had never
been possible in Imperial Russia, which is why Lenin and others were able
to have such an impact on events inside Russia. Last, but not least, with the
Soviet regime retaining effective power for much longer than had seemed
possible in the beginning, the old political leadership in exile was decimated
by sickness and death, and the new generation had neither the interests nor
the means to carry on their fight. True, attempts were made to create new
political organizations and to establish new programs that would take into
account the lessons and realities of Soviet rule and propose alternatives. The
Mladorossy (Young Russians) spoke of a "monarchy with soviets," and the
Natsionalnyi trudovoi soiuz (NTS—National Labor Union) hoped for a corporatist state combining Soviet social changes with a nationalist and authoritarian political and economic structure. The outbreak of World War II cut
short these efforts, whereas the plan of the NTS to take advantage of the
Soviet-German conflict proved misguided from the start and further illustrated
émigré political impotence.[6]

For these reasons, it seems to me, it is not very profitable to try to disen-
tangle the complicated and sterile political factionalism of Russia Abroad.
Neither the heated discussions about past actions and responsibilities, nor the
personal and ideological quarrels over the best tactics or programs in response
to happenings in the Soviet Union or the world at large, had anything but
limited and passing interest. Of course, a historian should be interested in
every aspect of past reality; but one also must be selective. Because it is the
purpose of this book to sketch a picture of and to offer a background for the
cultural life of Russia Abroad—a life of creative significance for modern culture in both the West and the Soviet Union—it seemed wise to avoid becoming mired in the political bogs. Only rarely did political developments in the

host countries give rise to important reactions on the part of émigrés; these instances have been covered by others.[7]

Emigré political organizations and parties, and their publications, naturally devoted much attention and space to developments in the sovietized homeland. After all, these developments validated their exile and alternately justified or dashed their hopes for return. In fact, however, only the liberal and socialist publicists had anything of interest to say in their analyses of events in the Soviet Union. The conservative and reactionary monarchists thought only in terms of a restoration, whatever its specific forms. But insofar as developments in Soviet Russia also affected some aspects of émigré cultural life, they will have a place in our story.

My intention in this book is to account for Russian cultural life in emigration—its institutional framework and its basic traits. But what is culture in this context? We do not speak of culture in the technical, sociological, or anthropological sense here; nor do we mean those aspects of culture that are nowadays the subject of the histories of daily life and of popular artistic, religious, or festive expressions. In these respects there would be little to say about Russia Abroad, for its denizens shared the material circumstances of their hosts. Nor did the émigrés manage to take along, let alone to preserve, a significant amount of the cultural objects with which they might have been surrounded in prerevolutionary Russia. Only the Cossacks had a well-defined social organization and "popular culture"; for most other émigrés, their past lives in a Westernized urban Russia had prepared them to accept the material culture of the cities of their exile.

Culture, for the Russian émigrés, was an essential aspect of their national identity, of their identity as educated, at whatever level, Russian people. It consisted of all those manifestations of what at times, erroneously I think, is called "high" culture: the literary, artistic, and scientific or scholarly creations of the nation, which are promulgated by such institutions as church, school, theater, books and journals, informal clubs, societies, and organizations. In all of these manifestations, however, there was a specifically *Russian* identity.

And what was this unique Russian identification? It is difficult to define. It was an amalgam of pre-Petrine and folk elements—largely, but by no means exclusively, expressed by the church in its ritual and teachings—and of the imported and post-Renaissance cultural trends and achievements of Western and Central Europe. In this sense Russian culture was displayed in all the arts as well as in scholarship and science. For a number of reasons to which we shall return, the predominant expression of modern Russian cultural creativity, roughly since the reign of Peter I, had been in the form of literature. In its manifold modes, the word was the mainstay of Russian cultural identity and the most prominent elements in the consciousness of its intelligentsia. In emigration, literature became even more crucial to the émigrés' collective identity, for language is the most obvious sign of belonging to a specific group. The Russian language, both written and oral, bound the émigrés together despite their geographic dispersion. For this reason, too, the cultural life and creativity of Russia Abroad was preeminently, if not exclusively, verbal. Other artistic and intellectual expressions of culture for which a national linguistic form was not essential could, and frequently were, integrated and assimilated by the international or host cultures.

It is also true that the written record constitutes the basic documentation for any kind of study of Russia Abroad; this is especially the case for our purposes. Russian society in exile was relatively well educated, and it was primarily verbal in its cultural manifestations. It was no accident, as we shall see, that for the Day of Russian Culture the poet Alexander Pushkin was selected as its symbolic personification. Of course, nonverbal arts—sculpture, painting, music, ballet, science—were also vital, and no one writer can treat all of these modes competently. Each historian focuses attention on areas in which he or she is best qualified. Although I shall not concentrate on painting, sculpture, music, or the sciences, I will touch upon the means and institutional frameworks through which these creative activities found expression in Russia Abroad. Since a mere listing of names and cliché labels would be tedious and uninformative, I shall try to describe the general conditions of émigré artistic and scientific achievements, and attempt to suggest the broad trends of which they were part.

The task of assessing the history of all Russian belles lettres written in exile is an immense one, which has stirred intense scholarly activity in the West on both shores of the Atlantic as well as in the Soviet Union; every month sees the publication of monographs and articles on individual émigré authors or on specific works. These specialist studies concentrate, quite rightly so, on the formal as well as symbolic aspects of the works they analyze. So far only the cream of émigré literature has been featured in these studies, which is a clear indication of the literary brilliance in Russia Abroad. A first step toward a just appraisal of this literary effort has been the publication of the second of a three-volume work on the history of Russian literature in the twentieth century (itself part of a seven-volume history of all Russian literature), in which émigré writings are treated as part of the whole fabric of Russian literature.[8] But neither the detailed studies nor the general treatments have so far endeavored to describe and understand the existential and institutional setting in which émigré authors lived and worked, and in which their works were read first. My own task here will be to sketch in this setting, giving a synoptic analysis in preference to enumerative description.

Since I have mentioned the existence of an ever-growing and already quite voluminous body of critical and biographical work on émigré literature, let me say a few words about the historiography of Russia Abroad. Besides books and articles on individual writers or specific works, we have a small number of studies on individual artists and musicians, pride of place being given to those who have greatly contributed to the contemporary artistic scene in the West, for example, V. Kandinsky, M. Chagall, M. Larionov, N. Goncharova, and the host of Futurist and Dadaist painters and sculptors, I. Pougni, the N. and D. Burliuk brothers, A. Arkhipenko, C. Soutine, and so on. One also finds treatments of Russian émigré scientific contributions in the relevant histories of particular fields, but only, and quite justly so, as part of the history of these specific fields. A few articles concerning individual political figures or organizations treat only limited aspects of their subjects' activities. Several biographies deal with personalities prominent before 1917 who continued to have a public role in exile (e.g., Peter Struve, Paul N. Miliukov, Alexander Kerensky), while studies of socialist leaders are usually part of the histories of their party organizations (Theodore Dan, Victor Chernov, Iulii Martov, Pavel Akselrod). But in all these cases, as may be expected, the focus is on the eventful and productive years preceding the emigration; the years of exile provide only a somewhat melancholy epilogue.[9]

To my knowledge only two monographs try to chronicle the history of a center of the Russian diaspora in the 1920s and 1930s. Concentrating on a single center, they also deal with the political history of the emigration as a whole. Unfortunately, the results are not fully satisfactory, as the approach is from the outside, as it were, and they do not provide either a good understanding or a complete and balanced description of émigré existence.[10]

If we are short on the historiography there is no dearth of documentation. This documentation, it should be stressed, is not only voluminous and varied, but also quite uneven and selective—some episodes, places, activities, and periods (the 1930s) are not as well represented as others. Let us characterize this material in a few words. The sources divide, naturally, into published and unpublished materials. The unpublished documentation consists of official materials of the host countries and the papers of émigré individuals and organizations. The host countries' official documentation is important in establishing the rules and practices that governed the existence of émigrés and refugees in the respective states. In addition there must, presumably, also exist extensive police files on individuals and organizations that, for some reason or other, attracted the concern of local authorities. Police archives have not been combed systematically. In the case of Germany, especially Prussia, most records appear to be lost, although thorough search in local and East German depositories might yield interesting data. The French police archives have been used by French and Canadian historians, but a systematic investigation is still in order. To date, the archives of countries within the Soviet bloc have been mostly inaccessible. It should be noted, however, that this type of material usually only adds detail to a picture that can be well reconstructed on the basis of other sources. Of course, for the story of political intrigues in which Russian émigrés participated, the police files would be of great interest— for example, FBI files were used for a preliminary history of Russian Fascist organizations.[11] Eventually, when the history of the Russian emigration for every land of asylum is written, this official and police documentation will be put to proper use.

The unpublished documentation of Russia Abroad has been preserved in extremely fragmentary form. Although the turmoils of World War II and its aftermath resulted in many losses, some records are coming to light again. Thus the archive set up in Prague was turned over to the Soviet Union where it is now just beginning to be consulted by scholars. Papers of individuals (e.g., P. Miliukov, I. Fondaminskii) and institutions (Poslednie novosti, Turgenev Library) that were seized by the German occupation authorities appear to have been lost in the last stages of the war (although rumor has it that some of this material wound up in the Soviet bloc). Many individuals lost their papers in the course of flight, bombing, and repeated evacuations or migrations during and after the war. It should of course be remembered that many people do not keep papers—especially when they live in straitened circumstances or must run for their lives. The precedent of losing all possessions in Russia during the revolution and civil war no doubt prevented many an émigré from collecting and preserving libraries and papers in what was always hoped to be a temporary sojourn in foreign lands. A glimpse of this attitude is afforded by the difficulties that the Paris agent of the Prague-based Russian historical archive encountered and which are documented in his correspondence.[12]

Apart from small individual collections of personal papers in private hands or in Western libraries, there are two major émigré archival depositories in the United States: the Hoover Institution at Stanford University and the Bakhmeteff Archive for Russian and East European History and Culture at Columbia University. Each has a large number of records of individual émigrés—correspondence, drafts of works, and so on—of organizations, usually in incomplete states. These archives should be investigated systematically and thoroughly, something impossible for one individual alone. To date they have been mined primarily for specific events before 1917 and during the revolution and civil war, as well as for the life and works of the most prominent émigré writers. I have culled from these two archives a number of facts on émigré activities and organizations; letters and manuscript reminiscences suggest the intellectual, cultural, and material atmosphere that permeated Russia Abroad in the 1920s and 1930s.[13]

The published sources also fall into two broad categories; memoirs (and autobiographies) and periodicals. There are practically no monographs, let alone general treatments, on the Russian emigration by the émigrés themselves; data along these lines can be found in personal biographies (e.g., obituaries) and memoirs, most of them in serials. Memoirs have great limitations as a source, as we all know. They tend to concentrate on the early years or the most striking events in a career, and they usually idealize the past. The majority of the memoirs of the denizens of Russia Abroad were written by representatives of the older generation, those active in prerevolutionary Russia, and they devote much more space to the years before 1917 than to the years of exile. The younger generation also contributed a few memoirs, published after World War II, and they suffer—even more so perhaps than those of their elders—from inaccuracies of recollection and gaps in chronology.

This is quite understandable, for one prefers to reminisce about momentous occurrences and eventful years, but the experiences of the younger generation before the outbreak of war were generally quite bleak and humdrum.

It is, however, in the incredibly voluminous output of the periodical press—daily and weekly newspapers, journals of all kinds, bulletins—that Russia Abroad lived creatively and registered its experiences. We now have good bibliographic tools that help us gain access to this vast outpouring.[14] The difficulties in exploiting this source stem from the dispersed, scattered, and ephemeral nature of so many of these publications. They appeared suddenly as the need arose and disappeared as rapidly for lack of support—mainly financial, but also intellectual and moral. The squabbling among émigré personalities contributed to the insecure and short-lived existence of many of the journals. As the emigration was scattered, so were its journals, and the local libraries were hardly aware or interested in obtaining them. No systematic effort was made to collect and safeguard this enormous, dispersed, and ephemeral production. The library attached to the Prague Archive did try to be systematic in its acquisitions, but its interests focused on the period of revolution and civil war, so that less money and effort were invested in collecting the publications of fellow émigrés. Nor did the publishers themselves think of sending copies of all their publications to Prague. While we have nearly complete listings of the publications, frequently only partial runs are in library holdings, so that they must be pieced together from the holdings of several depositories, often quite far apart. For the purposes of this book, a fair sampling was deemed sufficient, since my goal is to provide a context and a framework, rather than an exhaustive account, of what the émigrés accomplished or thought, in each place of their exile.

The aim of this book is quite modest; for a comprehensive history of Russia Abroad much monographic spadework is still necessary. As noted, such work has been and will be carried out by a number of scholars in the fields of literature and the arts, but more historical and sociological study is still needed, so that Russia Abroad ceases to be somehow suspended in mid-air, independent of the existential circumstances and the host environment of Russian émigrés in the 1920s and 1930s. It is precisely the institutional and intellectual context of life in Russia Abroad that I hope to provide. By concentrating on the broad circumstances, both émigré and local, and by stressing the ways in which the exiles set up institutions that enabled them to go on creating and preserving the cultural traditions that they brought from Russia, I hope to make it easier to situate more accurately specific individuals or events of the Russian emigration between the civil war and the Second World War.

This goal explains the synoptic approach that I have adopted; more important, it justifies—at least in this writer's opinion—the selective character of this work. Yet it is hoped, the approach will help to clarify and to explain how it was possible for poor, displaced exiles to have such an intense, meaningful, and creative cultural life. It is precisely this vital cultural life—despite the complaints about the passivity, indifference, and material stinginess of the émigrés in supporting an exhilarating milieu—that was the hallmark of the émigré experience and justified the name "Russia Abroad." It was a society in exile, to be sure, but a society that made remarkable contributions to the host countries as it nourished its own cultural tradition. With the emerging Soviet curiosity about the Russia beyond the borders of the USSR, the émigrés' contributions to their homeland is more and more manifest.

If this book helps us to understand how an exiled group can carry on a creative existence, in spite of dispersion and socioeconomic or political handicaps, it not only will contribute to the eventual writing of a history of Russia Abroad but it will also help explain the process of cultural exchange, dissemination, and interaction. Such a process constitutes a key aspect of the formation of any significant culture—as was the case at the end of classical antiquity, for example—and it is perhaps the most significant feature of our own twentieth century. The miseries of war, revolution, civil strife, persecution, and displacement have forged the culture which is at present a most significant component of our world culture, in its material, intellectual, and spiritual dimensions.

2

The Humiliated and the Insulted: Exile

Russians who found themselves beyond the boundaries of the former Russian Empire after 1919 were in a real sense refugees. In the first place they were seeking refuge from military defeat (which in most cases entailed retribution at the hands of the victors), from hunger and deprivation, as well as from threats to life and liberty on political grounds. But they quickly became émigrés, in the sense of the word that had gained acceptance with reference to the Frenchmen who left France after it became obvious that the ancien régime had collapsed. A Russian émigré was a person who refused to accept the new Bolshevik regime established in the homeland. This refusal became irreversible—at least for most—when the Soviet decree of 1921, repeated and reinforced in 1924, deprived them of their citizenship and made them into stateless persons—*apatrides* in French and in the League of Nations' categorization.

The total rejection of the Soviet regime, of the revolution itself in many cases, and the expectation of returning home when the hated system would end, sustained the refugees in their émigré identity. This aspect of self-definition determined their behavior and cultural activities, and provided a sense of cohesion, despite political disagreements, as a "society in exile" that only waited to go back home. Of course, as time went on and the Soviet regime showed no signs of disappearing, the hopes for repatriation faded.

The patterns of emigration and resettlement had an impact on the émigré experience in their new countries. With the exception of a few individuals who left Russia in 1917, and a few more (mainly from St. Petersburg) who left immediately after the Bolshevik seizure of power in October 1917, the Russian emigration was the direct consequence of the course and outcome of the civil war. The military personnel who crossed the border, or were evacuated by sea after military defeat at the hands of the Red Army, were the major contingent of the first wave of refugees. They were accompanied or joined by civilians associated with them and who managed to follow them into exile. In some instances, crossing the border, or evacuation by sea, was deemed only a temporary expedient—a time to recoup their strength and obtain supplies from the Allies to resume the struggle against the Soviet government.

These circumstances meant that the first place of refuge rarely became permanent. This fact also explains why from the beginning it was not always clear who was an émigré, in the sense of *not wanting* to return, and who was merely an interned soldier or a prisoner of war awaiting repatriation. An additional complication stemmed from the fact that the borders of the freshly created states to the west of Soviet Russia (Poland, the Baltic republics, and Romania, often called collectively the *Limitrophes* or Border States) included a native Russian population, mainly peasants, who had lived there continuously for generations and who, although outside the territory of the RSFSR, did not always enjoy full citizenship status in their new country. In this situation refugees could often merge with these Russian minorities or use their presence to escape Soviet control after active fighting ended. In the years of famine and during collectivization, until tight control could be enforced, the border zone permitted escape from the Soviet Union and its disastrous conditions.

Let us survey the various places of exit and try to determine the main characteristics of the Russian exiles in each case. The most important areas of exit were the shores of the Sea of Azov (Novorossiisk) and of the Black Sea (Crimea, Odessa, Georgia). Thus Constantinople—Istanbul by then—became the first major locale of émigré existence. The armies of General Anthony Denikin and General Baron Peter Wrangel were evacuated to Istanbul from their last-ditch defense lines with the help of Allied naval vessels. Accompanying the military personnel were civilians: families of officers and soldiers, and others who managed to board the ships. The vessels did not always dock in Istanbul; some proceeded farther to the islands in the Sea of Marmora, in the Aegean, or to the Gallipoli peninsula.

Naturally, neither Istanbul nor the islands could accommodate the large number of refugees, many of whom were in appalling physical (and emotional) condition. Most could be placed temporarily in former army camps and hospitals, but they could not remain there for long unless the authorities (Turkish and more particularly the Allied commissions that provided the main material support) were to bear permanently the burden of their upkeep. In the interests of both the local authorities and of the refugees themselves, the Russians had to move to a place where they could settle and find employment. At this point we should note that, first, Istanbul and the nearby islands had the largest single concentration of refugees from Russia. Second, the overwhelming majority were men who had been fighting to the last moment and whose commander, General Wrangel, endeavored to preserve their military organization intact in the hope of returning to the battlefield shortly. Third, the relatively large number of civilians included many professionals, members of the bourgeoisie and commercial class, as well as a fair sprinkling of intellectuals and personalities from the former imperial court and administration (among the latter, some had held positions in the government set up by Wrangel in the Crimea, for example, P. Struve, G. Vernadsky, and N. Tagantsev).

The military character of the main refugee groups enabled local authorities, Turks and representatives of the Allied powers, to settle the groups in orderly fashion and to distribute assistance in a fair way. This was not, however, the case of the civilians clustered chaotically in the area of Istanbul, and who required massive help from foreign rescue organizations. But it is also important to note—and this disproves, or at any rate qualifies, the Russians' reputation for inefficiency and organizational incapacity—that the refugees themselves created voluntary organizations to assist women, children, and the sick. They set up hospitals, nurseries, and orphanages, and obtained contributions from their rich compatriots and Russian authorities abroad (diplomatic missions and Red Cross chapters), as well as from foreign philanthropists and sympathizers.

Countless memoirs and eyewitness accounts describe the odyssey and the plight of the Russian refugees who found their way to Istanbul in 1919 and 1920. The story of the military personnel was quite simple and pretty much the same for all: after several defeats on the Don, and an initial evacuation from Novorossiisk under tremendous hardships, they regrouped and regained strength in the Crimea. But the rapid advance of the Red Army broke through the weak defenses of the peninsula and forced their evacuation by sea. Allied naval vessels at the last minute refused to support continuing resistance and helped evacuate the White Armies from Odessa, Sebastopol, and Batum. In the process the Russians had lost their equipment and personal belongings, the sick and the wounded had grown worse and more numerous, while lack of food and hygiene had brought about epidemics, typhus being the most common scourge. The scramble to board the ships (or trains) was both undignified and heartrending. It was at this stage that civilians tried to join the evacuation, and their plight, already difficult, was made worse by the lack of space on the naval vessels and the need to rely on the goodwill of private boat owners. Many perished at sea or were shipwrecked on the Russian coast. Those who managed to cross the Black Sea did so under unspeakable conditions that brought about disease, many deaths, starvation, and total despair. It was at this time that many families were separated, sometimes forever.

Even before the final collapse of the Crimean defenses, and the evacuation of General Wrangel's forces and government in December 1920, civilian refugees had been arriving in Istanbul—many were the wives and children of officers still fighting on Russian territory. The few who had managed to take along some funds, usually some jewels and heirlooms, as did Princess Shakhovskaia and her daughters, maintained themselves for a while and helped set up shelters, schools, and hospitals.[1] These few lucky ones were soon flooded by masses of refugees who arrived, after weeks of anguish, with nothing but the clothes on their backs, many of them seriously ill. Groups of children, orphaned or separated from their parents, swelled the ranks of these wretched refugees—among them was the future émigré writer Gaitan Gazdanov. They all were scarred by the horrors they had gone through, witnesses to a brutal and bloody civil war; many had seen the suffering and death of loved ones, and were separated from other members of their families, ignorant of the fate of parents, friends, and relatives. And as always and everywhere, the unfortunate victims were still further exploited, forced to sacrifice their only possessions, transported in boats barely seaworthy in unsanitary and overcrowded conditions. Nor did their hardships end in crowded Istanbul. There opportunities for employment were few—at best in restaurants, entertainment, petty hawking—and the last possession had to be sold at derisory prices. The Turkish authorities, especially once Kemal Ataturk's government regained control, were less than hospitable. Saddled with their own refugees repatriated from Greece and the social and economic dislocation brought about by the recent wars, they were eager to get rid of the Russian refugees as expeditiously as possible.

On their part, the Allied military and diplomatic authorities that held administrative authority on the Bosphorus reluctantly assumed the care of the Russians whom they had supported in the civil war. They did this not only out of humanitarian considerations; the rapid resettlement of the refugees was a necessity on economic and public health grounds. The Russian refugees were a burden on Allied resources as well as a threat: anarchy born of demoralization, deprivation, and idleness lurked in the crowded and dingy camps and shelters housing thousands of Russians around the Bosphorus (or so it was feared, with the specter of mutinies and political disorders in postwar Europe vivid in the minds of government officials.

All the efforts, Russian and foreign, were to achieve two goals: provide immediate relief on the spot to the sick, the wounded, and the children, and to move the refugees to a location where they would find opportunities to achieve economic independence. With respect to the military and their dependents, General Wrangel at first balked at the Allied plan to disband his units and have their members resettle individually. He still hoped to resume the fight against the Bolsheviks, with or without Allied support, after a period of recuperation. The Allied decision to give up further efforts at dislodging the Bolsheviks by force, and England's ending of the blockade and resumption of trade relations with the Soviets, dashed these hopes. The officers and men of the White Armies began to be resettled in early 1921, although they frequently managed to stay in more or less organized and coherent groups. In this manner, some units, the Cossacks for example, were able to preserve their identity for a while longer as they moved on from the refugee camps around the Bosphorus.

With the help of various humanitarian organizations, individual civilians managed to leave Istanbul for Western and Central Europe where other refugees, in many instances their relatives and friends, had already established some sort of existence. Thus the Shakhovskois left early for Paris; the Socialist Revolutionary leader Mark Vishniak was helped to Paris where he was to become the driving force behind the major quarterly of the emigration, *Sovremennye zapiski*. Those with some means (or good connections) were the first to depart. The crews of Russian warships were directed to the French naval base at Bizerta (Tunisia) where they were eventually allowed to proceed to France. The steamship *Rion* carrying refugees was shipwrecked and those rescued found shelter on the island of Corsica; they later moved to Marseilles and neighboring cities. Out of a sense of Orthodox solidarity, Greece agreed to admit some Russian refugees, but it could not provide much employment, burdened as it was with its own refugees from Asia Minor. Several thousand Russians did settle in Greece, however, mainly in Athens, Piraeus, and Thessalonika.

In spite of its own difficulties, but much in need of manual laborers (in mines) and scholars (in universities and schools), Bulgaria was willing to take in Russian refugees. By the end of 1921 about 12,000, and by 1922 an estimated 30,000, Russians had been settled in the kingdom. Young men from the military units of General Wrangel's armies, after recovering from wounds and disease in camps near the Bosphorus, were put to work in coal mines near Pernika. They were housed in makeshift barracks where their condition was far from enviable: they were not accustomed to the heavy physical labor that they had to perform. Most did not remain for long and either moved to Sofia or other cities in Bulgaria where they found employment or educational opportunities, or left Bulgaria altogether.[2] Bulgaria also took in several scores of professionals and academics who significantly contributed to the scholarly and scientific development of the fellow Slavic nation. However, Bulgaria's insufficient resources, the establishment of diplomatic relations with the Soviet Union, and the heightened nationalistic atmosphere prevailing in the late 1920s and early 1930s again drove many of the Russians to other places. As a result, Bulgaria never developed into an active center of Russian émigré culture, despite the presence in Sofia of such well-known scholars as N. Trubetskoi, the young G. Florovsky—both of whom moved on early—and P. M. Bitsilli who became professor at the University of Sofia.

It was the newly established Kingdom of the Serbs, Croats, and Slovenes, future Yugoslavia, that eventually played host to a majority of Russians who had been stranded in Istanbul. Out of both "sentimental" (if such an adjective may be applied to government decisions) and pragmatic considerations, the authorities of the kingdom opened the gates of their land to entire military units, as well as numerous civilians, and helped them to resettle in the major cities and countryside. The sentimental consideration was based on the gratitude that the Serbs felt toward Russia for coming to their defense in 1914, and the pro-Russian, virulently anti-Bolshevik personal attitude of King Alexander I, who had been partly raised at the imperial court of Russia. The pragmatic consideration was the new country's need for professionals. Many new educational, technical, and administrative institutions were just being established, and there was a shortage of adequately trained native cadres to staff them. Serbian nationalism was an additional factor: the Serbian establishment, which dominated the public life of the multinational kingdom, had more faith in the loyalty of Russian émigrés, who depended on its benevolence, than in that of representatives of the other nationalities in the state.

The technical personnel of the former White Armies, and civilian refugees with academic and administrative experience, provided the needed manpower. The closeness of the languages and the same religion encouraged the Russians' assimilation. In addition, the Serbian patriarch, who had received his education in prerevolutionary Russia, offered the hospitality of his church to the majority of the Russian bishops and higher clergy who had been forced to flee the Soviet persecution of the church. Finally, the great devastation and loss of population experienced by Serbia in the First World War offered opportunities for settlement on the land. Thus Cossack units resettled in the kingdom were able to set up their own communities and resume their traditional agricultural pursuits. We shall return to the situation in Yugoslavia in other contexts. Here let us simply note that as a result of all we have mentioned, Yugoslavia, particularly Belgrade, became an active cultural center of Russia Abroad, although, for reasons explored later, it was much less sophisticated and creative than Berlin, Paris, or Prague. We should also mention here that the newly born Czechoslovak republic also gave permanent refuge to some Cossack and other peasant groups who set up their agricultural communities there. In this manner the bulk of the refugees stranded in Turkey moved on to Slavic and Balkan lands.

Farther north and west of the Black Sea a second escape route from the Russian Empire emerged as a result of the chaotic conditions that accompanied the final political settlements in the region. We need not recount the complicated events that affected these settlements. It suffices to note the following: many prisoners of war (from the First World War, the Soviet-Polish War, and the accompanying conflicts between various Ukrainian regimes and the Germans) were concentrated in reborn Poland and Eastern Germany. Most of them were eventually repatriated, but many decided to remain outside Soviet control and became refugees-émigrés. The prisoner of war camps thus provided the nucleus of Russia Abroad in this area.[3] Originally there were only single men of military age, but the refugee population was expanded as civilians—women and children—managed to rejoin their husbands, fathers, or sons.

Moreover, taking advantage of the unsettled situation at the border, many crossed into Poland—and from there into Germany—to become exiles, while those who had property, or who had resided in places now a part of newly formed national states, were granted permission to leave by the Soviet authorities. These people, too, swelled the population of Russia Abroad, sometimes after short-term status as members of the Russian national minority of these states. The more ambitious and active intellectuals, professionals, and younger people seeking to complete their education, did not stay long amidst the national minority and either settled in the capital of the respective new state or moved on to Central and Western Europe, or beyond. In this way Poland, the three Baltic republics, and Finland acquired significant groups of émigrés who considered themselves part of Russia Abroad. But the existence of a national Russian minority in these countries—mainly peasants and frequently Old Believers at that—meant that the émigrés were neither encouraged nor supported in their efforts at developing an active cultural life there. Nor should we forget the understandable anti-Russian feeling that predominated among the native elites in the new states whom tsarist authorities had long repressed and discriminated. They could not be expected to be particularly well disposed toward a flourishing cultural, social, and political life for members of the former imperial establishment.

In some instances (for example, in Estonia and Lithuania), the need for highly qualified academics and professionals resulted in invitations to Russion émigré scholars and appointment to newly created institutions of higher education and technical services. But, as occurred in Bulgaria, the burgeoning nationalism and the political authoritarianism that came to the fore in the late twenties—in Poland, Lithuania, Latvia—rendered the situation of émigrés more difficult; many left for such dynamic centers of Russia Abroad as Prague, Berlin, and Paris. It explains why in the Border States, despite a sizable number of Russian refugees, no truly creative centers of émigré culture arose. But the émigrés in these states did constitute a grateful audience for Russia Abroad's production, so that books, journals, lecturers, theater, and music found much needed moral and material support. Ivan Bunin's visit to Riga after receiving the Nobel Prize for literature was a festive occasion for the Russian colony there, and it also helped him financially. Such writers as A. Amfiteatrov were almost wholly dependent on their essays and novels being published or reprinted in the daily Russian press of Warsaw and Riga.[4]

The last large group to escape from Soviet-controlled Russia was in the Far East, centered in the Manchurian town of Kharbin. Kharbin had been a Russian city from its foundation in 1898 as the administrative and economic center for the Eastern Chinese Railway, a Russian enterprise. A truly Russian town had grown up alongside the original Chinese fishing village on the River Sunhuatsin (Sungari). The various governments and armies that were defeated by the Red Army and pushed to the eastern border of the former Empire crossed over into Manchuria, which was under China's sovereignty, and added to the Russian population of Kharbin. In their wake came civilians—members of the imperial establishment or of the other temporary regimes in Siberia, Cossacks, merchants, and even peasants. The last of these waves came in 1922 with the fall of Vladivostok in the Far Eastern Autonomous Republic to the Red Army. In this way Kharbin became part of Russia Abroad and remained so throughout the 1920s. Kharbin rapidly declined when Japan began to displace the Chinese authorities, however, and its cultural creativity came to a virtual standstill with the outbreak of Sino-Japanese hostilities in 1931.

In comparison to European centers Kharbin suffered two handicaps: in the first place, dynamic cultural elements were overshadowed by the technical and administrative personnel of the Eastern Chinese Railway, and a highly unstable situation resulted from the vagaries of Chinese, Soviet, and Japanese policies. The fact that the culturally active elements were made up mainly of "provincials" (mostly from Siberia) was not as significant as the political frictions and economic hardships experienced by the Russian colony. The second, and probably most important, handicap was the distance that separated it from the creative cities of the Russian diaspora in Europe—Berlin, Prague, Paris. The difficulties and costs of communication and transportation precluded satisfactory contacts and active exchanges. As a consequence, the publications of the Russian Far East did not easily reach an audience in Europe, and European publications were expensive and took a long time to reach Kharbin. Visits by leading émigré personalities invigorated the "provincial consumer" centers in Europe, such as Belgrade, Riga, Sofia, Kaunas, and the like, and made for sustained exchanges with the "capitals": but such tours did not include the Far East. This is not to deny Kharbin's contribution to the culture of Russia Abroad, but it does explain why it did not have the impact it might have had under conditions of today's technology. Only with the renewed emigration of many cultural personalities from Kharbin to the United States (or Australia) was the full value of its contribution appreciated. This, however, occurred on the very eve of the Second World War when Russia Abroad, in our sense, was about to come to an end.

The different patterns taken in the formation of Russia Abroad helped to determine the particular character of each of the main cultural centers and of their production. We should keep this background in mind as we consider the nature of the émigré population and of its cultural history.

So far we have been speaking of waves of refugees and whole military units escaping from Soviet-ruled territories and settling down all over the globe. How many people were involved? Unfortunately, we do not have precise numbers. In the first place, the chaotic circumstances of escape and exile made accurate counts and records quite impossible. We should also remember that illegal entry and domicile, due to difficulties in obtaining passports, visas, and residence or working permits, leave no records. Second, the administrative machinery both of refugee institutions and of the lands of asylum was relatively primitive and as yet unaware of the value of accurate and complete numerical-statistical data. The most comprehensive, and on the whole reliable, figures are given in the survey undertaken at the behest of the Royal Institute of International Affairs in London in 1937 and published by Sir John Hope Simpson in 1939. Simpson and his collaborators used all available documentation—and nothing new has surfaced since—specifically, Red Cross rolls of persons assisted, records of refugee organizations, and official statistics of the countries of asylum and the League of Nations, as well as the research of specially appointed correspondents. In the summary that follows, the data are neither complete nor accurate, and there are serious discrepancies.

The German historian Hans von Rimscha estimated the total of Russian émigrés in 1921 at 2,935,000, while the American Red Cross reported 1,963,500 refugees as of 1 November 1920 and two independent estimates gave 1,020,000 as of 1 January 1921 and 635,600 to 755,200 on 1 January 1922. In 1930, however, the Sub-Committee of Private Organizations (of the office of the High Commissioner for Refugees at the League of Nations) estimated for Europe a total of about 500,000, while figures supplied to the same office by various governments amounted to a total of 829,000. In addition, there were approximately 50,000 Russians in the Far East registered by the Russian Red Cross as needing assistance. Later waves of refugees increased this figure so that by 1934 there were about 130,000 Russian émigrés throughout all of the Far East.[5]

As may be seen from these numbers, except for the Far East the Russian émigré population declined precipitously between its start in 1920 and the first years of the 1930s. One reason was the demographic constitution of the émigré groups, as will be discussed later. Another reason was the fact that many émigrés became naturalized citizens despite difficulties in such countries as France and Germany. Nevertheless, most naturalized émigrés still considered themselves "citizens" of Russia Abroad. Furthermore, in many countries, children born in the country of asylum were considered native citizens (unless they opted otherwise at the time of their majority, which was quite rare) and were not counted as émigrés. And though the rate of birth was low among the émigrés, even the small number of children recorded as native births affected the overall statistical picture of the population of Russia Abroad. But in the dynamic centers of émigré culture the children born to refugees were raised as Russians, even though they attended local schools, and many felt that they also belonged to Russia Abroad. For instance, many well-known members of the French intellectual and academic (or even political) establishments today are these very same children who have preserved their Russian cultural heritage while being French citizens *à part entière*—we need only think of French Slavists (V. Vodoff, and A., Al., and V. Berelowitch, and V. Lossky), scientists (A. Abragam, I. Prigogine), writers (V. Volkoff, H. Troyat), and political figures (P. Beregovoy).

Our previous remarks have hinted at some characteristics of the refugee group that constituted itself into a Russia Abroad about 1920–1922. Since a majority of its members had gone (or had been compelled to go) abroad because of their defeat in the civil war, there was a disproportionately high percentage of single (which in this case does not mean unmarried, but without a spouse at the time) males of arms-bearing age, i.e., between the ages of eighteen and forty. Naturally, the pattern of exile made this feature more prominent among those who came through Istanbul and settled in the Balkans (especially in Yugoslavia), as well as among those who had been prisoners of war in camps in Germany and the new Poland. It was less obvious among refugees in the Baltic states and Manchuria where we find large numbers of civilians and soldiers' families. Moreover, in the early years of the Soviet regime, under Lenin's New Economic Policy (which began in the Spring of 1921), some émigrés already settled in the centers of Russia Abroad were able to bring their families to Europe from the USSR.[6]

According to an investigation made in 1921 in Yugoslavia, 69 percent of the Russian émigrés there were men, 66 percent were between nineteen and forty-five years old, and 70 percent of the men were single, though most women were married.[7] These figures explain marriage and birth patterns. The poor and unstable finances of the majority of the refugees discouraged marriage, and those who did marry could not afford to have many children in the face of unpredictable and mediocre economic prospects. Also important was the preference for a mate of similar religion and language. There were few marriageable females among the émigrés, even if we include those girls who came to maturity in the late 1920s and early 1930s. Practically all female émigrés of marriageable age were married or widowed. The single émigré men lived in great social isolation, often in barracks; they were reluctant to assimilate and become acculturated, since they always hoped to go back "home." Moreover, women of the host countries were reluctant to become engaged to outsiders who had such insecure financial and legal prospects. Significant exceptions occurred, as might be expected, among émigré groups that settled on the land in Yugoslavia and Bulgaria where closeness of language, religion, and occupation made binational unions easier.

A natural consequence of the situation in the "marriage market" was the very low proportion of children in Russia Abroad. As time went on, the disproportion grew as the children of binational unions lost their commitment to Russian culture. Yet it was precisely this low rate of natural increase that stimulated émigré parents to give their children a Russian education. They made great sacrifices to "keep their children Russian"—especially as long as there remained a glimmer of hope that a return to Russia would be possible. They sent them to private schools, spoke Russian at home, and tried to stem the children's natural inclination to adapt to their non-Russian environment. Such educational enterprises will be discussed in Chapter 3.

The mortality in Russia Abroad was extremely high; even a higher birth rate would not have compensated for the death rate. Many of the émigrés were already older adults at the time of exile, and the hardships of revolution and civil war—wounds, disease, famine—and the stresses of penury and legal disabilities in foreign lands also made for poor health and rapid aging. The émigré community and its supporters constantly faced the problem of securing aid for a rapidly aging population that also had many sick and disabled. Many of these aid programs had a religious dimension, which in turn reinforced the revival of religious commitment on the part of the émigrés.

The demography was only one aspect of a broader sociological picture of the Russian émigré population. Movies and novels have popularized the stereotype of the Russian exile as a former rich nobleman (preferably prince or count) who must earn a living as a taxi driver, a waiter or a doorman at a nightclub.[8] Reality was far from this simple and sadly humorous picture. Emigrés of former wealth, title, or high social position were proportionately no more numerous than they had been at home, perhaps even less so. On the other hand, the members of Russia Abroad displayed a much higher educational level than the statistical average of prerevolutionary Russia. About two-thirds of the adult émigrés had had some secondary education, practically all had received basic elementary education, and one-seventh had earned a university diploma.[9] There was also a higher representation of professionals, academics, the intelligentsia, and various comfortably situated urban classes (many of the latter were also Jewish). And it is also true, as had been the case in Russia before 1917, that these elements, especially the intellectuals and professionals, were both quite visible and active in Russia Abroad.

Besides the educated elites, the majority were urban bourgeoisie, small landowners, skilled workers (e.g., typesetters), and agriculturalists (primarily the Cossacks). The traditional Great Russian peasantry constituted a tiny minority—the absolute reverse of what had been the case in Russia before 1917. Among the young men who fought in the White Armies most came from the urban and small landowner classes, and many had interrupted their studies at the secondary or higher levels. Some of these men were unwilling to resume their studies or to enter the ranks of the semiprofessionals in the land of asylum. On the other hand, however, a larger number of them apparently were eager to take up their studies and to acquire skills or professions that they hoped would be of use in a Russia freed from the Bolsheviks. Their commitment and demand stimulated the creation of a whole network of educational and cultural institutions in Russia Abroad.

The overwhelming majority of the Russian émigrés belonged to the Russian Orthodox Church; the significant revival of an active religious life that occurred in the diaspora affected many of them. But there were also small groups belonging to other denominations: Protestants, especially among those with Baltic antecedents and the so-called Russian-Germans, bicultural and bilingual. Some had only recently become Russian Orthodox, others converted during emigration. The number of Roman Catholics was negligible; and there was a scattering of Moslems and Buddhists among a few émigrés from the Caucasus and Central Asia. This brings up the question of nationality in the sense of ethnicity. Among the "Russian" refugees there were also sizable numbers of Jews, Ukrainians, Armenians (from Rostov-Nakhichevan or the short-lived Republic of Armenia, not the victims of Turkish persecutions), and Georgians, as well as a small group of Kalmyks.

These national and religious groups included many individuals (sometimes even a majority, as in the case of Georgians in France and practically

all educated Jews) who felt also Russian by culture. They actively participated in the cultural enterprises of Russia Abroad, and often provided a
most significant share of financial and moral support: they subscribed and
contributed to journals and other literary efforts; attended and financed theatrical, musical, and artistic events; and participated in educational institutions as faculty or as students. Some were bicultural and bilingual, others
spoke and read only Russian, though they later also acquired Western European languages. This was the case of many intellectuals and professionals
of Jewish or Ukrainian (i.e., Eastern Ukraine) background. But all of these
groups participated passively or actively in the cultural life of Russia Abroad.
And except for some of the diehard chauvinist reactionaries and the bigoted,
they were accepted by all educated Russian émigrés as fellow citizens of
Russia Abroad. They are an inseparable part of our story.

Anyone who looks at photographs of refugees taken when they reached
the first stop on their road to safety notes their tattered clothes and their
bodies showing hunger and sickness, their scared faces bereft of hope. The
Russian refugees who reached the haven of exile from civil war combat
zones needed assistance in practically all respects. A number of philanthropic
organizations, private and public, offered such help. World War I had
activated many international associations that could help them, and various
governments were aware that the refugee problems had become more acute
during the war and because of the sociopolitical dislocations in its immediate
aftermath.

First among the international organizations prepared to bring assistance,
for it had done so already during the war, was the International Red Cross
and its national societies, especially the American and Russian ones. They
were involved most actively in the evacuation of civilians and military personnel from the Crimea to Istanbul, and in the areas of Poland and the
Baltic where the armed struggle had lasted until 1921 and 1922. The International Red Cross took major responsibility for bringing material aid to
prisoners of war, and also assisted those refugees who had been housed in
the prisoner of war camps under its care.[10] Closely related to the physical
care of prisoners of war and sick troops was the concern for their intellectual
and spiritual well-being, the preservation and furthering of what had been
acquired in school in preparation of their future civilian life. This was
the main function that the American Young Men's Christian Association
(YMCA) and the World Christian Student Movement assumed during the
Great War. But in providing reading and educational materials to soldiers,
prisoners of war, and evacuees, these organizations were automatically involved in showing concern for their material needs as well. For this reason
the YMCA took on, albeit on a more modest scale, the distribution of food
and clothing to repatriated prisoners of war and to refugees streaming out
of Russia. As we learn from the letters the young YMCA representative in
Riga wrote to his mother, this involvement marked the beginning of his own

and the YMCA's commitment to help the exiles from Russia in their cultural endeavors.[11]

The war, and especially the first year of the Bolshevik regime and civil war, had brought about large-scale famine to vast areas of European Russia. The American Relief Administration (ARA), organized for civilian assistance during the Great War by Herbert Hoover, played the chief role in extending help to the stricken population. The ARA also became involved in assisting refugees fleeing the areas of famine, which were often the battlegrounds of the civil war. But the ARA's work had to be complemented by local efforts, for which end committees headed by leading Russian personalities were formed. This brought about Lenin's decision to expel about a hundred intellectuals, many of whom had been involved in a cooperative association to further famine relief. Thanks to Lenin, therefore, Russia Abroad received at one stroke a group of prominent academics and intellectuals whose work, supported largely by the YMCA, was to be seminal in the creation of émigré culture.[12] We shall encounter the names of many from this group in our account.

Of course, there were also private initiatives by foreigners who had an interest in or connections with the Russians. Committees to help various categories of refugees were set up in the United States and in England, as well as other countries. For example, the efforts of Thomas Whittemore (restorer of the mosaics of Hagia Sophia in Istanbul) proved an invaluable addition to the assistance given refugees in Turkey and Bulgaria—especially to children and young people. Eventually, Whittemore was able to raise money to provide several hundred scholarships for émigré youngsters. The Russian exiles who had access to money or influential foreigners contributed for specific purposes, for example, in Germany the Amerikanischer Hilfsfond für russische Schriftsteller und Gelehrte (American Fund to Assist Russian Writers and Scholars).[13]

Besides the substantial aid of all these organizations and individuals, government participation remained of crucial importance, for governments alone could resettle the refugees and provide employment opportunities. In Istanbul the military exiles received assistance from the French government, which felt committed to support them, especially after England renounced its involvement in protest over General Wrangel's formation of a government and plans to carry on the struggle in the Crimea. English help, however, was forthcoming in the north when the evacuation of the anti-Bolshevik government in Arkhangel under N. Chaikovskii brought 15,000 Russians to England—they were soon resettled on the Continent. England also assisted the former White Armies that had retreated into the newly formed Baltic republics, especially Latvia and Estonia, where they had been disarmed. The United States, following its unsuccessful intervention in the Far Eastern fighting, had to share the burden of aiding the refugees who streamed out of Bolshevik Siberia at the end of the civil war.

While the British and U.S. governments disengaged themselves quickly from the refugee problem, France remained active, for it had to deal with great numbers of émigrés who were to settle there permanently. France's need for labor, after the bloodletting of the war, led the government to allow recruitment of laborers among the Russian refugees in Istanbul, the Balkans, and North Africa.[14] Germany, responsible for former prisoners of war, as well as for those who had been evacuated after the Armistice and in the wake of German disengagement from Ukrainian affairs, provided assistance and relief for these men, primarily as the agent for such organizations as the International Red Cross.

The international organization of states set up in the aftermath of the Great War, the League of Nations, immediately confronted the major refugee problems—first the Russian, then the Armenian, and finally (at least until the 1930s) the Greek and Turkish—all resulting from the political and military upheavals that accompanied the peace settlements. The Norwegian Arctic explorer, Fridjof Nansen, who had become prominent in refugee work during the war, was appointed High Commissioner for Refugee Affairs entrusted with finding ways for assisting and resettling thousands of people left without a country and in penury. The material aid, rather paltry in proportion to what the sovereign states could have afforded, was channeled through the International Red Cross. The main tasks of the Nansen Committee—later replaced by the League of Nation's Commissariat for Refugee Affairs attached to the International Labor Bureau—were to offer legal protection, to help transport refugees for permanent resettlement, and to extend a helpful hand in the first stages of their establishment in new lands. As far as the Russians were concerned, the Nansen Committee's chief contribution was legal help, as we shall see shortly.

Several governments were actively involved in settling Russian exiles on their own territory. This naturally entailed extending legal and material help as well, for the émigrés had to travel to the new destination, and the costs of settlement had to be borne by the host country. This was the case of Bulgaria, Yugoslavia, and Czechoslovakia. For instance, the Kingdom of Serbs, Croats, and Slovenes (Yugoslavia) arranged for the railway transportation of thousands of former White Army men and their civilian dependents from Istanbul, the Greek Islands, and Gallipoli to a new home in Serbia or Croatia (sea transportation was usually provided by the French). The government then allocated a significant sum from its own regular budget to Russian émigrés as a direct subsidy, although the amount decreased sharply in the second half of the 1920s.[15]

But as the proverb "aide-toi, le ciel t'aidera" (God helps those who help themselves) has it, the Russians realized that they also had to help themselves to obtain permanent security. The Russian Red Cross, which had been very effective in assisting the wounded and sick during the war, now extended its aid to the refugees, especially in the most crowded centers. For this purpose it drew on funds held in reserve abroad or money that it had managed to evacuate with the White Armies. Additional monies came from the International Red Cross and from bank accounts in the name of Russian embassies abroad, accounts that remained accessible to the former ambassadors as long as the country to which they were accredited did not recognize the Soviet government. The Russian Red Cross came to concentrate on assistance to the sick and disabled, especially former military personnel. After the refugees had settled in the various countries of asylum, the Russian Red Cross continued to maintain hospitals and homes for invalid military personnel and their dependents, and orphanages.

Another Russian civilian organization that had proven its usefulness and efficiency during the Great War was the Zemgor, the Union of Zemstvos and Towns; it had assisted civilians behind the front lines and on their evacuation from the regions of military operation. After 1918 the Zemgor reconstituted itself in Paris, with executive offices in Prague and other major émigré centers, and resumed its work by aiding émigrés, particularly in matters of health and education. Its funds came largely from the assets of Russian embassies abroad that were managed and distributed by the Conference of Russian Ambassadors sitting in Paris, under the chairmanship of V. A. Maklakov (the appointee of the Provisional Government). The Zemgor gave emergency help to people stranded in Istanbul and on the borders of the RSFSR; later it regularly maintained clinics and sanatoria for émigré children and enabled them to attend Russian schools abroad. The Committee of Help to the Russian Child raised money for the Zemgor from private donations, especially in the United States, by organizing drives and benefits.[16]

As was to be expected, veterans of the Great War and the civil war organized their own associations. Originally the main purpose was to preserve the cohesiveness of their former military units. General Wrangel set up the umbrella Veterans Union (Rossiiskii obshche-voennyi soiuz) precisely in order to maintain contact with his former troops, in case of recall to active service should an occasion to resume fighting the Bolsheviks arise. We need not follow the avatars of this union and similar veterans' organizations of individual regiments or branches of service because their primarily political activities are not of concern here, although the veterans' associations certainly played a role in extending help to their members and their families. They collected membership dues, launched fund drives, organized charitable events, and solicited contributions from rich members of the émigré colonies, in particular from members of the imperial family and court. The associations assisted individuals with cash outlays and by maintaining hospitals, veterans' homes, orphanages, and schools.[17]

Civilian associations were founded mainly along professional lines, to protect the rights and welfare of their members; but they also helped a larger circle of émigrés. Each professional association of writers and journalists, lawyers, former court personnel, taxi drivers, engineers, and so on aided members in need and assisted them in solving legal and practical problems connected with their émigré status. The latter was a particularly important function, for the survival of members literally depended on their obtaining working and residence permits, or assistance in administrative red tape. Closely connected with the professional associations were the clubs and organizations of graduates or former members of various prerevolutionary Russian educational and academic institutions such as the Union of Former Students of the Imperial Aleksandrovsk Lyceum, or the Society of Graduates of the Smolny Institute, or the Russian section of the International Federation of University Women.[18]

Naturally, such professional associations came into being only after a number of émigrés had settled and obtained employment. They played no role in the relief efforts at the moment of exile, but once organized they were ready to help fellow professionals who made their way abroad later in the 1920s. They also could be counted upon to contribute more or less bountifully to charitable and cultural drives for Russia Abroad. Along this same vein we may mention the Action Orthodoxe, a significant self-help movement launched in the early 1930s in response to the émigrés' needs in the Depression years. As its name implies, it was an organization that drew its inspiration and set its goals on the basis of a recommitment to religious values.

Scores of organizations had limited purpose and even more restricted funds, and most had but ephemeral existence. It is significant that although the major sources of support were non-Russian in origin, the Russian émigrés themselves displayed great ingenuity and organizational energy, tenacity, and skill in finding ways to help their fellows in acute need. We turn now to a description of the ways the settlement of Russian refugees took place in various countries—their organization, legal status, material circumstances, and the forces that made for solidarity or conflict within the larger community of Russia Abroad.

Those refugees who sought asylum in organized groups—military units, political parties, and the like—often also settled in groups, at least in the first stage of their exile. The military formations of General Wrangel, evacuated through the Black Sea and the Bosphorus, endeavored to stay together as they moved on to settle in Bulgaria and the Kingdom of Serbs, Croats, and Slovenes. Those who had been interned in the army encampments on the Gallipoli Peninsula moved later, also often in groups, to Yugoslavia and Czechoslovakia. Even after the subsequent dispersal in search of permanent employment, veterans of Gallipoli stuck together, and wherever a few of them congregated they formed an Association of Gallipoli Men (*gallipoliitsy*) to minister to both their social and material needs. The Cossacks from the Don, the Kuban, and Siberia, following their centuries-old pattern, left Russia in traditional formations headed by their *atamany*; they also did everything possible to stay together. They managed to settle in agricultural communities in the Balkans, in the Czechoslavak Republic, Western Europe (southern France), and in South America, retaining their paramilitary organization and their elective hierarchy. Best known to the outside world were the sev-

eral Cossack choirs founded in emigration, which toured under the leadership of their elders.

The evacuees from the Crimea who wound up in Bizerta (Tunisia),
where they were interned for a while, also formed a group that later moved
on to France where it eventually dispersed, most settling in Provence and
the Paris region. The army units that crossed into the Baltic states also
preserved their organization for a while, a fact that facilitated their existence
in those relatively poor countries. The refugees who congregated in Kharbin
were also at first made up of distinct groups—military units, entire villages
of Siberian Cossacks or Old Believers. In addition, and this was a particular
feature of the Russian émigré Far East, they found asylum in a city that
already had numerous and active organized groups—employees of the Eastern Chinese Railway, former members of the administration and defense
units of the railway, church congregations, schools, and hospitals—all established before the revolution. These groups account for the preservation of
Kharbin's Russian character and the easy integration of the newcomers,
refugees from the civil war, into the city's social patterns and life style.[19]

The availability of remunerative work generally determined where and
how the refugees settled abroad. In the early 1920s, the first years of exile,
there were several employment opportunities that groups of émigrés could
take advantage of, since it was in the interest of both the refugees and their
prospective employers to deal with groups rather than with scattered individuals. This tendency was the reason for the large-scale settlement in "group
formation," so to speak, that took place in the Kingdom of Serbs, Croats, and
Slovenes. The Serbian authorities—Croats and Slovenes played a subordinate
role in this—went one step further: they encouraged the formation of émigré
communities, especially of agricultural villages in the provinces (but not
exclusively so), by allowing them to form autonomous, self-governing communes. The members of these communes elected their own officials and
could settle disputes among themselves, and they were responsible for the
upkeep of order and the payment of all taxes and dues. In case of difficulties
or unsolvable conflicts, the elected communal officials were to request the
intervention of local authorities and subject the matter to the latter's final
jurisdiction. Apparently the system worked quite well, although internal conflicts between personalities or on political grounds could not be avoided. It
remained in force until the end of the 1930s in the countryside; in urban
areas, however, the Russian "collectives" tended to dissolve early, and their
members merged into the general population administratively speaking.[20]
It may also be worthy of mention here that several army units, cadet schools,
and girls' "institutes," which had been evacuated *in corpore,* found refuge
in Yugoslavia and retained their administration and rules for admitting new
members. They were able to do so thanks to the financial support they received from King Alexander I and his wife, as well as members of the
Russian imperial family living in Denmark and Germany.

Czechoslovakia was also willing to take in Russian émigrés. The most prominent group consisted of the faculty and students of the newly founded Russian educational and research institutions in Prague.[21] Although students and professors came as individuals, they did constitute a cohesive group with a specific purpose, and they were financially supported by the Czech government to reach their educational goals. As long as the educational institutions of Russia Abroad were active and flourishing, i.e., in the mid-1930s, their group identity and solidarity continued, and in some instances lived on even after their dispersal to other lands. The Czech government also settled a Cossack group in an agricultural community in Moravia; these people simply moved their agrarian community en masse from southern Russia.

In great need of labor after the Great War, France organized the hiring of Russian refugees abroad. Agents of French factories and mining concerns traveled to Belgrade and other places in the Balkans (e.g., Sofia), as well as to Bizerta, to hire laborers for their enterprises. The French consulates in these countries served as a labor exchange and had instructions to issue visas and to facilitate travel arrangements of those hired to their places of employment. Once in France, these émigrés settled near the enterprises in groups—single men lived in barracks and ate at factory-run canteens. Small communities of Russians thus sprang up all over France, but mainly in the north, the east, and the southeast, where some form of Russian church and cultural life could be preserved, at least in the beginning. The harsh conditions in which they labored and lived quickly decimated their ranks, however, and resulted in apathy and tensions that frequently undermined the sense of community. The Depression hit these men particularly hard; they were to be the object of the particular solicitude of the Orthodox Action.

Whether they maintained some form of group cohesion and organizational ties or tried to make a go individually, all Russian émigrés needed assistance to cope with the legal and material complexities of the lands of asylum. Existing institutions and new organizations ministered to these needs. In the first years of emigration the Russians had still an official protector in the old embassies and their staffs. Indeed, most countries did not recognize the Soviet government and continued to extend diplomatic status to the ambassadors that had been appointed by the tsar or by the Provisional Government.[22] The embassies issued identity papers and passports, certified official documents, and offered legal counsel and assistance to their compatriots. Most ambassadors had some funds at their disposal, and in some instances they could also draw on the credits that had been extended to the imperial government, or from state properties abroad. A Conference of Ambassadors convened regularly in Paris to decide the priorities for these funds. To the embassies also fell the task of identifying and extending legal protection to former prisoners of war, interned military personnel, and individual Russians who had escaped from Soviet-controlled territories. The ambassadors had to plead for and disburse those monies that foreign governments allocated for refugee relief.

This simple situation was drastically complicated at the end of the civil and Polish wars as a result of two developments. First, the evacuation of General Wrangel with his army and administration from the Crimea meant that a "government" in exile, recognized by several powers—notably France and the Kingdom of Serbs, Croats, and Slovenes—could claim to be the legal heir of the imperial state and extend its authority to all Russians in foreign lands. Moreover, as we have seen, General Wrangel hoped not only to keep his own troops together, but to rally under his command all other Russian military formations or individuals who found themselves abroad, whether in internment or resettled. In short, as head of the last effective non-Soviet government and as commander in chief of the anti-Bolshevik fighting forces (although acknowledging Grand Duke Nikolai Nikolaevich as the representative abroad of the imperial family), General Wrangel claimed the loyalty of all émigrés. To enforce this claim he delegated his own representatives (members of his army staff or of his administration in the Crimea) to the major capitals of Europe. These representatives were to set up their own offices—unless the ambassador recognized them as part of his embassy—to register all Russians abroad, coordinate the activities of all refugee institutions, extend assistance to those in need, and to establish direct official contacts with the authorities of the respective host country. Friction, even outright conflicts, with the ambassadors and their staff were unavoidable. The officials of the host countries concerned with Russian émigré matters now had to decide whose authority to recognize. Where the Wrangel delegates had no significant community of former Crimean troops (for example, in Paris), they remained in the background and played a subordinate role, primarily organizing associations of war veterans. These delegates also had to accept the leadership of those top White Army commanders residing in that country (in France, this meant General Miller and General Nicholas Iudenich, for example).

In countries where the units evacuated from the Crimea formed solid blocs in the émigré community (Bulgaria and the Kingdom of Serbs, Croats, and Slovenes) General Wrangel's delegates played dominant roles. They were in a position to organize the émigré community according to Wrangel's views, and enforce his policies, pushing the tsarist ambassadors into the background. Only the direct intervention of local authorities could preserve the functions and practical status of the former ambassadors. This was possible when the ambassador had direct access to, or even held membership in the government committee in charge of the Russian émigrés, as in the case of V. N. Shtrandman in the Derzhavnaia kommissia (State Commission) of the Yugoslav government (which was directly subordinated to the office of the prime minister and in control of the funds allocated Russian exiles in the national budget). However, even in this situation, as we learn from the voluminous archives of S. N. Paléologue, Wrangel's Belgrade delegate played a major role in the day-to-day life of his refugee compatriots in the kingdom. The German government had a direct hand in Russian émigré affairs, deriving from its obligations toward former prisoners of war. Some of the ministries in Berlin had great expertise in Russian matters. Ambassador S. D. Botkin, representing the Conference of Ambassadors, was successful in acquiring the principal role in Berlin. The Wrangel representative, A. E. Rimsky-Korsakov, was forced into a subordinate role.

A second event that drastically disturbed the original simple situation was the diplomatic recognition of the Soviet government by European governments in the wake of the initiative taken by Germany as part of the Rapallo Treaty in 1922, which established economic and military ties with the Soviet government. France followed suit in 1924; and it is worthy of note that neither Yugosalvia nor Czechoslovakia recognized the Soviet Union before the 1930s. The particular makeup of the Russian emigration in Czechoslovakia and the democratic nature of the Czech government precluded General Wrangel's delegate from playing any role except in the internal affairs of veterans' and invalids' organizations. On the other hand, the refusal of Yugoslavia to recognize the legitimacy of the Soviet Union until after the assassination of King Alexander I (1934), and the king's personal sympathies for the Russian monarchy, gave Paléologue, Wrangel's delegate, the opportunity to play an important part in émigré affairs; his own bureaucratic talents, which helped to secure his files for posterity, were no doubt a significant factor in his success. Once diplomatic recognition of the Soviet Union had been granted, the former ambassador had to vacate the embassy's premises, disband his staff, and cease all activities. This left the émigrés without any representation and protection, since the Soviet embassies refused to deal with them.* This obliged the host countries to find a channel of communication between the exiles and local authorities.

The solution that was devised consisted in setting up a special office for Russian refugee affairs—usually under the direction of the diplomatic representative of the pre-Bolshevik regime. In France, former ambassador V. Maklakov became the head of the Office russe in Paris, while the former consuls in Marseilles and Nice were in charge of the regional offices. The offices certified the validity of imperial documents, issued such papers as certificates of birth or marriage for people who had lost them. These documents were recognized by the French authorities and courts. In case of need, the Office russe made representations on behalf of émigrés before French civilian courts and ministries. Thanks to his personal talents and wide connections in French circles, Maklakov continued in fact to be the ambassador of Russia Abroad to the French administration. Thus when a deranged Russian, P. Gorgulov, killed the French president Paul Doumer in 1932, Maklakov extended apologies and condolences on behalf of the

* Many de facto émigrés had Soviet passports, some retained and renewed them periodically. This was the case of those who had been expelled, or those who had decided not to return to Russia while they were abroad on a visit or on an official mission. In the eyes of the Soviet embassy and the host country's authorities they were émigrés, but they frequently earned moral condemnation in exile circles.

Russian community to the French Parliament and people. When the French imposed new dues on passports, or issued draconian regulations to expel Russians who were unemployed and without valid residence permit, Makla-kov succeeded in mobilizing deputies—in particular the socialist Marius Moutet, himself married to a Russian, and Edouard Hérriot, the radical socialist president of the Chamber of Deputies—to have these measures re-scinded or softened.

After the Rapallo accords, the *Vertrauensstelle für russische Flüchtlinge* (Trust Office for Russian Refugees) was set up in Berlin to exercise func-tions similar to those of the Office russe in Paris—until the advent of Hitler, who had all Russian émigré institutions put under the control of pro-Nazi émigrés. But before then, the Trust Office not only assisted the émigrés in their legal and administrative problems, but also helped to finance and administer material assistance (hospitals, schools, labor exchange). The office had a direct line of communication to the Ministry of Foreign Affairs in the person of State Secretary Ago von Maltzan. For example, it secured the intervention of the government on the occasion of a dispute with the City of Berlin (and the government of Prussia) involving some real estate it held and in making arrangements for the ministry's recognition of the instruction given in the Russian school.[23]

The de jure recognition of the Soviet government raised the question of the émigrés' legal status with respect to travel documents for crossing state boundaries. In response, the Nansen Committee, under the auspices of the League of Nations, undertook a new task: a special document, the so-called Nansen passport, was issued to all Russians claiming émigré status (and subsequently also to Armenians and refugees from the Saar). The document certified the holder's identity and category of statelessness. The Nansen passport could be used to apply for visas and to obtain permission to travel abroad (outside the host country); and as long as it was valid it also entitled the holder to petition for permanent residence. The land of asylum recognized the Nansen passport as a valid document on condi-tion that the holder satisfied all requirements for obtaining a residence per-mit and paid a set fee for the passport and its periodic renewal. The proceeds from these "Nansen stamps" were split between the international office in Geneva and the local refugee offices. By subscribing to the League of Na-tions Declaration of 1928, renewed and revised in 1933, a country acknowl-edged the validity of the Nansen passport, extended its own protection, and granted residence and employment permits to the holder, on conditions more favorable than those enjoyed by other foreigners. As noted earlier, the Rus-sian offices set up to minister to the needs of the émigrés after de jure recognition of the Soviet Union automatically became local Nansen offices administering the passport system, responsible to the High Commissioner for Refugee Affairs of the League of Nations, the successor of the Nansen Committee.

In a century of intense nationalism and state control over many aspects of life, the policies of the countries of asylum varied greatly with respect to the Russian refugees. The policies were determined in the first place by the economic situation and, second, by domestic political considerations. In all instances, however, we may distinguish roughly the following three periods: from 1920 to the late 1920s, with, in most cases, something of a caesura in 1923–1925; from about 1929 until 1935; and a brief epilogue extending from 1936 to the outbreak of war in 1939, or absorption by Germany, as in the case of Czechoslovakia and Austria. For reasons explained earlier, at first Germany had the largest number of Russian émigrés. Their number reached a high point during the German inflation when the cost of living for foreigners was lowest, while the cheap publishing and printing allowed great opportunities in publicizing their creative efforts. With the stabilization of the mark after 1924, the cost of living rose dramatically and led to a mass exodus. Additional departures occurred as the domestic political situation in the Weimar Republic became more and more ominous, jeopardizing free expression and personal safety (especially for the numerous Russian socialist, liberal, and Jewish émigrés). At the same time, growing unemployment during the Depression after 1931 brought about restrictive regulations for the employment of foreigners, so that many Russian émigrés were forced to go elsewhere. As we have seen in the statistics adduced earlier, the Russian émigré community in Germany, which had about 230,000 to 250,000 people in 1922, dropped to about 90,000 in 1930. Hitler's accession to power further stimulated the exit of liberal anti-Nazi and Jewish émigrés, even though employment opportunities improved, albeit under the strict supervision of Nazi-appointed organizations. For example, F. A. Stepun, the philosopher-sociologist with Slavophile leanings, was discharged from his teaching post at the Technical University of Dresden. He remained in Germany to the bitter end, maintaining himself by freelance work, lecturing and writing articles published abroad. For 1936–1937, the Nansen office estimated at 45,000 the number of Russians in Germany.

Except for working permits, the French were very liberal in their attitudes toward the émigrés. They granted long-term residence permissions, and for those who had means there were no further restrictions. The Russians enjoyed the free and exciting atmosphere of the Parisian cultural scene, and in some measure also contributed to it. Not surprisingly, Paris became the true political and cultural capital of Russia Abroad, with representatives of all shades of political ideologies and all trends of style. The labor situation, however, with its economic implications, was the major problem. At first, as has been mentioned, the French were eager to obtain laborers for mining and industry, and to work on rebuilding regions devastated by war. The dearth of workers led to the entry of a large number of Russians whose ranks were further increased when residence in Germany became more expensive and difficult.

In the first half of the twenties, working permits were granted rather liberally in France. This did not apply, however, to the so-called liberal professions—lawyers, doctors, teachers. Here the requirement of French citizenship (or veteran status in the French army), as well as the passage of French examination and possession of French diplomas, proved to be an almost insuperable barrier, though the requirements could sometimes be circumvented by émigrés working as assistants or under the cover of a French colleague. This situation did not change throughout the whole period of Russia Abroad, although naturalization became easier and more frequent in the 1930s, and this permitted a few younger émigrés to enter the professions.

As France was hit by the Depression early in the 1930s, although a bit later than Germany, the need for foreign labor declined, too. Government decrees made obtainment or renewal of working permits more difficult; these measures hit particularly hard those who had to renew their papers after losing employment. The Minister of the Interior ordered the expulsion of all those who did not have a permit or who had violated French law, even simple traffic violations. Those so expelled had nowhere to go, since other European countries would not accept them and resettlement overseas was too difficult and costly. We can read of innumerable cases of Russian exiles being arrested, transported across the border where the neighboring authorities refused to receive them, sent them back to France where they were arrested again and given jail terms; then the same scenario was repeated. No wonder some took up illegal residence or even committed suicide out of sheer desperation or became illegal residents. Finally, in 1936 the government of Léon Blum put an end to these practices and relaxed the policies in favor of the émigrés. As a matter of fact, with the Front Populaire government, émigré workers became entitled to the same social benefits as the French and were readily enlisted by the trade unions—the Confédération générale du travail (CGT, the largest national labor union) even created a Russian section whose members it protected on par with the French.[24]

The harsh legislation adopted in the early 1930s reflected not only the economic difficulties of France, but also the political rapprochement that Premier Pierre Laval had negotiated with Stalin. Moreover, it was not so much the fact that a Russian émigré had killed the president of the Republic, but rather the social and political crisis (e.g., the Stavisky affair, the riots of 6 February 1934) that produced a xenophobic backlash. The aggressively chauvinistic, proto-Fascist *ligues* (Croix de feu, Camelots du roi) clamored for stern measures against the many foreign *apatrides* living in France. The fact that most foreigners provided much needed labor to fill places the French would not take was, of course, ignored by the rhetoric in a heated atmosphere. However, none of these developments directly affected the cultural life of Russia Abroad in Paris or in France at large, although both producers and consumers of cultural "goods" suffered from the poor economic situation: books and journals were bought less readily and cultural events were not attended or supported as well as in the past.

Yet, as the celebration of the centenary of Pushkin's death in 1937 showed, the emigration's cultural life remained vibrant, in spite of the impoverished circumstances of many of its members.

The pattern in Czechoslovakia was not unlike that in Germany and France, though political considerations played perhaps a larger role. The so-called Action russe that began in 1922 in Prague saw the rise of a whole cluster of Russian academic institutions. But these could not be maintained at the same level of government financial support from the late 1920s onward. The potential users (students, researchers) of these institutions declined from natural attrition, departure to other countries, and the steadily increasing integration of the younger émigré generation into the educational system of the lands of asylum. The Czech government, and foreign philanthropies, grew more reluctant to put scarce money into these institutions to support the faculties and students, for most graduates left Czechosolvakia for better opportunities elsewhere. Most crucial for the decline of the Action russe, however, was the realization on the part of both Czechs and Russians that the émigrés' chance of ever returning to Russia was rapidly waning. A major justification for the Action russe was thus disappearing, and this raised the question of the worth of its survival. Finally, in the mid-1930s Czechoslovakia was more and more under siege. Its own national minorities were dissatisfied and displayed their disaffection ever more openly; the economic crisis, especially in the industrial centers and in the Sudetenland, added fuel to the increasingly hostile and inflammatory nationalist propaganda pouring forth from Hitler's Germany. The very survival of the Czechoslovak Republic was in jeopardy; naturally the Russians in Prague were last on the list of Czech concerns. The Munich agreement of 1938 spelled the end of liberal, democratic Czechoslovakia; many Russians left of their own accord, and the remaining institutions were closed following upon the republic's demise a year later. It should be said that the Czech-Soviet accord of 1935 that followed upon the de jure recognition of the USSR in 1934 affected neither the Russian émigrés nor their institutions, although in a subtle manner it made their usefulness even more problematic in the eyes of an ever-larger number of Czech public figures.[25]

Conditions in the Kingdom of Serbs, Croats, and Slovenes did not change appreciably during the existence of Russia Abroad there. The government remained friendly, and its refusal to recognize the USSR until very late in the 1930s, practically on the eve of the war, forestalled distrust of and pressures on Russian exiles. The government's need of professionals for the army, the administration, and public services made it possible for many Russians to enter the work force on a permanent basis. True, for a while, the Russians were discriminated against by not receiving "tenure," i.e., regular civil service status, remaining on a precarious and less-well-paid contractual basis. Total integration into Yugoslav government service, however, occurred with greater frequency as time went on; yet, by and large, the Russians were kept on a lower pay scale (or not promoted to top positions) compared to their native counterparts. On the other hand, they were not discouraged from having their own associations and public activities, as we have seen earlier. Natural attrition, as well as increasing rates of naturalization and assimilation, resulted in a smaller number of Russians working for public services by the end of the thirties. In other respects the situation remained stable, so that the Second World War saw Russian émigré units fighting in the ranks of the anti-Communist forces of General Mikhailovich. When the Red Army and Marshal Tito took control of the country, most Russians became refugees a second time.

In Bulgaria the original hospitality became more reserved when Bulgaria established diplomatic relations with the Soviet Union. Working conditions and opportunities, especially in the larger cities, deteriorated as Bulgaria came to feel the impact of the worldwide Depression. As there were no further additions to the émigré community—on the contrary, many left to seek better opportunities—and since death rates exceeded births by far, the Russian community shrank constantly, with far fewer than the 15,000 estimated by the Nansen office at the time of the outbreak of World War II. As far as I know, the Bulgarians continued to extend protection to émigrés even under German occupation and at the end of the war.

The Baltic republics, at first quite hospitable, became more restrictive, especially where employment was concerned, when ultranationalist and authoritarian governments, such as that of K. Ulmanis in Latvia and A. Smetona in Lithuania, came into power in the 1930s. National minorities and foreigners were increasingly discriminated against in public employment and even in private occupations, especially in the liberal professions. This trend greatly affected the prosperity, even the existence, of émigré and minority educational institutions. But the very need for highly trained academics forced Lithuania, for example, to call upon Russian émigré scholars. There were conditions, however: émigrés had to learn the local language and lecture in it within a reasonably short time. The University of Kaunas appointed Professors I. I. Lappo, A. S. Iashchenko, and L. Karsavin to permanent chairs in their respective fields. To be fair, I should point out that the situation in the Baltic republics was always complicated by the presence of a significant Russian ethnic minority, mainly peasants, in the regions adjoining the Soviet Union.[26] Consequently, the policy for the émigrés was closely intertwined with the policy for minorities, so that the chauvinistic, antiminority moods of the 1930s had immediate, negative repercussions for the emigration. But we should remember that in spite of their ethnic, linguistic, and religious similarity, a wide cultural gulf separated minorities and émigrés—similar to the great differences that had separated the educated classes from the peasantry in Imperial Russia. The application of minority legislation to the émigrés was doubly resented by the Russians.

The policies directed against national minorities (in spite of treaty commitments) deeply affected the situation of the émigrés in Romania and Poland. Without going into details, we may say that the Russians in Romania were not really part of Russia Abroad. The émigrés there (many were former landowners in Bessarabia) kept a low profile and had almost no cultural life of their own. Harsh discriminatory legislation directed against the Russian minority in Bessarabia was extended to apply to most émigrés in cultural matters.[27] In Poland the government supported a few political factions and their publications in the hope of using them in its anti-Soviet policy. Otherwise, however, the Poles were not friendly to the Russian émigrés in their midst, some of whom did recover their estates in the eastern part of the country. The cultural life of the emigration in Warsaw was far less dynamic than the numbers and makeup of the Russian émigré population might have led one to expect. The Russian academics and professionals who found employment there endeavored to integrate into Polish society. However, émigré publications from elsewhere were a permanent part of the literary scene and visiting lecturers were frequent and welcome guests.

Our preceding remarks have shown that the economic circumstances of the overwhelming majority of the denizens of Russia Abroad were far from brilliant. Most émigrés had to fend for themselves from day to day, in occupations for which they were not prepared. More stressful than the poverty was the insecurity of being foreigners on sufferance. The threat of unemployment hung like a sword of Damocles over their heads. Emigré wives often earned money as seamstresses or domestic workers, or by doing handicrafts or piece work. In Joseph Kessel's novel, two sisters eke out an insecure living designing and making flower decorations; a family I knew depended almost exclusively on the crochet work (removable collars for ladies' blouses were in high fashion in the thirties) taken in by the elderly mother and her married daughter; an active member of the Political Red Cross (which assisted prisoners in the Soviet Union) earned her living making handbags.[28] Naturally, the émigrés were also the object of shameless exploitation by their employers, whether from their own midst or native-born. It is true that in countries with a social welfare legislation, the Russians could claim some benefits—but not always on par with the native population. Political preferences at times made things more difficult for the Russians: in industrial enterprises, native workers, sympathetic to the Soviet revolution and regime, viewed with distrust the exiles in their midst. The émigré workers might have turned to the trade unions to protect their interests, but some refused to do so or resented the compulsory membership in them. Their reluctance stemmed from their own political views, shaped by their experiences of Russia, which were opposed to any form of trade unionism. Moreover, since the local unions were often avowedly pro-Communist, or in favor of a socialist reconstruction of society, they held little appeal to men whose very raison d'être was rejection of these aims.

But when all is said and done, the main reason for émigré insecurity was not so much the generally parlous economic situation in all countries of refuge—and it grew steadily worse in the early thirties—as the legal restrictions to which the Russian exiles (and other refugees, of course) were subject in a foreign land. These constraints were enforced with greater severity when social and economic conditions deteriorated, and when the political atmosphere became saturated with xenophobic, nationalistic moods. It is not easy to say whether xenophobia was the result of economic distress or the latter a consequence of the autarkic nationalistic policies pursued by the governments of that time. In either case, the Russian émigré paid a heavy price, psychologically and materially, to overcome the administrative barriers.

Naturalization was rarely a solution. First, none of the countries of the Old World had the policy and tradition of automatic naturalization prevailing in the United States and in some Latin American countries; second, the Russians themselves believed that naturalization was a betrayal of their Russianness, of their émigré mission as representatives of an alternative to the Soviet Union. They made no serious efforts to acquire new citizenship, especially as long as the dream of returning home lived on. And when naturalization was possible, nay practically necessary, it presented a moral dilemma; some were ready to accept it as a mere formality, which would not change one's loyalty and identity as a Russian, but such an attitude could not please the authorities who were willing to grant naturalization.[29] As noted previously, the raison d'être of emigration was the expectation of a return to the homeland, and fear of *denationalization,* as assimilation was called, was an uppermost concern of all Russia Abroad; subjectively the idea of new citizenship reinforced the objective obstacles that the host countries placed in the path of naturalization.

Not surprisingly, to overcome the material and legal difficulties we have just sketched, the Russian exiles formed associations and communities that constituted cells, as it were, in the body of Russia Abroad. Basic to émigré efforts to achieve community or solidarity was the underlying feeling of belonging by virtue of a common homeland, of a never-questioned refusal of the Soviet system, and of a nostalgic dream of returning to Russia. In short, it was the sense that a common fate had brought them together in spite of the socioeconomic, political, or professional diversity of their previous existence. As in any political diaspora, an unwillingness to give up past identity, and the hope of resuming it at some time in the future, constituted the strongest bond. This "homesickness" is what lay behind all efforts at mutual aid, whether narrowly focused on a group defined by professional, religious, or political criteria, or aimed at all members of Russia Abroad. It was precisely through these endeavors that the émigrés created and preserved the sense of a mutual community among widely dispersed individuals.

Veterans' groups celebrated special events and days, bringing together their scattered members to reaffirm their commitment to a common past and hope for a better future for their homeland. In the major centers of Russia

Abroad, church services, at regular Sunday mass or on special occasions, were attended by veterans parading in their uniforms and carrying their flags. Schools, summer camps, and scouting groups for émigré children not only contributed to the intellectual and physical development of the young, but also reaffirmed the solidarity of the parents. And as we shall see in a later chapter, the organization and celebration of commemorative days bound together—in spirit as well as in body—exiles of various persuasions and backgrounds. The church also affirmed this historical-cultural identity, especially in view of its dependence on a common language and knowledge of traditional ritual. Praying together was more than an act of devotion, it was also a public commitment to a unique national and cultural tradition that set off the worshippers from the host society.

As is the case with people who find themselves in an alien milieu, personal contacts and individual ties played a considerable role in preserving the émigrés' identity as well as enabling their material survival. In countries where the Russians did not settle in more or less closed communities and where they lived more isolated lives in large cities, personal contacts helped in obtaining employment, selling products, arranging for admission to educational or medical institutions, and in coping with local authorities. Chance encounters between émigrés brought about unexpected help in times of distress and the reunions of families. The columns of the émigré daily and weekly newspapers with wide circulation carried notices of individuals seeking lost family members or contacts for specific purposes. Personal acquaintance at the time of evacuation, or at the first place of exile, might lead to more permanent associations and possibilities of mutual aid. Individual contacts generated some common economic enterprises, not always successful, such as renting farms, setting up small trading, manufacturing, or sewing businesses, and the like.[30] By and large such enterprises attracted other refugees as customers—again this illustrates the importance of personal contacts and the sense of common identity. This behavior, common among immigrants, often maintains separateness instead of encouraging integration.

The root of the feeling of isolation from the surrounding milieu for the Russian émigrés—unlike the situation of the genuine immigrant—was the everlasting belief in return, of resuming one's life in the homeland once it was free from the Soviet regime.[31] In European countries, the host societies were reluctant or even refused to genuinely accept the émigrés. Fears of denationalization may have been exaggerated for this reason. Even the children of émigrés had some difficulty in integrating fully into the society of the land of their parents' asylum; despite their fluency in the language and their attendance at native schools, they remained outsiders. This was particularly true in France, Germany, Manchuria, and to a lesser degree, perhaps, in Yugoslavia, Czechoslovakia, and the Border States. The Second World War brought about a radical change in this respect, especially in the case of France.

In any event, the sense of isolation was reinforced by the unique experiences, in Russia and on the road to exile, of the members of Russia Abroad. Even when they spoke the local language well, and were fully acquainted with the history and culture of the host nation, they were still outsiders; their newly acquired language skills and knowledge were not integral parts of themselves. This kind of isolation is difficult to convey, perhaps, but it created an invisible, sometimes imperceptible, yet ever-present and unbreakable, emotional barrier to genuine and truly satisfying contacts with the host society. Of course, economic circumstances and legal status gave palpable form to the differences that separated the exile from all others. Nor did the external circumstances disappear as time went on, unlike the situation in other countries of immigration, such as the United States, Australia, and Canada. For the émigrés lucky enough to have families of their own, and those who were part of a Russian community, there were few incentives to overcome their isolation, since their own small world bestowed emotional and material support.

Yet another important factor deepened the isolation of Russia Abroad. Many émigrés, as noted earlier, had lost their families, either in Russia or on the way to exile. These people were still emotionally committed to their lost relatives and friends, which inhibited active search for new bonds, especially since they held fast to the hope of repatriation. The fact that single male émigrés had a poor chance of finding mates or beginning families only intensified their loneliness. This isolation was compounded in the case of men who worked in the provinces where they lived in barracks and dormitories, exhausted by unaccustomed physical labor, with few opportunities to meet the local population, let alone make genuine contacts. To preserve some sense of identity that stemmed from a common past and fate became the prime imperative, and this determination precluded serious efforts at integration.

The strong sense of solidarity and common identity did not preclude, however, wide divergences of opinions among individuals and groups. The most noticeable and dramatically displayed source of strain and conflict derived from political differences. The political spectrum duplicated that of the Russia they had left, with the obvious exception of the Bolsheviks. The spectrum ranged from the extreme left—anarcho-syndicalists, Left and Right Mensheviks, Left and Right Socialist Revolutionaries, and liberals of all stripes—to the extreme right, ultrareactionary monarchists and Fascist-oriented groups from the 1930s on. These political divisions obviously affected the normal operation of many institutions. We have noted the conflict between the representatives of General Wrangel and of the Conference of Ambassadors. These conflicts were not just over administrative "turf," they also involved political preferences for a future Russia: the Wrangelites were avowed monarchists, while the refugee offices of the ambassadors refused to commit themselves to a restoration and sympathized with a moderate liberalism. And the same kind of division affected the associations of students and teachers. An illustration of how political disagreements could damage the work of an institution was the opposition of Paléologue's office to the Zemgor in Yugoslavia. Political differences also cut through the same organization, even those that on the surface seemed immune to them. For example, the All Russian Veterans Union almost collapsed over the question of whether its members had to renounce publicly all political commitment, except for a vague support of monarchy in general.[32] Similar disagreements resulted in the creation of two student associations, two unions of taxi drivers in Paris, and so on.

Another source of conflict with a political dimension originated in a split within the Russian Orthodox Church abroad. The question arose as to who should wield spiritual authority over the Russian churches in the diaspora, the patriarch of Moscow or the Synod of Bishops in exile at Sremski Karlovci (in Serbia). We shall discuss this split later in detail. The controversy gave rise to conflicting loyalties that disturbed or curtailed the activities of many other organizations that maintained close ties to the church. It manifested itself, for example, in summer camps, schools, and youth organizations, and even in special celebrations. But it should be noted, in defense of the emigration, that the political divisions did not result in the kind of ugly diatribes, mutual recriminations, and unseemly personal quarrels in church activities, as they did in other areas. This irenic state of affairs, paradoxically, was largely brought about by the Soviet government's insistence that Metropolitan Evlogii and other bishops in western Europe publicly pledge that the church abroad would not engage in any anti-Soviet activities or issue anti-Soviet statements. Metropolitan Evlogii refused, since this would have committed the church to taking a political position, which he believed was against tradition and contrary to the interests of Orthodoxy. His refusal resulted in a partial de facto reconciliation, or at least mutual tolerance in practical affairs, between the Bishops' Synod at Sremski Karlovci and the metropolia of western Europe. The conflict was resumed openly and with greater violence after World War II under very different political circumstances.

The émigrés had frequent occasion to fear conflicts of loyalty. In many instances they could resolve such dilemmas by accepting a "dual citizenship" or double loyalty.[33] In other cases such a duality was deemed incompatible with membership in Russia Abroad. For example, as noted, some exiles refused to accept another citizenship through naturalization, believing that this would betray their former allegiance to Russia as a state and of their Russianness as émigrés. Others, for obvious practical reasons, accepted naturalization as a double "nationality": they were citizens of the new country, but Russians in cultural terms and in their concern for the fate of Russia. Such an accommodation, however, rarely went so far as to accept membership in a political party of the land of asylum, although it did not preclude service in the army of the host. Some may have believed that by serving in the army they worked for the ultimate "liberation" of Russia.

As noted earlier, similar considerations applied with respect to joining a labor union of the land of refuge, though in many cases union membership was accepted, since it clearly provided economic safeguards. Finally, for fear of denationalization, émigrés refused to join actively a foreign Orthodox church.

Given the difficulty and variety of circumstances, and the great number of organizations that were the source of strains and conflicts, it is the more remarkable that Russia Abroad managed not only to preserve, but also to contribute creatively, to Russian culture. It is to this dynamic aspect of the history of Russia Abroad that the following chapters will be devoted.

3

To Preserve and Transmit:
Education in Exile

The Russians who sought refuge abroad and decided to stay in exile, rather
than return to a Russia ruled by Bolsheviks, did so not only out of consideration of personal safety—although the latter did play a role in the
aftermath of the terror campaigns of War Communism (a drastic regime
instituted in 1918 by Lenin)—but mainly because their homeland no longer
conformed to their idea of what Russia should be. If they remained in exile
and established a Russia Abroad, it was to preserve and pass on to their
children their own notion of what constituted genuine Russian culture.
While there were divergent opinions among the émigrés as to what in fact
should constitute the very essence of Russia's culture and traditions, these
divergences were overcome for the sake of preparing the young to play a
constructive role in some future, free Russia.

The first task was to restore the refugee children to physical and psychological normalcy. Many children had lost parents and family, and had not
known a normal environment throughout all the years of civil war and
their evacuation abroad. Even those who had the good fortune of staying
with a parent had lived through traumatic experiences. In extending material help to the Russian refugees, special attention was paid to the needs
of children and adolescents. Everything we have said of the assistance extended to the refugees streaming out of Bolshevik Russia in the previous
chapter applies even more to the children: besides food and medical care,
orphanages, schools, and kindergartens were established at every center of
evacuation and at the first stations of exile. These first measures were largely
successful because sizable numbers of the émigrés had been active in the
fields of education and child care, especially in the Zemgor institutions.
They took the initiative or were consulted for their special skills and experience; some examples are of A. V. Zhekulina, Countess S. V. Panina,
and V. V. Zen'kovskii. Many teachers who had fled Russia were eager
to resume their work for émigré children. Finally, as we have mentioned,

several orphanages and boarding schools—cadet corps for boys and institutes for girls—had been evacuated in entirety. These became the focus of financial and material assistance for children from émigré and foreign institutions.

All those involved with the refugee children realized the necessity of healing the "souls" of youngsters bruised by their experiences in the turmoil of revolution, war, and civil strife. One approach was to allow the children to express their feelings and recount their experiences as a way of helping them to a catharsis that would restore their psychic health. Several projects were set up to enable the children to express their thoughts and feelings—either by direct questionnaires, interviews, or setting up child communities. In this connection, it should be noted, émigré educationalists were continuing the kind of work and experimentation with advanced psychological and pedagogical theories and techniques that had been a prominent feature of the progressive intelligentsia's outlook on the eve of the Great War and the revolution. Russian pedagogical theories were remarkably well developed, in the direction of a modern, individualized approach to the care of the child's psychic health during World War I. Workers in child psychology confronted the problems created by the absence of parents (fathers in particular) and the trauma of evacuation from the war zones, and deteriorating material circumstances. Their previous experience in Russia, and the body of extant literature were of great help in exile, serving as guideline for the organization of émigré educational institutions. Research had already yielded a graphic picture of children's reactions to the traumas of the Great War, and these results were summarized and discussed in émigré publications. True, this research—which had its parallels in Soviet Russia in the first years of the Bolshevik regime—did not have the methodological sophistication, especially theoretical conceptualization and statistical rigor, that we expect of similar investigation today; but the material gathered in the form of autobiographical essays offers much insight into the refugee children's emotional and intellectual condition.[1]

The émigrés were determined to preserve the children's knowledge of traditional Russian culture so that they could acquire skills that would allow them to play a constructive role in a future free Russia. The educational efforts of Russia Abroad were directed to prepare the émigré young to fulfill this double assignment.[2] This mission explains why so many Russian parents preferred to have their children taught in émigré schools rather than in local ones. But practical considerations, including cost, often precluded this, so that other arrangements were made—they were more modest in scale but proved quite effective nonetheless. Under the circumstances, the humanities—language, literature, history, geography—were the major concern of émigré educational enterprises. Sciences, including mathematics, being transnational by definition, were not required for the preservation and development of a Russian identity, which was the main goal of émigré schooling, so that science courses could be handled in the manner prescribed by the host country's educational system. It was natural, therefore, that beyond the elementary grades the old Russian *gimnaziia,* with its emphasis on the humanities (classical languages and Russian literature and history), provided the model for the schools established in the diaspora. No sooner had the great waves of refugees found a place to settle than a network of schools—primary and secondary—appeared in the main centers of Russia Abroad.

The émigré schools on the elementary level imparted the three Rs and religion in Russian; then there followed the old curriculum of the *gimnaziia,* and where the émigré group was large enough, a *real'noe uchilishche* (patterned on the German *Realschule*) that gave priority to the sciences was established. In all instances the aim was to inculcate a thorough command of Russian language, grammar and composition, literature, history, and geography. The emphasis on religious instruction, which usually had received only perfunctory attention in the prerevolutionary schools, may be considered an innovation over the old pattern in that it stressed the spiritual-historical aspects of Orthodoxy, rather than the mere ritual.

The few figures we have on the number of émigré schools and their population are far from complete, and the reliable numbers involve only those establishments that were supervised (and supported, in part at any rate) by the Zemgor. In 1924 there were ninety secondary schools with 8,835 day pupils and 4,954 boarders.[3] This amounted to about 20 percent of children of school age in emigration.

The émigré condition imposed a new perspective and approach to the teaching not only of religion but of the "Russian" disciplines—language, history, literature, geography. Unlike their predecessors in the homeland, émigré children did not have a firsthand acquaintance with the *realia* of Russia. In the early years of emigration there were pupils who still remembered what life was like in Russia—its landscape, its people, its ways; but with emigration lasting longer and longer, a new generation was growing up that only knew a foreign land, without a direct experience of Russia—and this ignorance had to be remedied in the classroom. It required making greater use of illustrations and examples to bring the realities of Russia closer to the understanding and capacity of the émigré pupil. This need demanded modifications in the traditional pedagogic approach and the contents of instruction. What and how to modify was the subject of much discussion, and émigré instructors looked to foreign experiences for guidance and inspiration. The "case study" approach that was having a great vogue in the United States and Germany caught the attention of the teachers in Russia Abroad and was taken up wherever possible. As in the German *Heimatkunde* classes, the case study approach involved the reconstruction (since actual visits were impossible) of a specific village (or region) graphically, and its history traced with the help of literary, artistic, and oral sources. The instrumentalist pragmatism of John Dewey, the child's direct involvement in the learning experience through doing, was an approach that many émigré teachers adopted with good results.

Modifications in traditional programs and methods in response to the abnormal situation of emigration triggered discussions and controversies that highlighted the difficulty in defining what was the "truly" (or traditionally) Russian to be preserved and transmitted to the young. Like any émigré group, the Russians abroad were conservative in the sense that they wanted to preserve the past, as they knew and understood it; they feared that an *aggiornamento* would betray their children's Russian identity. It explains the heated controversy over orthography that agitated Russia Abroad throughout the 1920s and directly affected the educational community.

The modernization of Russian orthography had been prepared by the Academy of Sciences on the eve of the revolution. As with the reform of the calendar, the changes would have been accepted without much resistance, or further discussion, had they been promulgated before February 1917. The implementation of the recommendations, however, was postponed until the end of the war. Thus it was the Bolshevik government that gave legal force to and implemented the reform by immediately demanding that everything be published according to the new rules of spelling (and dating). The mere fact that the Bolsheviks applied the reform, even though it had been thoroughly discussed and formulated by recognized specialists before the revolution, was sufficient to identify it with the evil regime and make it anathema to most émigrés. Whether children should be taught according to the old or the new orthography was the subject of numerous conferences, articles, and polemics in Russia Abroad. As long as the overwhelming majority of the reading material accessible to émigrés was in the old orthography, the latter prevailed. But as time went on, and more books and journals were printed in the new orthography and Soviet publications were becoming more widely accessible in Russia Abroad, the traditionalists were bound to lose ground. Some schools, for example the Russian lycée for girls in Paris, devised the following solution: a quarter or half point would be deducted for each error in old orthography, while each mistake in the new would carry the penalty of a full, or even two, points. Naturally, the pupils preferred the slighter penalty, even though it involved greater risk and learning a somewhat more complicated set of rules. Eventually émigré publications also began to drop the "hard sign," for instance, and modern spelling came to be adopted more and more widely, and the issue died of itself.[4]

With respect to such subjects as history, geography, and religion, serious problems arose only in history. As a rule, contemporary history was not taught, so that contentious issues could be easily avoided (this was also the normal practice, for example, in French schools). The schools that were openly monarchist and conservative naturally stressed the goodness of the last rulers, especially Nicholas II, whose reputation was now enhanced by an aura of martyrdom because of his and his family's "execution" by the Bolsheviks. By and large, however, the teaching of history followed the old prerevolutionary scheme, stressing dynastic, military, diplomatic events, and treating domestic political problems from the perspective of the central government's efforts to modernize (Peter the Great) and reform (Alexander II). The role of Moscow in bringing about the unification of the Russian lands, in creating a centralized administration, and in acquiring a huge territorial empire received pride of place and positive evaluation. The most popular and widely used history textbook in émigré schools was the brief history of Russia that S. Platonov had written for use in secondary schools in the first decade of the twentieth century. It was familiar to the old generation, moderate and liberal in its nationalism and monarchism, and frequently reprinted abroad. Such an orientation was quite understandable when we remember that at the same time, in the 1920s in Soviet Russia, the teaching of history had been displaced by "social studies," which dealt with sociological and economic processes, at the expense of factual knowledge of concrete historical events and of the role of individuals. When at Stalin's behest Soviet schools returned to more traditional history and stressed national glory and past achievements, the émigré and Soviet perspectives on Russia's past began to converge, despite continuing philosophical and methodological incompatibilities. At times, émigré teachers did depart from the Platonov scheme in that they were more critical of the Petrine revolution than Platonov had been, and they manifested a proclivity for a Slavophile interpretation. Thus the children's almanacs—*Russkaia zemlia, Russkii kolokol*—and pamphlets and books issued in connection with important historical events, as for example the conversion of *Rus'*, displayed fervent national patriotism and suggested that the Slavophiles had come closer to defining the true essence of Russia's historical path and future role.[5]

One type of literature of paramount importance for the devevolpment of children in prerevolutionary Russia was, strangely enough, rather deficient in Russia Abroad; namely, journals and books exclusively for the young. This lack was all the more striking, since in Soviet Russia this tradition was dramatically revived at the end of the civil war, and children's books and magazines were not only published in great number but also attained a high level of literary and graphic sophistication. Russia Abroad's failure to carry on this valuable tradition is to be accounted for by its economic situation, as well as by the demography of the entire community. Publishing was expensive and the émigré were scattered across many borders; there was an inadequate system of distribution, and most potential customers were too poor. Most Russians abroad had difficulty in finding money to purchase a daily newspaper or quarterly journal, let alone books. Recall, too, that the young were proportionately underrepresented in emigration, and publishers could not count on a large youth market. All these circumstances deterred authors from producing for the young.[6]

In its efforts to preserve traditional national culture and to prepare its young generation for an active role in the free homeland of the future, Russia Abroad could not forget that it had to work in a foreign environment, and under conditions that were radically different from those either in the old regime or in Soviet Russia. The foreign environment demanded that the young be also prepared for gainful employment abroad, regardless of what they might do if they returned to Russia. Times, too, were changing rapidly

and many new subjects had to be introduced (or updated) if the young were
to have a chance of surviving either abroad or upon returning "home." For
example, more attention had to be given to the natural and physical sciences
in general education, whether elementary or secondary, designed for young
émigrés. Furthermore, the scientific preparation had to be practically oriented
to include awareness of the technological advances made since 1914. It is no
wonder that émigré educational literature displayed great interest in the
methods devised in the West for teaching science and technology at all levels.
The models developed in the United States attracted the greatest attention,
for schooling there had always been practical and flexible, so as to accommodate different interests and career levels. Another source of inspiration came
from Germany where, during the Weimar Republic, much effort had been
given to the modernization of education for a greater emphasis on practice; but
even more important, to make the educational system accessible to pupils of
working class, peasant, and other "popular" background. Reports in the pedagogical journals and conferences of the Russian emigration recount the endeavors to introduce scientific and technological subjects and to teach them
with modern methods. Given the limitations of numbers and resources, such
efforts were usually restricted to the earlier grades, since neither equipment
nor competent teaching staff were easily found for higher levels of instructions.[7] Moreover, the most serious handicap for émigré efforts at a "Russian
schooling" was that technical education was better obtained in local schools,
for only their certificates and diplomas made immediate practical application
possible.

The diplomas issued by Russian émigré schools at each level of the curriculum had to be acceptable to the local authorities for admission to their
own schools at the next level, or for professional licensing. This meant that
Russian curricula had also to include the basic requirements of the local educational system. Inclusion of these subjects eventually resulted in their being
taught in the local language, so that most émigré schools became in fact bilingual: the general subjects were given in the host country's tongue, while
Russian language, history, literature, religion, and geography were taught in
Russian. Another formula, exemplified by the Russo-German school in Berlin,
consisted in alternating the language of instruction from one day to the
other, all subjects being thus taught in both languages. Such practices encouraged the pupils to become fully bilingual, but competent teachers, capable
of giving bilingual instruction were scarce. As the years went by, it became
increasingly difficult to preserve the bilingual practice. By the 1930s the overwhelming majority of émigré children attended local schools, although many
also took additional classes or tutorials in Russian subjects outside the regular
school hours.[8]

The young generation's experiences on the path of exile, and the example
of the countries of asylum, called attention to the importance of caring also
for the health and for the character of the pupils in the process of imparting
knowledge. In the case of children brought up in the "natural" environment

of family and homeland, health and morality had been the responsibility of parents and various nonschool institutions. But when the child was either taken out of the family environment, placed in a boarding school, for example, or worse still, thrown into the totally alien and confusing environment of emigration, then this task fell to the schools. The youngsters' poor state of health and emotional damage led émigré schools in the early 1920s to pay particular attention to hygiene and mental health. But even later on, as many of the émigrés lived on the margin of poverty, the schools were frequently the only place where a child could receive a full meal daily and adequate attention to physical condition. Pedagogic theory and practice stressed the need for attending to the pupils' physical needs; whenever possible, the amount and quality of physical exercise were increased. In less innovative manner, greater attention was also given to the moral and spiritual development of the children by stressing the ethical side of Russian subjects—especially history and literature—which also was intended to raise the level of the children's national and cultural consciousness. In this context, too, in part also because of practical considerations of finances and space, the question of coeducation had to be tackled. We should remember, however, that this was not a purely émigré problem, it was an issue debated among educationalists and parents in the twenties in Germany and in the thirties in France. Naturally, the example of the United States and Scandinavia, and to a lesser degree England, showed the positive results of coeducation, especially, it was thought at the time, for the healthy emotional development of the young.

All these problems were closely related to teaching methods. Here, too, the émigrés had to face the fact that the prerevolutionary methods and schools had not contributed much in avoiding either revolution or the anarchic violence that swept Russia after 1917. For many émigrés, the major culprit of the revolution was the traditional progressive intelligentsia: the educated elite had lacked the flexibility of mind necessary to understand and adjust to the new needs faced by Russia after 1905, or even after 1914 and 1917. One of the reasons for this failure, many thought, lay in the inadequacies of a school system that had been too rigid and out of date, thus encouraging rebellion and an unhealthy skepticism about the basic social and moral values and of the country's traditions.

Whatever the excellence of the contents of its teaching, the methods of prerevolutionary official education had been unquestionably antediluvian, much too rigid, bureaucratic, and formalistic, inhibiting creativity, self-sufficiency, and independence. The situation was well understood by enlightened and progressive educational leaders before 1917, and their awareness presided over the transformation that the school system was undergoing in Bolshevik Russia. This very fact, however, gave rise to a quandary for the émigré educational leadership: the modernization of curricula and progressive methods could—banish the thought—easily be identified with Bolshevism. It was better to turn to Western progressive theories and methods. The journals for émigré teachers carried much information on Montessori schools, on the ideas of

who had become involved in providing religious (as well as Russian) instruction for children whom the parish did not reach. Religious education groups were set up in Paris under the leadership of individuals closely associated with this bureau. The bureau also helped direct the religious education offered at the summer camps of the Russian Christian Student Movement. With the help of the YMCA and a Rockefeller grant, Zen'kovskii, and his pupil Sophie Koulomzin, made a trip to the United States to study the methods of religious education outside school.[10]

Let us now turn to a brief description of the schools in Russia Abroad. Institutions existed on all three levels of instruction, as we have mentioned: primary, secondary, and higher; but not all levels were represented uniformly everywhere. Small colonies of émigré settlement could afford only a rudimentary primary school, whereas a few large centers boasted all three levels. Moreover, we should keep in mind the fact that the emigration did not reproduce itself, and as time wore on, the children born in emigration were sent, more and more frequently, to the local schools, receiving additional instruction in Russian subjects privately. Unfortunately, we do not have full and reliable statistical data on the numbers involved, for only the information accumulated by the Zemgor, and covering only those under its direct care, is readily available.[11]

Information on émigré schooling on the primary level is incomplete, largely because so much of it was carried out in the homes (and orphanages) and informally, as circumstances permitted. From the second half of the 1920s on, most émigré children went to local schools in the first grades and received their Russian religious instruction from the parish church. Aside from a few progressively experimental groups or schools in Berlin and Paris where the methods of Montessori or Dewey were applied, primary education was quite traditional, taught in Russian and in the language of the country of asylum. The Russian primary schools generally continued after the 1920s only in fairly large, isolated refugee communities, for example in Yugoslavia. Elsewhere, the task in elementary grades consisted in developing the children's knowledge of Russian: learning the alphabet and the catechism. We have little information on the teaching staffs of these schools. Apparently in most cases they consisted of the priest and his family—as had been the case in the villages of prerevolutionary Russia—or volunteer laypersons.

The secondary school was central for achieving the double goal of the émigré educational project defined earlier. At that stage the children were mature enough to be receptive of the tradition that was to be preserved and of the skills needed to play an active part in case of a return to the homeland. As mentioned previously, the basic curriculum of the secondary schools in Russia Abroad was that of the *gimnaziia* (or the *real'noe uchilishche*) of prerevolutionary Russia. In addition, the program of sciences was enlarged to satisfy modern requirements. Also added was the study of the language, history, geography, and literature of the host country.

Financing secondary schools was a major problem, never adequately solved, except in Czechoslovakia (at Třebov) and in Yugoslavia (in Belgrade) where the schools were fully recognized and received government support equal to what was given to local institutions. In the Border States, particularly Latvia, the émigré schools were identified with those for the Russian minorities and considered part of the regular school system; they were under the administration of the section for minorities in the Ministry of Education, which supervised the hiring of teachers and financed the schools. Elsewhere the émigré secondary school had to struggle on its own, with very little, if any, support from the local authorities, as for example in Berlin where the Prussian Ministry of Education subsidized the Russian *gimnaziia*. In Paris, under the directorship of V. A. Maklakov's sister, a secondary school for girls had been established with the financial support, maintained throughout the period, of Lady Detterding, herself a Russian, the wife of an oil magnate. None of these schools could forgo tuition, although a number of scholarships were available; practically all their pupils came from families who had managed to secure a comfortable economic situation. High tuitions were a major obstacle, for local schools were much cheaper, even at a time when secondary education in Europe was mostly subject to tuition fees (which in France were abolished only in 1932).[12] The situation in Kharbin was a little different because none of the émigrés could or would attend Chinese secondary schools. The three levels of instruction in Russian schools were available in Kharbin; although in the later years there was also an English school that attracted Russian exile children, for it offered instruction in a language and in subjects that seemed better adapted to employment, especially as the necessity of moving away from war-threatened Manchuria approached in the 1930s. The English-speaking world, whether in China proper or beyond the ocean, seemed to be the only alternative region of resettlement, and an English or American schooling was attractive to the refugees.

In addition to the secular open schools, there existed a small number of private boarding schools similar to the prerevolutionary corps of cadets for boys and institutes for girls. A few such establishments existed in Yugoslavia. As far as I have been able to determine from accessible sources, these schools had few pupils and did not play a notable role in Russia Abroad, except in Yugoslavia. Quite a few graduates of the cadet corps there entered Yugosalvia military and government service.

In view of the demographic, financial, and social difficulties faced by émigré secondary education, it is not surprising that the number of its schools and pupils declined sharply over the span of two decades. To my knowledge, on the eve of the Second World War in France there was only one Russian lycée left in Paris, while the Russian *gimnaziia* in Berlin and Czechoslovakia had closed. The number of Russian schools dwindled drastically in the Border States as a result of discrimination against national minorities. For those émigré families who wanted their children to preserve the Russian cultural heritage, other ways, outside of school, had to be found. The most obvious and relatively simple way was to have courses in Russian subjects offered on a voluntary basis within the framework of the local school system, but after regular hours. This was the case, for example, in France. Some secondary schools, mainly in Paris, offered Russian subjects on Thursdays—the day free from regular instruction since 1905 to enable pupils to receive religious instruction. Emigré teachers and scholars, specially licensed by the authorities, taught these courses, for example, P. E. Kovalevsky, T. Rostovtseff, and Madame T. Rafalsky.[13]

Finally, there was the option of private tutoring. Many a child of the emigration, especially in the larger centers of the diaspora, received instruction in Russian language, literature, and at times also history, from émigré scholars for whom such lessons supplemented the poor remuneration they received elsewhere. Sometimes the tutoring was done by a well-educated member of the family, or an acquaintance. In some instances, several families hired a teacher to tutor their children in Russian subjects. The success depended largely on the qualities of the tutor. Thus Professor N. Struve and the author of these pages remember gratefully the stimulating tutorials of K. V. Mochulskii, who was not only an outstanding literary scholar but an enthusiastic and gifted teacher who imparted information in such a way as to encourage moral and intellectual development as well. Of course, the qualities inherent in so much of Russian literature facilitated his task. Even the setting of his lessons had this effect: he lived in a small maid's room on top of an apartment building in a modest section of Paris (the 15th arrondissement). One walked up the last flight to a small room whose walls were lined with volumes of the classics of French, Italian, and Russian literature; beneath an icon corner were a couple of small paintings and several family photographs. It was clearly the abode of someone totally dedicated to the life of the mind, and serene in his faith.

More formally organized were the Russian courses for children in Prague which imparted Russian language and literature, and some history, geography, and religion. It was a cooperative venture, in which parents provided the teaching staff. In Paris, with the help of the YMCA, and under the auspices of the Russian Christian Student Movement, a sort of "Sunday school" was established at the movement's headquarters at 10 boulevard Montparnasse. Groups of émigré children, divided according to age, gathered to hear and read Russian literary works, listen to lectures, and carry on discussions on historical and literary topics; they also presented theatrical and musical events based on Russian cultural heritage.[14]

If preservation and transmission of Russian culture were the main goals of elementary and secondary émigré schools, preparation for future active service in a free Russia was the main mission of the institutions of higher learning created in Russia Abroad. Such a purpose, of course, also entailed ongoing creative effort to further Russian cultural and scholarly development—a development that in the early 1920s appeared to be badly distorted and aborted by the revolution and the Soviet regime. Emigré scholars felt it was incumbent on them to continue the surge of creativity of the Silver Age (ca. 1900–

1914) which had been brutally interrupted by war, revolution, and civil strife. The first impression of a Bolshevik-created cultural desert began to pale in the heyday of the New Economic Policy, when a renewal of intellectual life in a spirit of experimentation and innovation seemed to announce a cultural renaissance. In the thirties, when Stalin's regime rehabilitated Russia's historical past and extolled its classical cultural tradition, the émigrés felt vindicated in their original stance, and many became reconciled to what was happening in the Soviet Union in the domains of scholarship and science. But whatever happened in the Soviet Union, the émigré intellectuals set themselves another major assignment, namely, to help bridge the gap between past Russian tradition and modern Western achievements. After 1928 the task of bridging the gap had become clearly impossible for those in the Soviet Union; however, the effort, which had originated with Peter the Great, had seen some progress in the last decades of the imperial regime. Russia Abroad wanted, therefore, to keep the process going, in the hope of an eventual "feedback" to the homeland.

The institutions of higher learning, both teaching and research oriented, in Russia Abroad had a double goal: first, to prepare the younger generation professionally for an active career, either in a free Russia to which they would return, or in the country in which they had found asylum; second, to enable the mature exiled scholars, scientists, artists, and thinkers to pursue their creative work, further Russian culture, and acquaint the society of refuge with Russia's contributions in their respective fields. In the long run, the creative work of émigrés faded as a result of the natural attrition of their ranks, or of their becoming integrated into the professional life of the country where they had settled—this was especially true of those who eventually went to the United States, England, and France. The dream of preparing the young for their future activity in Russia also vanished gradually as the return to Russia became more and more problematic and younger émigré scholars and scientists joined the academic and scientific institutions of the host countries. Of course, in so doing they helped to acquaint the world with Russian accomplishments, and by their own contributions added a special, Russian element to the Western cultural and scholarly scene. This contribution almost exclusively touched the humanities—philosophy, literature, history—and the social sciences only marginally; and it had no particular meaning in the natural sciences.

Not surprisingly, it is in the fields of Russian literature, art, history, and perhaps philosophy, that the younger generation, partly trained in émigré institutions, have made a significant contribution, carrying on the work begun in Russia before the revolution, and serving to disseminate the work done in the Soviet Union in these fields. But their own original contributions and impact came only after World War II, so they will not be a part of our story here. (A partial list of that generation would include critic V. Weidlé, philosopher A. Koyré, art historians A. Grabar, and B. Lossky.) Only after 1945, primarily in the United States, did the remaining older representatives of the émigré scholarly community, and members of the younger generation, help develop what is now called Russian studies. Except for some attention paid to the analysis made by émigré economists of Soviet economic performances, for example in the works of V. Woytinski, A. Yugov, N. Yasny, and S. Prokopovich, between 1919 and 1939 émigré scholarship on Russia was hardly taken notice of by foreign colleagues. Indeed, as we shall see, some émigré scholars offered courses in academic institutions of host countries, but these ad hoc events had little impact on the latter's understanding of Russia (or of the Soviet Union, for that matter). This did not preclude, of course, occasional significant inputs through personal and informal connections.

As soon as scholars and scientists reached the West, and Kharbin, after their odyssey of exile, they set about to realize the two major goals we have mentioned, to educate the young and continue their own creative work. The initiative came from England where, under the chairmanship of medievalist Sir Paul Vinogradov, a committee of English well-wishers and émigré scholars (e.g., P. Miliukov) formed to collect funds to help academic refugees. It was the beginning of a far-flung enterprise that led to the restarting of an academic life in Russia Abroad. The English initiative was taken up in Paris where a number of Russian scholars and intellectuals resided, some of whom had been living there since before 1914 and had good contacts with French academic circles. The enterprise finally took concrete practical shape in Berlin. With the help of monies collected in England, and some further support from the YMCA, academics in exile there formed the Russian Academic Group. The group immediately established the Russian Institute to serve as framework for a series of courses intended to enable young refugees, some of whom had been prisoners of war, to resume their studies. The German authorities were well disposed to the enterprise, and thanks to the intervention of such personalities as Professor Otto Hoetzsch, well connected with the Foreign Office, the Russian Institute was given space and logistic support in close association with the University of Berlin and other institutions of higher learning (e.g., the Technische Hochschule). The Russian Institute's offerings were recognized as German university "credits" and its certificates were accepted for admission to German institutions.

At first, the formal, pedagogically oriented courses were well attended, but with the dispersal of many young émigrés to other cities, demand for such formal courses declined. On the other hand, more informal lectures directed at a larger audience continued to be popular and were a noteworthy element in the intellectual life of Russian Berlin. Expelled from Soviet Russia in 1922, N. Berdiaev and his philosopher friends settled first in Berlin, and with the help of the YMCA, they founded the Free Spiritual and Philosophical Academy. The academy offered lectures and discussions on religious and philosophic topics, and enjoyed popularity as long as Berdiaev remained in Berlin. As a matter of fact, both the Russian Academic Group and Berdiaev's Free Academy made it possible for some of the émigré scholars to remain active in Berlin, even after the closing of formal courses. Thanks to their connections they continued to serve as an institutional umbrella for lecture tours in Germany for F. Stepun, S. Frank, and others.[15]

The Russian Academic Group in Berlin also took the initiative in setting up a special series of publications, so that its members had a forum for the dissemination of their scholarly writings. The several volumes of the *Trudy* (Works) of the Academic Group, edited by A. I. Kaminka, who was also co-editor of the Russian-language daily *Rul'* (Rudder; the other editors were V. Nabokov and I. Gessen), constitute the repository of the ongoing scholarly creativity of Russian intellectuals in the first years of their exile. The Berlin Academic Group, too, was prominently active in organizing conferences of representatives of all the Russian Academic Groups that had sprung up in the major centers of the diaspora. The first meeting was held in Prague, in 1923; it not only enabled contact between those who had been separated by circumstances and geography for many years, but also created a regular and active network of communications and mutual cooperation in several projects. The first conference also affirmed publicly that the Russian academic world in exile constituted a single entity, intent on continuing its creative efforts in a foreign environment for the mutual benefit of Russia Abroad and the host countries. Furthermore, the Prague conference restated its members' responsibility toward the younger generation and committed them to helping members to finish their formal training and to further their intellectual development.[16]

The last-mentioned goal was implemented after President Thomas G. Masaryk and the Czech government founded the so-called Russkaia aktsiia (Russian action, or Action russe) in 1922. The government was not simply interested in helping refugee scholars—the chief goal was to prepare cadres for a future Russia cleansed of the Bolshevik bacillus—Masaryk, along with many others, believed that the Bolshevik government would fall in the near future. It was also meant as an expression of gratitude for previous Russian help in furthering the national aspirations of the Czechs, Slovaks, and other Slavs. Masaryk himself had been a student and junior faculty member in Russia before the war; the Czech legionnaires who had returned home (via Siberia) also had much sympathy and goodwill toward a people that had helped to free them from Austrian rule (and many Czech soldiers had married Russians, as did, for example, the influential conservative politician Karel Kramař). With the approval of his government, in particular that of Eduard Beneš, the foreign minister of the young republic, Masaryk drew on the funds of the Presidential Chancellery and secured additional American monies with the help of U.S. Ambassador Charles Crane (himself married to a Russian). Finally, the World Christian Student Movement and the YMCA also pledged their assistance, since it was a kind of enterprise that was very much in line with their priority of helping students and faculty to return to normal activity after the turmoil of world war, revolutions, and civil wars.

The Action russe provided for the creation of a Russian university, with faculties of law and humanities, as well as for a number of specialized institutes, of the Economic Cabinet to follow trends in the Soviet Union, and for the support of the already existing Seminarium Kondakovianum for the history of art and medieval studies. Lenin's expulsion of more than a hundred academic personalities, including such luminaries as the historian A. Kizevetter, the philosopher N. Lossky, the economist S. Prokopovich, the jurist P. Novgorodtsev, and the availability of others already abroad (N. Kondakov, V. Miakotin), staffed these institutions with some of the outstanding scholars of prerevolutionary Russia. In addition, the Czech government offered 1,000, later increased to about 2,000, fellowships to émigré students. While the scholarships were not very lavish, they did enable the students to live in modest dormitories and take meals in student cafeterias (*mensa*). The Russian faculty had full authority to select the recipients of fellowships, and they were also responsible for the supervision of the students' work and progress. Lastly, the Russian institutions were fully accredited by the Czech Ministry of Education: they certified the validity of prerevolutionary diplomas, and issued their own diplomas upon fulfillment of examinations and requirements identical to those of pre-1917 Russian universities (a representative of Charles University of Prague sat on each committee for examining and promoting students, as well as on those that made appointments to the faculties).

In Prague the Russian University was established with two faculties in law and humanities ("historico-philological faculty" in old Russian terminology), a Technical Institute, and a School of Agriculture. The latter two had a distinctly practical orientation and graduated engineers and agronomists who, it was hoped, would be useful in reconstructing Russia after the Bolsheviks, but who, as it turned out, had to find employment in Europe and overseas.* Thanks to the existence of the Russian University, Prague attracted numerous and frequent guest lecturers: from Berlin came the philosophers S. Frank and F. Stepun and the economist B. S. Izhboldin; P. Struve came from Belgrade; and P. Miliukov and others traveled from Paris. The students at the university and the Russian academic community in Prague were at the center of the most lively scholarly life and exchanges in Russia Abroad.

Since the Bolshevik regime did not collapse as expected, it is not remarkable that the number of students eventually dwindled, at least the number of those seeking degrees from the Russian University. This decline in enrollment converged with the increasingly difficult economic situation in the world, and in Czechoslovakia in particular. In addition came the growing political conflicts that were to undo the Czech Republic. Foreign institutions in the country suffered in the process and declined. For all intents and purposes, the active role of the Russian University in Prague came to an end a couple of years before the Munich agreement in 1938 sounded the death knell of independent Czechoslovakia. Until then, lectures continued to be attended by a number of outsiders, including some who came for advanced

---

* There was also a Ukrainian university in Prague. Thus the Czech capital had four universities: a Czech-, a German-, a Russian-, and a Ukrainian-speaking institution throughout the 1920s and early 1930s

training under such renowned scholars as Kizevetter, E. Shmurlo, V. A. Frantsev, V. Zen'kovskii, N. Lossky, and others, for example, in the mid-thirties, M. Karpovich of Harvard). A small number of graduates went on to have distinguished careers, especially in history, for example, G. Katkov, S. Pushkarev, G. Florovsky, and A. Fateev.

The university was not the only creation of the Action russe. The Seminarium Kondakovianum was founded by the outstanding art historian and byzantinist N. Kondakov. The Kondakov Seminar was primarily a research institute, although special seminars and discussion groups enabled advanced students to receive further training and gain experience in the fields of Russian icon painting, Byzantine art and history, and medieval Slavic studies. Until his emigration to the United States in 1928, G. Vernadsky was its active secretary; one of its graduates, also a prominent medieval historian, N. E. Andreyev became its last de facto director. However, the Kondakov Seminar achieved worldwide recognition through the publication of its scholarly series, *Archivum Kondakovianum*. In spite of a generous subsidy from the Czech government, the Kondakov Seminar and its publication did not have an easy time of it—its problems, well documented, were paradigmatic of all scholarly enterprises and publications. We learn from the correspondence of G. Vernadsky that the financing and distribution of the series required outside help from private individuals, and special arrangements for the dissemination of the publications. Despite these difficulties, and the years of conflict on the eve of and during World War II, the Kondakov Seminar left a significant mark on the development of Byzantine and medieval Slavic studies in the West. The careers of G. Ostrogorsky, H. Grégoire, G. Vernadsky, and N. Andreyev owe much to their association with the seminar.[17]

Another specialized research institute was the Economic Cabinet founded and directed by S. Prokopovich, the prominent economic statistician of pre-revolutionary times. After his expulsion from Russia in 1922, Prokopovich set up a research institute for the study of the Soviet Union, especially its economic and social development, in Berlin. The Action russe sponsored his move to Prague where he remained, until the eve of the Second World War. The Economic Cabinet closely followed events in Soviet Russia, collected all relevant printed materials, and periodically issued studies based on its materials and analyses. It was practically a one-man show, for budget problems did not allow Prokopovich to maintain his earlier collaborators. Moreover, he broke with some of them, for example A. Peshekhonov, when they joined the Change of Signposts movement and welcomed the October revolution and the Soviet regime. The publications of the Economic Cabinet, sometimes also undertaken on special assignment for other institutions, such as the Carnegie Endowment in the United States, as well as Prokopovich's own books, are still valuable for their information on economic and social trends in the Soviet Union in the 1920s and early 1930s.

There also existed in Prague a so-called People's University, with evening courses for those who could not attend a regular university. The lectures at this university, as well as its publications of a scholarly series encompassing all disciplines, provided a much needed forum for émigré scholars and scientists, and unabled them to make their research known to the academic world. The studies published in the series were often the continued or completed versions of work started in Russia before the revolution, so that they represented an organic extension of prerevolutionary Russian scientific life. The Russian Scientific Institute in Prague served as a kind of academy and umbrella organization for the lectures and publications on works in progress. The Scientific Institute was the main sponsor for visiting lecturers from other areas of the Russian diaspora. Prague was thus the academic and scholarly capital of Russia Abroad; until the early 1930s it was the core of the émigré university community. In the fields of Russian history, literature, religious and philosophic thought, and art the lectures (sometimes published in hectographic form, as was, for example, Shmurlo's course of Russian history) and publications of books and articles in the institutions' series, are still essential sources.[18]

Although Paris was the political, literary, and artistic "capital" of Russia Abroad, it was not its academic center. A major reason for this, aside from the direct support given by Masaryk which put the Action russe in Prague in the forefront, was the fact that the French university was powerfully entrenched and very conservative in its structure and approach. It did not easily make room for outsiders or new fields of study. Nor did the institutions beyond the university prove hospitable to émigré scholars, with the exception of the Institut Pasteur for biological sciences and the Musée de l'homme for anthropology; both maintained former Russian contacts and both had Russians as active regular members. Despite this unpropitious situation, however, a number of academic enterprises of the emigration flourished in Paris as well.

At the very beginning of the Russian diaspora in Paris, due to the initiative and energy of Jules Patouillet, former director of the Institut français de St. Petersbourg, and the Slavic scholars Paul Boyer and André Mazon, with the help of Eugène Petit in the French government, the Sorbonne agreed to have refugee scholars lecture on Russian literature and history. From the mid-1920s, Russian scholars occasionally offered special lecture courses at the University of Paris, particularly at the Faculty of Law where they taught Soviet law (B. Nolde, P. Tager), international law (B. Mirkine-Getsevich), and sociology and philosophy of law (G. Gurvitch), and contributed to the journals published under the auspices of that faculty. Some Russian émigré students took these courses, but to work toward a diploma they had to satisfy the regular French requirements. A number of émigré jurists were active in Paris as private consultants to individual clients or as expert witnesses in court cases, but only a very few became members of the French bar.

The Institut d'études slaves, founded by Ernest Denis in 1919 (officially recognized in March 1920 by the French government) as an independent, semipublic institution, also served as haven for a number of Russian émigré scholars. There they could give lecture courses, as well as participate in certain examinations. But in contrast to the situation in Prague, the academic activities of the Russians took place within the framework of the French academic establishment. The émigrés' work there was connected with Russia Abroad only in the sense that the people engaged in it were also denizens of "Russia beyond the boders." However, thanks to the involvement of émigrés in the Institut d'études slaves (and to a lesser degree in the École des langues orientales vivantes), a younger generation of French Slavists, some of Russian background, was trained to take over after 1945: this might have been the case of Michel and Raissa Gorlin had they not perished during the war, and it was indeed the case of B. Unbegaun, D. Stremoukhoff, D. Djaparidzé, to name only the better-known figures among those who came to full academic maturity on the eve of or during the Second World War.

Although Paris did not have a regular Russian university along the lines of the university in Prague, it acquired the reputation for the study and teaching of religious subjects when the St. Serge Theological Institute and Seminary was founded in 1925. We will discuss this institution in some detail in the chapter on religion and church. In addition, as did Prague, Paris had a People's or Free University where lectures and courses were given in the evening (or weekends) on a variety of academic and practical subjects to satisfy the hunger for knowledge, study, and intellectual activity of the many exiles whose days were spent earning a living and raising a family. The People's University gave refugee scholars the opportunity to communicate the results of their studies and research to a larger public. It also made special efforts to reach the younger generation, including adolescents, for whom special lectures were held on Thursdays (a scholar-free day in prewar France) and Saturdays. These lectures dealt primarily with history and literature, although there were also illustrated talks on natural history, geography, and art. In this way the People's University in Paris complemented the formal, school-connected efforts to preserve and transmit to the younger generation the traditions and achievements of Russian culture. Its work was further supplemented by the Technological Institute's curriculum by correspondence. A number of technicians and practical engineers graduated in this way and obtained more remunerative positions in the provinces as well as abroad.[19]

In Belgrade, Sofia, and Riga the situation resembled that of Paris and Berlin in the very first years of the emigration. Russian Scientific Institutes (and Academic Groups) brought together émigré scholars and scientists and gave them the opportunity to lecture on their subjects and their work in progress. Occasionally, émigré scholars were asked to give courses at local universities, especialy if they could do so in the native language (e.g., P. Bitsilli in Sofia, F. Taranovsky in Belgrade). In Belgrade, the Scientific Institute also published a journal with articles by members of the local scholarly community, as well as by those living in other centers. The number of Russian refugees in Yugoslavia was quite large, and theirs was a community of close-knit units, but on the whole they were not as intellectually inclined as elsewhere. A well-developed network of schools remained quite active throughout the entire period, but there was no comparable effort at the university level. The outside lecturers invited by the Scientific Institute invariably remarked on the "provincialism" and narrowness of émigré interests in Yugoslavia— perhaps this explains why they were so readily absorbed into the service of the Yugoslav establishment. Another reason partly lay in the makeup of this émigré community (military, Cossacks) and its strong pro-monarchist and conservative, if not outright reactionary, political preferences. Such attitudes repelled most émigré academics who were of mostly liberal and moderate socialist persuasions. The intellectual isolation of P. Struve in Belgrade provides a telling illustration: even though he became a conservative, moderate monarchist, and a committed churchman, the émigré community in Yugoslavia could not forgive his earlier associations with Marxism and the Kadet part or his role in Osvobozhdenie, the leading opposition to the ancien regime on the eve of the revolution of 1905.[20]

For Riga—and this was true of Sofia and Warsaw as well—we have evidence of only very occasional lectures by Russian émigrés at the university. Small informal groups of academics residing there tried, as often as possible, to invite speakers from other centers of the diaspora to stimulate the cultural life of these "backwaters." But, as we noted earlier, the presence of a Russian national minority did not help in this respect; on the contrary, the nationalist reaction of the early 1930s rendered scholarly efforts even more difficult. On the other hand, the local universities of these cities appointed émigré scholars to chairs for which natives were unavailable.

The last center of émigré higher education we should mention was in geographically isolated Kharbin. Immediately after the revolution and the influx of exiles to this Manchurian city, three institutions of higher learning and education arose. All three were concerned with meeting the practical demands of the administration of the Eastern Chinese Railway; they also wanted to be of use to the Chinese authorities and to their own younger generation. In the long run these goals were not reached, for a Sino-Soviet accord on the railway and then the Japanese invasion undermined the émigré community of Kharbin completely.

The three institutions of higher learning were established with some modest help from the YMCA. The Commercial Institute was a business school that focused on problems related to the railway and to the Chinese economy. The Technological Institute prepared personnel to administer and operate the railway and to assist Chinese elsewhere. The Faculty of Law taught history, economics, sociology, jurisprudence, and Russian and Chinese law. All three institutions had Chinese as well as Russian students; the language of instruction was primarily Russian and secondarily English. The Commercial Institute and the Technological Institute played a limited role, for the expert personnel they trained could not apply their knowledge after the Japanese invaded, although some of their Chinese graduates seem to have been active in China later.

The Faculty of Law trained not only Russians but Chinese as well. Its curriculum was strictly academic and paralleled the prerevolutionary programs of law schools in Russia, except that there were also courses in Chinese law and on economic problems of direct interest to residents of Manchuria. The Kharbin legal institution contributed to the intellectual life of Russia Abroad despite its isolation because it prepared young Russian émigrés to receive advanced education that many completed later elsewhere, primarily in the United States; they also disseminated the scholarly work of its faculty through a publication that circulated in the diaspora. The high quality of the contributions made them an indispensable research tool and they are of value to this day.[21] In addition to the journal, the Kharbin professors and their advanced students also contributed articles to foreign-language journals (mainly in English) and wrote monographs. The Law Faculty's location in the Far East prompted members of the faculty to study problems dealing with China, Mongolia, and Manchuria, both in their domestic and international dimensions. Thus Professors G. Guins and V. Riasanovsky made significant contributions in English to the fields of international relations, political science, and Mongol law. The accessible documentation does not throw much light on the numbers and nature of the student body at the Faculty of Law, or on its members' subsequent careers. Guins and Riasanovsky came to the United States where they continued to make marks in their field, while N. Ustrialov returned in 1934 to Russia where he disappeared during the purges.

Learning and study require the support of libraries. In the West, before 1939, only a few émigré colonies had extensive library resources dealing with Russia and its problems. The most extensive holdings were in the United States (Library of Congress, Widener Library at Harvard, Hoover Institution, Columbia University, New York Public Library), but they were practically inaccessible to scholars in Russia Abroad. Europe was much poorer in this respect than might be expected. The British Museum, the Bibliothèque nationale in Paris (and in the 1920s the Bibliothèque de documentation contemporaine), the university library in Helsinki, and the Prussian and Bavarian state libraries (in Berlin and Munich, respectively) were the only ones with important scholarly resources in Russian fields. They were accessible only with permissions that most émigrés could not or would not take the trouble to obtain; and for both financial and legal reasons, very few could travel to them. It should be added that throughout the 1920s and 1930s European countries made little effort to invest in the acquisition of materials from and about Russia. Of course, other academic institutions had useful holdings of Russian-related materials, but as a rule they were closed academic institutes, widely dispersed, and they acquired materials only for the direct didactic and research purposes of their own faculties and student bodies. Among them we may mention the libraries of the Institut d'études slaves and the Ecole des langues orientales vivantes in Paris; in Germany there were the so-called seminar or institute libraries of the Osteuropa institutes in Breslau and Königsberg. In short, the situation was quite unsatisfactory from a scholarly point of view, and even less so for the average émigré student. In practice, no library that was easily accessible had worthwhile Russian-related materials.

Russia Abroad proceeded to meet its needs in this respect on its own. Fortunately, some steps had been taken earlier, in prerevolutionary times, by exiles and visitors from Imperial Russia. Foremost was the Tourgueneff Library in Paris. Established in 1875 under the aegis of Ivan Turgenev, it had served as a rallying point for all Russians who came to live in France for personal, artistic, scholarly, or political reasons. It was administered by a committee chosen by the readers and a largely voluntary staff; it lent books for a small fee, and carried a fairly complete selection of the most widely read periodicals and literature. New acquisitions came from donations and modest purchases. The library served the emigration of the 1920s and 1930s as well. The influx of a large Russian population, with many outstanding creative personalities, permitted the expansion of the library and of its services. Writers and scholars abroad donated their works, while the library subscribed to as many émigré serial publications as its funds permitted. It received help from the former Russian embassy and the municipal authorities of Paris, but essentially it was a self-sustaining operation, relying on the abnegation and commitment of its staff and governing committee. It was not only the core of Russian intellectual life in Paris, it also had a wide audience in the provinces to whom books were lent by mail. A major cultural institution, it also participated actively in all the events and celebrations of Russia Abroad in Paris and France. The Germans hauled away the collection during the Occupation; some of its books have surfaced in second-hand shops or auctions. The library was restored on a more modest scale after the war in new quarters provided by the City of Paris.[22]

Other cities of Europe had a number of reading rooms, and some bookstores served as reading rooms and lending libraries. But they were widely scattered and their collections were quite limited, so that they did not play the unifying role of the Tourgueneff Library. Some of these reading rooms had been set up before 1914 by groups of exiled political figures or by students. This was, for example, the case of the Russian library in Geneva, much frequented by socialist émigrés of all stripes. Heidelberg University had a Russian reading room (now merged into the library of the Slavic Institute) founded by and for Russian students attending the university. The wave of refugees after 1919 gave rise to similar reading rooms and small lending libraries throughout the Russian diaspora, from London (the Pushkin circle) to Warsaw, Sofia, Riga, and Kharbin.

A new library was set up in Prague in conjunction with the Action russe. The decision was made to collect there all the materials—published and unpublished—relating to the Russian revolution, broadly defined. Thus arose the Russian Historical Archive and Library (Russkii zagranichnyi istoricheskii arkhiv), under the direction of a Czech librarian, Jan Slavik, and assisted by Russians. It was administered by a council of prominent Czech and Russian scholars, and financed by the Czech Ministry of Foreign Affairs. The library and archive had a network of "agents" in the centers of the Russian diaspora whose task was to locate, identify, assess, and acquire materials that could be of interest to the institution which was viewed as a "deposit library" for Russia Abroad, similar to the old deposit libraries of the Empire.[23] The archive appealed to the exiles and émigré institutions to turn over their papers and correspondence. At the same time it encouraged former participants in historical events to write their memoirs and deposit them with the archive. By 1939 the library and archive constituted the most extensive and valuable depositories of materials related to Russia's immediate past.[24] An effort to launch a publication series of these materials did not get off the ground, although the *Arkhiv russkoi revoliutsii,* based in Berlin and edited by I. Gessen, worked in close contact with the Russian Historical Archive and Library in Prague. Both library and archive survived World War II—the Germans did not take them over. Nor did the Red Army at first display any interest in them. President Beneš gave the archive to the Soviet Union as a gift in gratitude for its part in the liberation of Czechoslovakia. After a period of total neglect, during which much was probably lost or damaged beyond recovery, the remainder of the library's holdings were merged with the National University Library in Prague.[25]

Our brief account helps explain two major features of cultural life of Russia Abroad. It reveals, first, the great difficulties that émigré scholars faced in carrying on their work in the historical and humanistic disciplines as they related to Russia. Second, and more important, we can account for the large number of publications, periodicals, and books produced by the emigration. The population of Russia Abroad was poor and scattered, but it demanded access to reading matter. Such material was not adequately provided by existing libraries and reading rooms. Many small lending libraries, as well as private individuals, represented a market for whatever was published, regardless of where it was published; it was only a matter of finding out what was available and paying postage. The paucity of Russian materials in local libraries made it necessary to reprint or republish textbooks and classical authors. It is not remarkable that many émigré publishing houses printed selected or complete works of Russia's favorite authors. Conversely, however, these circumstances made it more difficult for new works, especially by younger authors, to find publishers.

One last aspect of the educational scene of Russia Abroad deserves brief mention. Some émigré scholars and scientists were able to carry on their work in association with institutions of the countries of refuge. This was possible for those who had acquired a worldwide reputation before going into exile and who could settle near such scholarly or scientific establishments. At times it was also possible for the ambitious, outstanding, and well-connected scholar of the younger generation to join an official institution in the host country, once his or her unusual qualities and contributions had been demonstrated. In the sciences this occurred readily in the Institut Pasteur, which had a long-

standing tradition of close ties with Russian scientists going back to I. Mech-
nikov. In Germany, several émigrés became adjuncts to Osteuropa institutes.
We have noted the appointment of exile scholars to university posts in the
Border States. The Université libre de Bruxelles took on Professor Alexander
Eck, the medieval historian, the University of Vienna invited N. Trubetskoi
to a chair in Slavic philology. In France outstanding younger scholars—e.g.,
A. Koyré, G. Gurvitch, and N. Shchupak—found employment within the
complicated framework of the Ecole des hautes études pratiques, as well as
such institutions as the Musée de l'homme (e.g., E. Schreider, B. Vildé,
A. Levitsky). Members of the faculty of the Russian University in Prague
were sometimes asked to offer courses at Charles University (e.g., Frantsev,
A. Florovskij). It should be stressed, however, that these were all exceptional
instances. There was no "regular" way of gaining full membership or even
part-time ties in the faculty of the state universities in most countries of
Western and Central Europe (and there were practically no private academies
except for church-connected ones). Most Russian scholars remained outside
the official intellectual and academic life of the host country, so that their activities were almost entirely directed to the needs of Russia Abroad.

Students are an integral component of academic life, of course. Unfortunately, it is impossible to generalize, as so much is still unknown about the
émigré students' daily life, their attitudes toward their studies and toward the
goals that émigré education held out for them. Pupils in the lower grades, by
and large, shared their families' problems of practical and cultural survival.
But it is impossible to say whether, on the average, they were better or worse
off than their counterparts in prerevolutionary Russia, or their contemporaries
in the Soviet Union and the host countries. To judge from personal, and of
necessity partial, observation and occasional statements found in the émigré
press, the main dilemma for youngsters was the ambivalence that arose over
continuing in a Russian school and remaining outsiders in the host society,
or integrating and adapting. How a child would resolve the conflict depended
on the parents' tact and their commitment to their Russian heritage. For children from intellectual families who enjoyed a positive home atmosphere (even
if destitute) with a strong commitment to Russian culture, and an understanding of their child's predicament, adjustments were worked out quite
easily. It seems that many children in Czechoslovakia, Germany, and France
managed to retain the Russian language and loyalty to its cultural heritage
while integrating into the host milieu. This was as true of pupils of Russian
primary and secondary schools as of those who took tutorials or special classes
in Russian subjects. In other instances, as reported in the press, the strain was
too great and the children rebelled—particularly when there was ambivalence
about the issue in the home, and when material circumstances were so penurious as to leave no energy for such concerns. In these cases, the children
strove with all their might to escape from such circumstances and to seek a
better life, which meant total assimilation.

For those studying in institutions of higher education, the problems were different. Of course, economic hardship and social and cultural isolation were factors. But once the hope of going back to Russia and being useful there had evaporated by the end of the twenties, most of émigré students concentrated on acquiring professional skills, finding employment, and integrating into the host society. Of course, our sources report only on those who were successful; probably, too, in overcoming their underprivileged condition émigré students made more of an effort to develop to the maximum all the talents they possessed.

From the very beginnings of émigré educational endeavors, students on the secondary and higher levels felt the need to organize. By cooperating they would not only help each other materially and intellectually, but also would create their own framework for any future role they could play in the home-land. With the encouragement of representatives of the World Christian Student Movement, they formed in 1922 the Union of Russian Emigré Students, (ORES—Ob'edinenie russkikh emigrantskikh studentov), with head-quarters in Prague. The union organized international conferences to exchange information and to discuss common problems, and to find ways of improving their status and material conditions so as to continue their studies. The union published journals with reports on student living conditions in the diaspora, on the émigrés' moral and intellectual problems, and other issues. Unfortunately, the organization could not maintain its unity: the question of political allegiances and plans for the political future of a "free" Russia split the partisans of the former White Army officers and those who had remained monarchists from the democratic, socialist, or nonpolitical intellectuals. In short time the organization collapsed. But on the basis of a religious commitment and eschewing political discord, another student organization, the Russian Christian Student Movement proved successful throughout World War II and later. It will be dealt with at some length in Chapter 6.[26]

Several organizations aided students, collecting and distributing funds for fellowships and scholarships, working closely with the Zemgor or the Association d'aide aux étudiants émigrés russes to help Russian students directed by M. M. Fedorov in Paris. They were successful in securing government and philanthropic funds, and organizing events to raise money. One fund-raising event was the yearly St. Tatiana Day, the traditional university feast in Russia; the occasion of a ball, concert, and tombolas at which money was collected from the guests, as had been the practice in Imperial Russia. The dispersal, isolation (often without any family ties), and poverty of the émigré students precluded any corporate life; for example, in Latvia attempts to create fraternities along the lines of the *Verbindungen* that existed among German-speaking students at the university of Dorpat (Iur'ev, Tallinn) in prerevolutionary days ended in failure.

In conclusion, the task of preserving Russian culture and transmitting it to the younger generation was fulfilled with remarkable success. To be sure, not all children remained faithful to Russia's pre-1917 traditions; the old cultural ties did loosen and integration into host societies did occur with ever-increasing frequency. Yet, the majority, it would seem, did retain essential elements of their parents' heritage: language, knowledge and love of Russian literature and history, and most important, a sense of loyalty or even identification with Russia itself. Many children of émigrés raised in "Russia beyond the borders" actively participate today in the ongoing life of Russian culture; indeed, their work enjoys acceptance in the Soviet Union. Nevertheless it should not be forgotten that the high mortality and low birth rates of the émigrés, along with the dramatic upheavals of the late thirties and early forties, curtailed the émigré educational establishment. The children of Russia Abroad who were born in the 1930s were fully integrated into the countries of asylum.

4

The Gutenberg Galaxy:
Publishing in Alien Lands

Any modern educational establishment and culture need printed literature—mainly books; and so do the educational and cultural networks. In Russia Abroad this need was particularly great, since émigré schools were arising virtually ex nihilo and lacked all material necessities. Moreover, beyond the needs of its schools, Russia Abroad had to shape itself, keep together its widely scattered denizens, assert and develop its identity. The printed word—newspapers, journals, books—was obviously the most effective means to this end. Nothing else would do, since the émigré groups scattered over the globe were too small and too poor to afford a radio station (which would not have had a very wide range at the time and for which government licenses were needed). Personal contacts were difficult, since they meant crossing state boundaries. We have already seen the problems of obtaining passports and visas. And so the major tasks of bestowing a sense of unity and coherence to Russia Abroad fell to publishing. And quite obviously, the possibility of printing and disseminating the Russian word enabled the émigrés to continue to create and maintain their intellectual and cultural life.

It is difficult to describe and to give a full history of the publishing activities of the Russian diaspora in the twenties and thirties as we lack much essential documentation. Most archives of Russian publishing houses abroad have disappeared—largely because in so many cases they had a very brief existence. In some instances we know that the archives were confiscated by Occupation authorities and most likely lost in the turmoil of the Second World War. For example, the papers of the successful and long-lived publishing house of Petropolis in Berlin (1923–1938) were hauled away by the Gestapo—they were not found again.[1] It is well-nigh impossible to find answers to such basic questions as the number of titles, print runs, and the patterns of sales and distribution. To complicate the picture, many émigré publishers moved from one city or country to another (for example, Petropolis moved from Berlin to Brussels), used another publisher's imprints, or omitted the place of publication while printing in another country.[2]

Since the late eighteenth century, Russia's most important creative cultural effort had been in the realm of the word. Literature, for a number of reasons, had served as the major vehicle for the cultural and intellectual life in prerevolutionary Russia. Even for the radicals and revolutionaries, the printing press had been the favored, as well as the most effective instrument, in preparing for revolution and the overthrow of the old regime. Not surprisingly, too, the creative explosion of the Silver Age (despite the great role played by arts and music) had been marked by an exponential increase in the number of publishers, print runs, titles, and readers of books and journals. Groups, movements, and individuals who made artistic or ideological statements had specific publishers and a stock of publications in serial or book form. Despite material hardships and social instability, the flood of printed matter did not subside during the early stages of the revolution and during the civil war. On the contrary, the new aims of propaganda, reeducation, and aesthetic experimentation made possible by the political upheaval could not have been achieved without printing presses.

It is little wonder, then, that the exiles beyond Russia's borders turned to Gutenberg's invention to accomplish the task they had set themselves by emigrating—to preserve and carry on the culture of their homeland in the hope of its use in a Russia freed from Bolshevism. There was no lack of potential authors, but given émigré circumstances and the world's economic condition, it was no small challenge to set up a publishing house and find a printer. It was even more difficult to organize the distribution to widely scattered and penurious customers. Prices had to be kept as low as possible; no easy task, for print runs were small and distribution complicated and costly. Advertisements were not very effective and played a subordinate role, even in newspapers. The best means of publicity for books were reviews in journals and newspapers, but this method encouraged in-group networks, mutual admiration postures, envy, and personal rivalries. The major handicap to an efficient distribution was the fact that bookshops could not stock many copies of books or journals, and the owners preferred to carry only those titles they were sure to sell. Unsold copies were returned to the publisher at additional mailing costs for the press. Attempts to create a publishers' syndicate to coordinate distribution failed for personal, political, as well as purely business reasons.[3] Nor was it easy to satisfy the great variety of tastes, levels of education and culture, and ideological—both political and aesthetic—preferences, for in good Russian intelligentsia tradition, each group belonged to separate, self-contained circles (*kruzhki*) not readily permeable to other trends and values. Every particular orientation represented only a limited market, and even titles of more general interest, like the classics brought out by several small houses, were competing for a restricted circle of readers and bookstores. These circumstances explain the failure of ambitious plans for large-scale publication of textbooks or collections of classical authors. At the beginning of the emigration, in the early 1920s, at the time of the onset of the New Economic Policy, there were hopes that some of the publications of Russia Abroad would be distributed in Soviet Russia too. The enterprising publisher Z. I. Grzebin in Berlin, with the help of Maxim Gorky, negotiated for the marketing of his reprints of Russian classical authors and selected new books (mainly of technical nature) inside the Bolshevik realm. The agreement did not work out, for the Soviet authorities would not relax their censorship restrictions and made it impossible to import large quantities of books printed abroad.[4]

The émigrés reproduced the basic pattern of publishing that had existed in prerevolutionary Russia, carrying on the innovations of the Silver Age. Pre-1917 Russia had relied more heavily on serial publications than on books for the transmittal of its cultural creations. This was also to be true of the emigration; the periodicals reflected the varied and splintered character, for every ideological and aesthetic group aimed at having its own voice. Moreover, as exile lasted beyond the brief period first expected, the younger writers increasingly resented what they perceived as the domination of the publishing media by the older generation. The young generation found it difficult to break into the establishment, which feared that unproven innovations might further reduce their all-too-limited market. Nor were the established writers of the older generation about to yield their hard-won foundation of material survival. Necessity thus forced the younger writers, thinkers, and critics to publish in their own journals or pamphlets. But financial support for these ventures was slim, and the revenue from the publications was hardly sufficient to cover costs. As a result, these efforts were short-lived and most reached only a small circle of "insiders." This explains why these publications are so hard to find; many are no longer available anywhere, and we only know of them from remarks or comments of contemporaries or from reviews in other publications. Lastly, émigré publishing suffered from rising tariffs and censorship imposed by nationalistic, authoritarian governments. It became increasingly difficult to send publications across borders, especially if they contained critical or unfavorable remarks about the country to which they were sent. By the end of the 1930s many émigré books and journals circulated only in the country where they appeared. Their reach, as well as their chances of survival, were quite small.

The inflation in Germany made Berlin the first and most active center of émigré publishing between 1920 and 1923. A further factor in favor of the German capital was the presence of a large number of Russian refugees with a professional and intellectual background, who provided both a ready pool of authors and a market for the many publishing houses. Finally, since Germany's flirtation with the Bolshevik government, Berlin had the best contacts with Soviet Russia; with the start of the New Economic Policy, Soviet citizens who could obtain permission to travel came to Berlin. Naturally, old contacts between German and Russian intellectual circles were resumed. The border between Russia Abroad and the Soviet homeland was not as delineated or as restricted in Germany, a situation that stimulated lively intellectual exchanges. That interchange was registered by the printing presses.

The curiosity of exiles about everything going on in the home country was more readily satisfied in Berlin than in any other center of the Russian diaspora. Berlin transmitted information about authors and publications both in Soviet Russia and in Russia Abroad. A former law professor, A. S. Iashchenko, created the journal *Russkaia kniga* (the Russian Book), later titled *Novaia russkaia kniga* (The New Russian Book) for that very purpose. His journal provided the most comprehensive, though by no means complete, survey of publications and authors in the diaspora (and selectively for the civil war years in Soviet Russia as well). Iashchenko's publications were instrumental in establishing contacts and exchanges between the émigré authors, and served as a first forum for the literary endeavors of Russia Abroad. A similar role in informing the émigrés about what was going on in Bolshevik Russia was played by the Socialist Revolutionary publication *Svobodnaia Rossiia* (Free Russia) in Prague; its rubric "novosti literatury" (literary news) summarized the major happenings in the field of literature for Russia Abroad.[5]

This informational role had particular significance as long as Soviet Russia was not sealed off from Russia Abroad. Indeed, thanks to Berlin's role as a center of Russian publishing, upon conclusion of the civil war many Soviet writers traveled abroad—a few stayed for good. Others made temporary visits, for example L. Pasternak, M. Gershenzon, A. Tolstoi, and I. Erenburg. Those who never returned to Russia are too numerous to be listed, especially if we include those who were expelled from Soviet Russia in 1922.[6] A. Remizov, V. Khodasevich, N. Berberova, M. Tsvetaeva were among the best-known littérateurs who visited Berlin. In the early 1920s V. Mayakovsky, S. Esenin, A. Belyi, and M. Gorky (who stayed abroad until the late 1920s) also came through Berlin. In this way, a modernistic strain was infused into the intellectual climate of the emigration. The modernistic impact was reinforced by painters, musicians, and dramatic artists who pursued the experimental aspects of contemporary Russian art and who visited Berlin. The first exhibition of contemporary Russian art was held in 1922. A number of galleries and artistic circles arose around that event.[7] This point about modernism is significant because, by and large, the writers in emigration belonged to the older naturalist and symbolist schools—I. Bunin and A. Kuprin to the former and Z. Hippius and D. Merezhkovsky to the latter—while the established intellectuals in exile, although friendly to the new trends in philosophy and religion, tended to be conservative in their aesthetics and viewed with much skepticism the modernistic experiments in Russia on the eve of and after 1917. True, this was not so much the case in poetry—symbolism, and its successor acmeism, received full *droit de cité* in Russia Abroad. Emigré poetry proved more innovative and experimental than émigré prose. The younger poets in exile were interested in the new movements of the twenties and eagerly absorbed what the writers, and especially the poets, coming from Bolshevik Russia had to teach them. In this way Berlin helped to make Russian modernism known in the outside world. This not only affected cultural life in Russia Abroad, but even more striking, it enabled modernism to survive in Soviet Russia by permitting its writers and artists to escape, be it only temporarily, from the constraints and hardships of Soviet life in the early 1920s.

Berlin thus could offer the greatest variety of publishing activities: variety of contents, as well as diversity of form—such as layout, typography, illustrations—which gave full expression to the innovative features of the Silver Age. The variety, however, receded quite notably when economic changes, the stabilization of the mark and resulting higher prices, forced most intellectuals, and their publishing outlets, to leave Berlin. Academics resettled in Prague, while most creative writers, artists, philosophers went to Paris; other intellectuals ended up in Belgrade and Riga. After about 1925, Paris became the focus of publishing for the rest of the emigration period, although Riga was a center for republishing popular and classical writers, and Prague was the headquarters of scientific and scholarly publications under the sponsorship of the Russian academic institutions there.

The extent and variety of Russian publishing in Berlin may be gauged by the fact that the attempt to identify and chronicle the émigré output there from 1918 to 1928 yielded a list of 188 enterprises. Many had but an ephemeral existence, and many had only a few titles to their credit. Yet the number is quite extraordinary and had no counterpart in any émigré center. The same volume that contains these data also contains an article that conveys a graphic idea of the imaginativeness and high artistic level of the Russian publishers in Berlin, not duplicated or matched anywhere else.[8] I. M. Iliazd-Zdanevich, who turned from writing to typographical creativity, set the tone for much avant-garde publishing in Paris, although his graphic production involved primarily works by non-Russians.

It is not easy to sort out the émigré publishers on the basis of the type of material they brought out. A specific focus or specialization would have been difficult to maintain over a period of time under conditions of emigration. Most presses published primarily two major categories of books: reprints of Russian classical writers and publications of new works by well-established émigré writers. Among the latter, popular writers such as Vas. Iv. Nemirovich-Danchenko (brother of the stage director), A. Amfiteatrov, and M. Aldanov, author of historical fiction, readily found publishers, and their works enjoyed relatively large print runs. The financial considerations suggested earlier also account for the fact that no writer in Russia Abroad had one particular publisher, and no publisher had an exclusive list of authors. Writers published with any publisher; often they gave the same book to several publishers at different times, for different geographic markets.[9] Attempts to bring about greater order and economic fairness for both publishers and authors by concerted action were failures: there was a great deal of piracy—works published in one journal or paper would be reprinted without payment elsewhere, or the same titles might be brought out by different publishers. The effort by an American to secure the authors' rights by forcing copyright agreements on all parties was unsuccessful.[10] Associations of publishers did not fare any better, since cutthroat competition for the few available channels of distribution precluded any effective arrangement.

One publishing house, however, was quite different. The YMCA established and subsidized the YMCA Press (still flourishing in Paris). For a while it operated under the name Editeurs réunis. It was originally founded by YMCA representatives in Europe to provide textbooks and (mainly religious) reading matter for prisoners of war. With the emergence of Russia Abroad came a realization of the émigrés' craving for reading material. At first, the YMCA concentrated on technical literature and began a vast program of textbook publication; but, too grandly conceived and poorly administered, this program failed. Reprinting old textbooks, or commissioning translations of foreign ones, was not feasible, for the émigrés did not buy that kind of literature. Even the popular Göschen series of scientific books for the layman in Russian did not prove successful; they petered out in the 1920s when expectations of admission of these publications into Soviet Russia proved a naive mirage. In 1925 the YMCA moved its operations to Paris, and from then on it was the primary publisher of books dealing with philosophy and religion, and the St. Serge Institute journal *Pravoslavnaia mysl'* (Orthodox Thought) and Berdiaev's Spiritual Philosophical Academy journal *Put'* (The Way). In addition, the YMCA Press published some fiction and general interest books, including occasional translations.[11] Its longevity, and the financial support of the YMCA, enabled the press to become the main source of high-quality intellectual fare for Russia Abroad throughout our period (a function that the YMCA Press is fulfilling even today, but on a different financial basis and with a more openly religious orientation). The press was in a position to remunerate its authors, especially for articles contributed to the journals, and thus it indirectly supported quite a few members of the émigré intelligentsia.

As mentioned, publication of textbooks or manuals that could be useful for the self-education or further training of prisoners of war had been the original stimulus for the publishing activities of the YMCA, and this applied to some other émigré presses, too. All Russian educational institutions abroad, especially schools, needed textbooks, since they were not available abroad and could no longer be imported from Russia. At first it seemed that this need would be a promising field for publishers. The YMCA, for example, had reprinted a number of such texts but was left with a large unsold stock that encumbered its finances for several years. The reasons for this venture's failure were not surprising, in retrospect: old textbooks could not satisfy the postwar generation of pupils; they were hopelessly out of date, for they did not take into account the scientific and technical innovations, discoveries, and changes that arose during and after World War I. Translations of the new textbooks published in the West were expensive and time-consuming; the relatively small market hardly made such effort and investment worthwhile. The market was small indeed, for the number of émigré children who attended Russian schools beyond the elementary level, was not very large. Moreover, the schools' curricula had become more varied than they had been in Imperial Russia, as they had to incorporate the requirements of each host country, and it was difficult to find or write a textbook fitted for use in all émigré schools. Since the émigrés were poor, textbooks had to be distributed virtually free, leaving the publisher with little expectation of profit.

At one point there was also hope that textbooks and manuals to be used in correspondence courses might prove both useful and profitable. The émigré publicist S. Tsion suggested a scheme for the publication of such a series to the YMCA and other presses, but nothing came of it, probably because the plan was too broad and speculative.[12] Indeed, this was the wrong approach, since the Russian refugees who wanted to acquire technical skills and new knowledge to bring their professional qualifications up to date, would be better off using the manuals in the language of the country where they expected to be employed. For example, the evening and correspondence school for engineers and technicians, mentioned in the previous chapter, set up in Paris under the auspices of the YMCA, relied on foreign literature that was more up to date than anything that could be produced in Russia Abroad.

A few publishers did put out textbooks for use in Russian schools, but this did not represent a significant share of émigré publications, although those that could be adopted for schools for Russian minorities in the Border States had a wider market. The reissue of some old Russian history textbooks (for example, S. Platonov's high-school history course) and literature was quite helpful to pupils in secondary schools, and these books were reprinted as far afield as Buenos Aires. The Pochaev Monastery specialized in reprinting and publishing little pamphlets (or broadsheets) with religious and moral themes which were widely disseminated in church schools and parishes. But these efforts were of importance only in the first decade of the emigration: in general, the exile publications were primarily belles lettres and a fair, though limited, number of monographic studies on historical, literary, or philosophic topics.

Among the first concerns of émigré publishers was to republish the works of Russia's classical authors—Pushkin, Gogol, Tolstoi, Dostoevsky, Chekhov—books that the exiles thirsted to reread. Petropolis and Slovo brought out multi-volume sets of selected works of these authors. These were not scholarly editions; they were simply handy and pleasantly produced books, mostly in the old orthography. On the occasion of an author's anniversary, special editions would appear, as, for example, was done for the centenary of Tolstoi's birth in 1928, or for the 1937 centennial celebration of Pushkin's death. Several presses of various countries brought out new Pushkin editions—the most beautiful was a leather-bound selection on bible paper, published in Paris. A special edition of *Evgenii Onegin* was published by Petropolis under the editorship of V. Khodasevich, illustrated by M. Dobuzshinskii. It was not until the thirties that Soviet publications of the classics became attractive enough and easily available to compete with the production of Russia Abroad. Although the Soviet books were much cheaper, many émigrés refused to buy (or even read) them, because they were in the new orthography and set the word *God* in lower case.

Second in importance were books of fiction by émigré authors. The most popular works were by Nemirovich-Danchenko, Amfiteatrov, Aldanov, and P. Krasnov. Most of these first appeared in partial serialization in journals. New works by I. Bunin, D. Merezhkovsky, A. Remizov, B. Zaitsev, A. Kuprin, and I. Shmelev always found a modest, market. Younger writers had greater difficulty in getting their books published. This was the case of V. Sirin (Nabokov), G. Gazdanov, and N. Berberova, to name only the most success-ful and slightly older ones. More frequently these works appeared only in journals. Still younger authors, who started to write in the mid-1930s, V. Yanovsky, Iu. Fel'sen, V. Varshavskii, were at a still greater disadvantage, in part because of their innovative, modernistic style and themes. The average reader in Russia Abroad was too exhausted by the struggle for daily bread to be an avid reader, let alone an adventurous reader. He preferred light novels or familiar classical and contemporary authors. As the critic-poet G. Ivanov observed, first of all a writer needs readers, and younger authors did not readily find them; it put a damper on the creative energies of the literary guild in exile.[13] Poetry, on the other hand, could be more daring, partly be-cause the "revolution" of the Silver Age was integrated into the émigré heri-tage, and partly because verse was easily published in journals and newspapers. Collections of verse, however, were more difficult to arrange; most were pri-vate publications with small print runs, and only the most enthusiastic criti-cal reviews in journals and dailies attracted a small number of buyers.

The situation was even worse for nonfiction. Religious and philosophical books, as we have mentioned, were published by the YMCA Press, which could afford to lose some of its investment. Biographies and memoirs, espe-cially of contemporaries, found an interested readership among the émigrés, because they dealt with familiar events or people. Memoirs of the civil war found a particularly wide audience, although they earned little money for their authors, unless they were translated by foreign publishing houses—and this was the case only with reminiscences by the most prominent personalities of the imperial court and White Army command.

Scholarly books and monographs could count only on purchase by libraries, academic institutions, or a handful of private individuals. This kind of pub-lication could, as a rule, be arranged only with additional subsidies and help. For example, P. Miliukov's *Ocherki po istorii russkoi kul'tury* (Essays on the history of Russian culture) had been a great publishing success before World War I; it went through several editions and printings and, according to some, except for V. Kliuchevskii's lectures, it was the most widely read book on Rus-sian history. A revised edition of the essays was published in Paris in the early 1930s, made possible by a special fund drive among the emigration and addi-tional monies provided by the governments of Bulgaria and Czechoslovakia.[14] As far as I am aware, all book-length monographs had to be subsidized, either by an émigré organization, for example, the Host of the Don Cossacks commissioned S. G. Svatikov to write *Rossiia i Don* (Russia and the Don), or through some form of public subscription. The small number of book-length monographs and the large output of learned articles in various journals (professional and general) is well documented on the pages of the bibliography of scholarly and scientific works by exiled authors published in two volumes in Belgrade in 1931 and 1941. The smaller number of pages in the second volume graphically shows the attrition of émigré scholars and scientists, either through death or integration into the host country's professional life.[15]

Only a limited number of translations into Russian were published in Russia Abroad. In the first place, there was the relatively high cost of translation rights and fees to the translators; second, most émigrés acquired some knowledge of the language of the host country, although not as readily as is sometimes believed. English was the language most frequently translated, for there was a rich body of good contemporary fiction in English, and it had the largest assortment of mystery and adventure stories. The latter were translated mainly in the daily press. Most Russian newspapers in the urban centers (*Poslednie novosti* in Paris, *Rul'* in Berlin, *Segodnia* in Riga) serialized English or American mysteries and popular fiction.[16]

As already pointed out, serial publications were the most readily available creative and scholarly outlet. Serials provided the framework and most effective venue for maintaining the cultural unity of Russia Abroad: journals were cheaper and faster to produce, and did not need the capital investment that book publishing required. They were also more easily distributed, even across national borders; they addressed a "targeted" audience and could be assured of a minimum demand. The hardships and complexities of émigré life often prevented exiled intellectuals or writers from undertaking long-range projects; they engaged in short-term projects that resulted in article or short-story-length pieces published in a journal or newspaper.

The bibliography of émigré serials published by the Institut d'études slaves shows that journals and newspapers appeared like mushrooms after rain in every center of the Russian diaspora—and like mushrooms, most had a short life span. There were publications for every taste, for every literary and aesthetic preference, for each political commitment, for any professional concern, as well as simply for information and entertainment. It would be impossible to review the whole spectrum here, especially since our documentation is so fragmentary. The archives of most serial publications have disappeared, so we cannot obtain even such basic data as the number of copies printed and distributed or the financing. And the "inside story" of editorial policy decisions is often lost as well. The following general observations and illustrations are drawn primarily from memoirs.[17]

The major categories of serial publications were informational (primarily newspapers, either local or diaspora-wide), political (mouthpieces of political groups, ranging from leftist anarchists and socialists to diehard reactionary monarchists), publications of various associations (professional, social, veteran, philanthropic, and the like), scholarly (sponsored by academic institutions), literary-aesthetic (representing various styles and trends), popular reading and entertainment, general "serious" reading, the so-called thick journals (on which more shortly), and religious-philosophical (discussed more fully in Chapter 6). In addition there were regular periodical information sheets, most of them only of local interest.

Except for the strictly technical or professional publications and those with an exclusively political thrust, the journals with the longest lives and greatest general appeal were edited by liberals or moderate socialists. Even though the overwhelming majority of the "average" Russian émigrés were conservative monarchists practically none of the right-wing newspapers or journals were as successful as the liberal publications. The explanation may lie, in the first place, in the fact that liberal and progressive intellectuals had had extensive experience with the written and printed word in prerevolutionary times. That experience stood them in good stead in running periodicals in the emigration. Second, members of the liberal intelligentsia were more balanced and tolerant in their judgments, and more critical of the information received and conveyed, than their conservative competitors. They could thus appeal to a broader segment of readers; for even among the monarchists there were deep-seated and emotion-laden dissensions that made for a great deal of intolerance and prejudice.

The major émigré dailies that lasted for over a decade were *Poslednie novosti* (Latest News) and *Vozrozhdenie* (Renaissance) in Paris, *Rul'* (Rudder) in Berlin, *Segodnia* (Today) in Riga, and *Novoe vremia* (New Times) in Belgrade. These papers had readers throughout the diaspora.[18] The other great centers of Russia Abroad—Prague, Kharbin, Warsaw—also had dailies, but they were relatively short-lived and do not seem to have been much read elsewhere. Both *Rul'* and *Segodnia*, although in many ways excellent newspapers, became more and more provincial over time, concentrating on local events, reprinting articles and stories from other publications, and relying on the local and international press for their accounts of current events. *Rul'* closed down in the early 1930s, largely as a result of the depletion of the Russian community in the last years of the Weimar Republic. *Segodnia* concentrated more and more on local Latvian affairs under pressure from the authoritarian regime of K. Ulmanis, and lost, therefore, much of its general attraction, even though it reprinted articles and "correspondences" from *Poslednie novosti* in Paris, and works by prominent émigrés.

By general consent, the *Poslednie novosti* of Paris was the most outstanding, respected, and widely read newspaper in Russia Abroad. Edited by P. Miliukov, it was published without interruption from 27 April 1920 to the day before the Germans entered Paris on 11 June 1940. It had a fair and objective coverage of international events; local French problems did not monopolize the paper's space, although they figured prominently in periods of crisis. It prided itself on following and fully covering conditions and events in the Soviet Union. This information received a very critical and negative assessment, although the paper duly noted and underscored all positive developments in the Soviet homeland, for example, its improved military and international standing, reforms in education, various social measures, and so on. It offered a thorough coverage of artistic, musical, and literary events in Russia Abroad and in the world at large, which made it particularly attractive to an educated readership. Every week, *Poslednie novosti* devoted several pages exclusively to poetry, fiction, literary criticism and literary history. Every day, its *feuilleton*, section (*podval*) carried political and critical essays or fiction, where émigré authors of various artistic and political persuasion found a forum. Inevitably, there was much envious criticism of the putative "conservative," unimaginative, timorous decisions of the editor, Miliukov, in matters literary and aesthetic. This was a very sore point, for the paper was practically alone in paying decent, by émigré standards, honoraria; to be published by the paper was not only important for authors' egos, but for their pocketbooks as well. Miliukov also serialized mysteries, usually translated from English.

At its beginning, *Poslednie novosti* apparently received subsidies from various sources, perhaps including foreign governments, but it soon became self-sustaining due to its large circulation. Advertisements, primarily local, did not play a significant role, either in the paper's finances or in the apportioning of its space. *Poslednie novosti* was consistently liberal in tone and strictly democratic in its politics. The paper had no political program or stance of its own, except for its uncompromising rejection of all forms of dictatorship. And the editor maintained a highly critical attitude toward a monarchic restoration in Russia—even though Miliukov had advocated preservation of the monarchy in March 1917. The newspaper never ceased to denounce in harshest terms the brutal terrorism and ruthless dictatorship of the Bolsheviks, but from the very beginning it also unambiguously condemned Mussolini, Hitler, and Franco; it took a clear antiappeasement line in 1938–1939. *Poslednie novosti* approved of democratic-liberal experiments to escape the Depression, such as the New Deal in the United States, Prime Minister Paul Van Zeeland's plan in Belgium, and especially the Popular Front government of Léon Blum in France. In spite of these political preferences, the paper was regularly read even by the monarchists, and it reached the high circulation figure of over 23,000 in the early thirties, which it maintained until its demise at France's collapse in 1940. The paper was denounced as a Judeo-Masonic and pro-Soviet organ by its monarchist competitors, particularly *Vozrozhdenie* in Paris.[19]

Vozrozhdenie was founded in 1925 under the original editorship of P. B. Struve and with the financial backing of the oilman A. O. Gukasov. It was to be a moderate, conservative, monarchist organ. As we learn from his fragmentary correspondence, Struve secured the collaboration of a broad array of contributors throughout Russia Abroad; he intended it to be a serious newspaper, with an important literary section. Soon, however, he fell out with Gukasov, who apparently did not like Struve's political orientation. Gukasov charged that Struve's editorial policies led to the formation of an exclusive,

snobbish circle (*kruzhkovshchina*) and that its high-brow fare and style repelled the ordinary émigré reader. Struve resigned in a huff. The editorship
passed to Iu. F. Semenov and the paper became outspokenly monarchist and
"reactionary," appealing to a less-educated readership, although it carried information on many social, professional, and political organizations and events
in Russia Abroad, as well as an excellent literary section that enlisted the
collaboration of, among others, Khodasevich, Zaitsev, Shmelev and, on occasion, Bunin. It lost readers, however, and the paper had to pay greater attention to events in France and the world at large than it had at the outset. In
the 1930s it openly rejoiced at the electoral victories of Hitler in Germany
and of pro-Fascist parties and organizations elsewhere (e.g., the Croix de feu
in France); it supported Mussolini's war in Ethiopia, vociferously acclaimed
Franco's rebellion, and defended appeasement. It was a bit more ambivalent
in its attitude toward the Front Populaire in France, for Léon Blum's government had done a great deal to improve the economic and legal security of
the Russian émigrés. A long sit-down strike at the printer's, and the economic
difficulties of the early 1930s, forced the paper to become a weekly in 1936,
and it remained such until its end at the time of the German invasion. Despite appeals to readers, fund-raising events, and advertisements, *Vozrozhdenie*
never reached the circulation of its rival, *Poslednie novosti*, which Semenov
ruefully noted in his memoirs. He blamed the "Masonic" and "Jewish" elements of the emigration for subsidizing the rival newspaper and preventing
Vozrozhdenie from having the readership and influence it deserved.[20]

The variety of journals, bulletins, and other forms of periodicals was so
large as to defy meaningful description. The bibliographic repertory published by the Institut d'études slaves, even though by no means complete,
gives a comprehensive listing. Many serials merely informed readers of conditions and requirements of specific groups and associations and addressed
only a narrow membership. The strictly literary and artistic journals, such as
Versty (Miles), *Vstrechi* (Encounters), *Verteno* (Spindle), *Zveno* (Link),
were quite idiosyncratic advocates of specific aesthetic or philosophic positions.[21]

Political, partisan, and ideological publications were totally self-contained,
exclusively preoccupied with their own organizational and ideological quarrels, and directed at those who shared their presuppositions and outlook. Most
of them did not last for long, since any political or ideological movement in
emigration is by nature fissiparous, constantly splintering into factions and
new organizations. This was, for example, the fate of the Eurasian movement—perhaps the only innovative historiosophical and political outlook to
arise in Russia Abroad. In the early thirties, the movement split into a "conservative" faction that remained primarily committed to ideological and theoretical historical problems and eschewed discussion of current events, especially developments in the Soviet Union, and into a "left" faction that was
politically committed to a position close to the ideals of *Smena vekh* (Change
of Signposts movement). This faction accepted what was going on in Soviet

Russia as a natural result of the basic character of the Eurasian civilization. Their reputation was badly damaged by the implication of one of its members, S. Efron (Marina Tsvetaeva's husband) in the Soviet-instigated assassination of Ignatius Reiss in Switzerland. In similar fashion, the political movements of the younger generation—the Mladorossy (Young Russians) and the Natsional'no trudovoy soiuz (National Labor Union)—which had distinctly corporatist and proto-Fascist leanings, were divided over the question of whether to take a defensive or a defeatist position in case of a conflict between Stalinist Russia and Nazi Germany.

Among the political journals, the *Sotsialisticheskii vestnik* (Socialist Courier) occupies a special place. It was the voice of the Menshevik party's "delegation abroad." Until the 1930s, it was dominated by that party's left wing, followers of Iu. Martov, who condemned the Soviet regime for its denial of personal and political freedoms, but considered the revolution, including the Bolshevik takeover, acceptable because it had put Russia on the correct path of a socialist reorganization of its economy and society. They welcomed the Five Year Plans of industrialization and the principle of collectivization, although they denounced its harsh implementation. The right-wing faction, which took control of the *Socialist Courier* in the mid-1930s (largely in response to Stalin's brutal tyranny), condemned the Soviet system as a perversion of socialism, and they were the first to brand it as "totalitarian."[22]

What makes the *Courier* interesting for the history of Russia Abroad is the fact that it was the longest living political journal in emigration. It was founded on 1 February 1921, in Berlin, and moved to Paris after Hitler's seizure of power. Ultimately the paper came to New York where it ended in 1963, victim of the mortality of its contributors. Its main historical contribution, was the contacts it managed to maintain inside Soviet Russia well into the 1930s. These enabled the *Courier* to receive important and—as it proved—reliable information on conditions in the country and on the actions of the government. With Stalin's effective control over all access to Soviet Russia, their sources began to dry up, although the contributors' thorough knowledge and keen understanding of developments in Russia preserved the *Courier's* value, so that many of its articles are of interest even today.

The so-called thick journals, however, were the major vehicles for the cultural life of Russia Abroad. These journals continued one of the most glorious traditions of modern Russia. Indeed, the "thick journal" (*tolstyi zhurnal*)—comparable to the *Revue des Deux Mondes* in France or the *Edinburgh Review* in England—had been the main agent in broadcasting belles lettres, ideas, and culture in the broadest sense to an ever-widening circle of readers in Russia throughout the nineteenth and early twentieth centuries. The format of the thick journals was fairly standard: every issue had about 300 to 400 pages and appeared regularly once every three or four months (more rarely every two months). More than half of each issue consisted of fiction, serialized novels, short stories, novellas, poetry, drama—both in the Russian originals and in translations from leading foreign writers. The remainder of the issue was made up of literary, art, and music criticism; political, philosophical or socioreligious essays; book reviews; and calendars of current events (with or without comments), both domestic and foreign. Depending on the censorship practices at a given moment, an issue would be provocative and innovative or more guarded. In prerevolutionary Russia, as a rule, each thick journal represented one or the other major ideological position: conservative, liberal, populist; none of the serials were outright reactionary or openly socialist mouthpieces. Whatever its particular orientation, a thick journal appealed to a relatively wide spectrum of readers and helped set the tone for a dominant aesthetic or intellectual trend. In the Silver Age, the influence of the thick journals was restricted largely to sociopolitical and public matters; purely literary and aesthetic movements found expression in special journals (e.g., *Mir iskusstva*, The World of Art) or in almanacs put out by various coteries.

Once they had settled down, the émigrés turned again to the nineteenth-century tradition and format of the thick journal. Two émigré journals can claim to be both direct heirs and skillful practitioners of this tradition. *Volia Rossii* (Russia's Freedom) in Prague lasted for about ten years, and the longer-lived and more influential *Sovremennye zapiski* (Contemporary Annals) was published in Paris. *Volia Rossii* began as a supplement to the daily newspaper of the same name; it was edited by a group of Socialist Revolutionaries in Prague, with the literary critic Marc Slonim as its most influential figure. Its main contribution in the field of literature was to open up its pages to the younger authors in exile, such as the modernistic avant-garde writers like Marina Tsvetaeva, Sirin, and others. The journal also argued the case of a "single Russian literature"—whether it was written inside or beyond the borders of the Soviet state. It regularly acquainted the emigration with the literary production of the Soviet homeland, hoping to maintain closer contact and communication between the two Russias. These ties faded when socialist realism was officially proclaimed the only aesthetic doctrine and practice in the USSR. The journal appealed primarily to the younger generation, as well as to those who were at least inclined to view the Soviet system as a natural product of history and the fulfillment—in however distorted and brutal manner—of Russia's crying need for modernization and social justice. The split within the Socialist Revolutionary party abroad, political dissent and developments, as well as the shrinking financial support from the Czech government, brought about the demise of the journal in 1932.

Contemporary Annals was clearly the most significant and respected thick journal of Russia Abroad, a position it held throughout its entire existence, from 1920 to April 1940, the eve of the German occupation of Paris. We know most about this journal compared to the others because complete sets are available in many libraries, and also because the secretary of the editorial board, Mark Vishniak, wrote memoirs of his experiences at the journal and left a file of correspondence. Let us attempt to describe the journal and its physiognomy, in full awareness of the fact that it is impossible to do justice to all its features and contributions, not to mention statistical data and the "inside" story of its editorial work.

Vishniak's memoirs were not written until after the Second World War, so some facts may be misremembered. According to Vishniak, in 1920 Alexander Kerensky obtained from President Masaryk and Beneš the funds to found a Socialist Revolutionary newspaper and journal. The Czechs were willing to offer money (in addition to that given later to the Action russe) because the Socialist Revolutionaries had been the Czech Legion's allies in Siberia, and in case of the expected overthrow of the Bolsheviks, the Socialist Revolutionaries, with their peasant mass following, seemed the most likely pillar of a new democratic regime. Whatever the Czechs' reasons—Kerensky's persuasive rhetoric should not be discounted—a sum sufficient for the establishment of two publications was secured. Socialist Revolutionary papers, under varying names, were founded and published in the subsequent years. A thick journal, *Griadushchaia Rossiia* (Dawning Russia), had been established in Paris with the support of an industrialist, but it did not fare well and folded just as the Socialist Revolutionaries obtained the Czech money. A committee of Socialist Revolutionary leaders decided to hire some of the writers and editorial staff of the defunct journal and set up their own publication under the name *Sovremennye zapiski.* The title was intended to remind the émigré readers of *Sovremennik* (Contemporary) and *Otechestvennye zapiski* (Annals of the Fatherland), the most prestigious liberal thick journals of the nineteenth century. An editorial committee of five—N. D. Avksentiev, I. I. Bunakov-Fondaminskii, M. V. Vishniak, A. I. Gukovskii, V. V. Rudnev—was formed, not without some difficulty, and the journal was launched in late 1920.

The five editorial board members belonged to the Socialist Revolutionary party. It is remarkable—according to Vishniak it was mainly thanks to Fondaminskii—that they obtained the collaboration of authors far removed politically from the Socialist Revolutionaries. At times the authors were even hostile to the party's past activities in the revolution and civil war. The editorial statement, however, clearly spelled out the purpose of the journal, a purpose to which it clung tenaciously and which indeed secured its success. The key passage of the statement stressed its liberal cultural mission, a mission that was also the rationale of Russia Abroad's existence:

> The *Contemporary Annals* are committed, in the first place, to the interests of Russian culture. Our journal is fated to appear under conditions that are particularly difficult for Russian educated public opinion (*obshchestvennost'*): The free and independent word has no place in Russia, while here, abroad, there is gathered a large number of cultural leaders forcibly torn away from their people and from active service to it. This circumstance confers special responsibilities on the only sizable Russian monthly abroad. For this reason the *Contemporary Annals,* disregarding an author's belonging to this

or another political group, opens wide its pages to everything in the domains of artistic creation, scientific research, or the search for the social ideal, which has objective value for Russian culture. The Editorial Board believes that the limits of an author's freedom of opinion must have wide latitude, especially at a time when there is not a single ideology that does not require critical verification in the light of the ominous events happening in the world.

As a sociopolitical journal the *Contemporary Annals* is a nonparty organ and intends to pursue the democratic program, the outcome of the Russian liberation movement of the nineteenth and early twentieth centuries, which was proclaimed and accepted by the peoples of Russia in March 1917. . . .

The Editorial Board considers it essential to state its basic point of view: the re-constitution of Russia is incompatible with the existence of the Bolshevik power, it is possible only as the result of the autonomous action of the Russian people's own forces, and that the accomplishment of this task is beyond the ability of any one single party and class, but requires the united effort of all those who have sincerely broken with the old order and taken their stand on the side of the people's revolution of 1917.[23]

The first issue's 2,000 copies came out in November 1920. Later the journal was printed in fewer copies; precise figures are lacking. Vishniak does not say how much money was secured from the Czechs, but mentions that shortly thereafter the subsidy decreased significantly, and eventually dried up completely. By that time, however, the journal was already on the road to success, but not to financial security, an impossible goal under the conditions of émigré economics. For example, the two members of the editorial board who worked almost exclusively for the journal took sharp cuts in salary (from 1,000 francs a month to 400, in Vishniak's case).[24] Various schemes were attempted to finance the journal; among these were special arrangements with *Poslednie novosti* (advertisement and coupons for reduced subscription rates), fund-raising events, and complicated deals with bookstores and dealers that proved unsatisfactory. A book-publishing venture also was undertaken by the journal. The books were to be based on articles and serialized fiction from the *Sovremennye zapiski* as a complement to its earnings. This venture was unsuccessful financially, though a number of valuable volumes appeared under the journal's imprint. In any event, with the help of individual gifts, the journal survived to its seventieth issue; the German occupation of France sounded its death knell. In a sense, the journal was reborn in 1942 as *Novyi zhurnal* (New Review) in New York, still published today, under very different conditions.

Although the members of the editorial committee were men steeped in the pre-1917 radical, positivist, and socialist tradition, the journal published authors and works quite remote from, even opposed to, this tradition. In an initial lucky coup, the *Contemporary Annals* obtained the help of the most prominent and popular émigré novelist at the time, Alexis Tolstoi, whose most recent novel, *Khozhdenie po mukam* (Torturous march), was serialized in the first issues of the journal. Tolstoi was followed by Andrei Belyi, also recently arrived from Bolshevik Russia and uncertain about whether to return home or stay in exile. Eventually both Tolstoi and Belyi returned to Soviet Russia, where the former became the "court novelist" of the Stalinist regime. On the other hand, the personal contacts of Fondaminskii secured the collaboration of Z. Hippius and D. Merezhkovsky—who were polar opposites of Belyi and Tolstoi, literarily as well as politically. Eventually all of the senior émigré writers were published in *Contemporary Annals*. The literary qualities of the journal created its reputation and popularity. But equally important for its role in the intellectual life of Russia Abroad were the essays—critical, political, informational—these high-caliber works represented a broad ideological gamut from the moderate socialist St. Ivanovich, a right-wing Menshevik to the moderate Kadet V. Maklakov, and the nonparty conservative B. Nolde.

Although the journal was anti-Bolshevik, its tone was never hysterical, and the journal gave quite balanced information on happenings in Soviet Russia. Moreover, in the 1930s, threats to international peace and social stability encouraged quite a few contributors, including some on the editorial board, to adopt a more conciliatory attitude with respect to the role Soviet Russia could play in the world, and to recognize that social changes wrought by the regime were irrevocable. This, in turn, resulted in a willingness to reconsider previous judgments about the causes, characters, and consequences of the revolution.

Many émigré writers, cut off from their homeland, were prone to brooding and self-questioning doubts. Personality conflicts among the exiles sometimes led to great strains. Another problem stemmed from a gnawing feeling that the journal's literary policy was too old-fashioned and rigid. Younger authors believed that they were not published frequently enough. The editors deemed it too risky to publish unknown writers or authors whose styles and themes might shock an older generation of readers. This was particularly true of prose; the poetry section was the domain of poet M. O. Tsetlin and F. Stepun, who were more hospitable to rising new talent, specifically the modernists and the so-called Paris school of émigré poets. Supported by the influential critical essays of G. Adamovich, *Contemporary Annals* had always given place to the verse of Marina Tsvetaeva, B. Poplavsky, G. Ivanov, V. Khodasevich, and many younger poets. Prose offerings, however, were almost monopolized by such recognized writers as Bunin, Zaitsev, Aldanov, A. Remizov, Shmelev, M. Osorgin, and the younger Sirin (V. Nabokov). On the other hand, in the 1930s the journal gave space to younger prose authors such as V. Yanovsky and G. Gazdanov, but many new writers believed that experimental writings did not receive their proper share of pages.

A second, more significant, disagreement grew out of the evolution of Fondaminskii's philosophical and religious views. He was the most active member of the editorial board, and received the support of V. Rudnev. He had been moving toward a growing sympathy for idealism and spirituality, a trend that was increasingly apparent among the émigrés. The articles of such religious thinkers as L. Shestov, S. Frank, G. Florovsky, and others upset several contributors, particularly M. Vishniak. They believed that the journal was opening its pages to reactionary and bigoted (*mrakobesie*) expressions of prerevolutionary thought, in clear opposition to the liberal, humanistic, and secular values proclaimed in the first editorial statement. On the other hand, I am convinced, this new trend was welcomed by many, for as we shall see in Chapter 6, the religious and idealist renaissance of the Silver Age continued abroad and attracted an ever-larger segment of the émigré intelligentsia. In any event, conflict over the publication of these authors led to the resignation of M. Vishniak. He became the editorial secretary of a new thick journal, *Russkie zapiski* (Russian Annals), which was founded partly in response to the needs of the Far Eastern diaspora and partly to accommodate the unreconstructed positivist radicals and secularists of the *Sovremennye zapiski*. *Russian Annals* lasted until the outbreak of the war; it featured many of the same authors as *Contemporary Annals,* becoming a kind of clone of the latter, but the articles were duller and never achieved great popularity.

Another kind of serial publication reached a wide émigré readership. These offered popular entertainment to less sophisticated, poorly educated readers. An illustrated weekly, modeled on the prerevolutionary *Niva* (Cornfield), was called *Illiustrirovannaia Rossiia* (Illustrated Russia). It was primarily a picture magazine, but it serialized popular romances and mysteries and carried special features for women and children. It was widely read, and although overtly nonpolitical, it displayed sympathy for the monarchical past (it reported on royalty in exile and at foreign courts). Like its predecessor *Niva,* it offered, at bargain prices, subscriptions to sets of Russian classical authors, handbooks, and the like. A more sophisticated version of this kind of publication was the magazine *Dlia vas* (For You), published in Riga in a similar format. *Dlia vas,* in view of the proximity and influence of Germany, gave increasingly greater prominence to happenings there in the early 1930s, especially after Hitler's seizure of power.[25]

It is fair to conclude that Russia Abroad carried on the basic features of the intellectual life of the homeland in prerevolutionary times. It should also be stressed that none of the émigré publications with a broad circulation appear to have been much interested in, or influenced by, the intellectual and cultural atmosphere of the countries of asylum.

The printing press was the most effective means by which widely scattered Russians could maintain their identity, exchange ideas, and disseminate creative work, but it was not the only one. As a society in exile, the émigrés endeavored to reconstitute the cultural institutions they had left behind. Since it was very difficult to penetrate the established circles of the host societies, émigré institutions acquired a life of their own. But because most of these exile institutions were somewhat private in character—as they had been in Russia before 1917—it is not easy to compile full catalogs or to trace their internal history or day-to-day activities. Many organizations did not keep records, and the archives of most individual participants cannot be retrieved. The following remarks indiacte the character of these institutions and point up the need to learn more about them.

The most characteristic form of association of the Russian intelligentsia in the nineteenth and early twentieth centuries was the intellectual circle, *kruzhok.* The practice went back to the eighteenth-century student and translator circles at the University of Moscow and the Corps of Cadets; it received its emotional coloring in the youth circles of the early nineteenth century; and it acquired its overriding concern for a comprehensive ideology in the idealist circles of the Westerners and Slavophiles in the 1830s and 1840s. The tradition was continued with different philosophical and aesthetic preferences and political commitments in the nihilist student associations of the 1860s, the revolutionary circles and direct action groups in the latter quarter of the nineteenth century. The circles demonstrated a renewed metaphysical, aesthetic, and religious dimension in the artistic and literary debating circles of the Silver Age.

Such circles appeared anew in emigration. As will be seen in connection with the religious life of the disaspora, young students, veterans of the civil war, came together and formed discussion circles. They did so in order to find answers to their emotional anguish and thirst for self-improvement, and to dedicate themselves to work for the common good of their homeland. These circles of young people, and the elders to whom they turned for spiritual guidance and enlightenment, gave rise to religious brotherhoods (*bratstva*) which served as seedbeds for the Russian Christian Student Movement and other church-oriented endeavors. The so-called Orthodox Action to relieve economic hardship, while giving spiritual succor, also had its roots in these circles and brotherhoods. In the 1930s in Paris the Krug (Circle) formed to discuss philosophical, religious, historical, and artistic questions. The Krug came to be closely associated with the journal *Novyi grad* (New City, discussed later), whose leading figures were Fondaminskii and G. Fedotov. The minutes of the meetings of the Circle were summarized in the journal *Novyi grad;* unfortunately they are only brief digests and the names of the participants and discussants are omitted, making it impossible to reconstruct their debates and ideas in full. The circle was a source of contacts, exchange of information, and new ideas for the younger generation of exiles in Paris.[26]

There was also a religiously oriented circle among academic personalities. It was modeled on the Priutino Brotherhood in which outstanding scientists, such as V. I. Vernadsky, had played leading roles. With the goal of combining scholarly and scientific concerns with religious ideals, the Brotherhood of St. Sophia was founded by S. Bulgakov in 1919 in Russia. It was revived abroad and brought together P. Struve, S. Frank, G. Vernadsky, P. Savitskii, and other émigrés. Their sense of togetherness was maintained, despite the geographic distance that separated them, by the simultaneous performance of the same religious rituals—prayer and communion, both in private and in church. Of course, such forms of association could be adapted to political purposes as well. Thus the Fraternity of Russian Justice apparently involved in some questionable political adventures in the 1920s in Poland and on the borders of the Soviet Union.[27] Similar circles, with more pronounced social aims, took the form of Masonic lodges. We know of Russian émigré Masonic lodges in Paris, but aside from bringing together several prominent exiles, these lodges do not seem to have played a significant role in Russia Abroad, some purportedly "revelatory" literature to the contrary notwithstanding.[28]

At the time of the revolution, Houses of the Arts or Literature arose to help writers and artists survive the hardships created by the breakdown of the economy and social structure. The émigrés, too, set up similar groups. The most lively, although short-lived, was in Berlin in the early 1920s. It served as a clearing house for practical information and assistance; the major function was to bring together the Russian writers, painters, artists, musicians, and their supporters in Berlin. The House of Arts organized discussions, readings, exhibitions, and the like. I have not found evidence of a similarly dynamic House of Arts elsewhere, although the bohemian Paris cafés on boulevard Montparnasse (the Rotonde, the Coupole) informally served a similar function.[29]

It had been the custom in prerevolutionary Russia for educational institutions to promote and guide student and youth circles for the pursuit of literary, artistic, dramatic, and musical achievements. Many a school in the diaspora apparently also had such circles, but they have left only vague traces in personal reminiscences. The group in Kharbin, however, which called itself Churaevka, proved extremely energetic. It published also its own journal, which allows us to trace something of its history. The sad story of this circle vividly illustrates how external events affected an exile enterprise, transforming and perverting its original cultural purpose. It was founded in the mid-1920s by advanced *gimnaziia* pupils, students, and young people interested in arts and letters. The society held meetings to discuss and study aesthetic, artistic, and literary questions, read works by its members, and to organize concerts and dramatic events. Its journal, *Churaevka,* printed members' works and accounts of the circle's activities. The main concern of the society was to preserve the Russian heritage of the members and to safeguard and promote Russian culture; it shunned political issues and tried to maintain intellectual and artistic sophistication. The very success of Churaevka showed that it had found a satisfactory answer to the crucial question of emigration: what is Russianness, what is exile supposed to preserve and carry on abroad?

The growing influence of Japan gripped Manchuria in the early 1930s, culminating, as is well known, in the proclamation of the Empire of Manchukuo. This led some members of Churaevka to advocate a narrow and exclusive definition of Russianness: they came close to identifying it with imperial tradition and monarchic sentiments. These chauvinists seized control of the organization and put a damper on the circle's creative spontaneity, which led to its rapid decline.

In its heyday, Churaevka expanded its activities as similar organizations, with the same name and purpose, arose in other émigré centers in China. Before their demise, Churaevka and its sister branches had provided a forum for the development of the literary and artistic talents of many young people of the Far Eastern emigration and even helped to establish some contact with the literary life of Paris.[30]

Russian Houses of the Arts, not as artistically oriented as in Berlin or in China, appeared in Prague, the Balkan countries, and Riga. They served as cultural centers for the entire local émigré population: they invited guest lecturers and guest performers, organized literary and historical celebrations, and sponsored concerts, discussions, charity balls, and the like. Sometimes they opened Russian libraries and served as a social clubs. Theirs was a passive, rather than actively creative, cultural role. Along with schools, churches, professional and social associations, the Russian Houses of the Arts organized traditional festivals.[31]

Leaders of Zemgor and the Association of Emigré Teachers initiated a Day of Russian Culture, a day when all émigrés, wherever they might be, would celebrate and reaffirm their heritage, and pledge to preserve it. The Russian language was the one form of cultural expression that all émigrés shared, and since the modern Russian language had been "created" by, and given its highest literary form in, the art of A. Pushkin, it was proposed that the poet's birthday (8 June, new style) be celebrated each year as the Day of Russian culture.[32] The initiative found ready and enthusiastic response and the Day of Russian Culture was celebrated wherever there were groups of Russian exiles.

The days was marked by public reading and enacting of the works of Pushkin, and other theatrical and musical performances. Scholars lectured in clubs, schools, church halls, or Russian Houses of the Arts on history and culture, addressing themselves primarily to the young. Younger members of Russia Abroad became acquainted with the best of their literary, artistic, and historic heritage. Accounts of these celebrations were circulated as special booklets, press reports, and the like throughout Russia Abroad.

The year 1937 was the centenary of Pushkin's death and became a high point of the celebrations. Berlin was already in the shadow of Nazism, and most other centers of the diaspora were impoverished and had declined to a "provincial" level, but in Paris the Day of Russian Culture was a grandiose affair. With financial support from such personalities as S. Lifar, and many French and Russian cultural and social organizations, the celebrations included several important exhibits connected with Pushkin and nineteenth-century Russian culture. There were performances—readings, plays, ballets, and operatic excerpts of works inspired by Pushkin at the Salle Pleyel and the Grand Opéra. Special editions of the poet's works were also published in that year. The centenary was given a lavish celebration in Soviet Russia, too, and in a way this reestablished a sense of a common cultural identity between the two Russias. Perhaps the émigrés' grand Days of Russian Culture influenced the Soviets to celebrate their Pushkin centenary with just as much pomp, on such a scale, and in such a spirit.

Alas, in a society in exile political conflict cannot be barred even from the most innocuous cultural enterprise. Celebrating the Day of Russian Culture on Pushkin's birthday did not sit well with those who felt that the culture that the poet exemplified was too secular, too modern. They wanted a celebration that recognized the religious and monarchist elements of Russia's tradition. Conservative circles in Yugoslavia, with the full support and blessing of Metropolitan Antonii (Khrapovitskii) of the Bishops' Synod at Sremski Karlvci, proposed an alternative Day of Russian National Consciousness to be held on 28 July, the day of St. Vladimir, the prince who "baptized" Russia (more precisely, Rus', the ancestor of the three eastern Slavic nations of Great Russians, Ukrainians, and Byelorussians). The proponents of the Day of Russian National Consciousness denounced the Pushkin Day as the work of Masons, liberals, and secularists who were most responsible for the revolution and the defeat of the White Armies in the civil war. In spite of a few successful celebrations of this day in Yugoslavia, and the publication of several collective volumes to illustrate the importance of Prince Vladimir in shaping the history of Russia, the Day of Russian National Consciousness never eclipsed the Day of Russian Culture.[33]

Russian "junior high school" in Istanbul, May 1922. (Vserosiiskii zemskii soiuz, Bakhmeteff Archive, Rare Book and Manuscript Library, Columbia University)

Group of boy soldiers from the Volunteer (White) Army in front of a Russian school in Bulgaria. (Committee for the Education of Russian Youth in Exile Papers, Box 57, Bakhmeteff Archive, Rare Book and Manuscript Library, Columbia University)

V. A. Maklakov (at head of table) and the Russian Emigré Committee in Paris, 1932. (V. F. Zeeler Collection, Bakhmeteff Archive, Rare Book and Manuscript Library, Columbia University)

P. N. Miliukov and the board of the Union of Russian Writers and Journalists in Paris. Seated, from left to right: V. M. Zenzinov, B. K. Zaitsev (Vice-President), P. N. Miliukov (President), A. A. Iablonovskii (Vice-President), V. F. Zeeler (Secretary-Treasurer). Standing, from left to right: K. S. Zaidler, B. S. Mirkin-Getsevich, M. A. Aldanov, Al. M. Mikhelson, M. V. Vishniak, S. M. Soloveichik, K. K. Parchevskii (Secretary). (V. F. Zeeler Collection, Bakhemeteff Archive, Rare Book and Manuscript Library, Columbia University)

Composer A. Glazunov at the Russian Conservatory in Paris. Seated, from left to right: M. N. Muromtseva, Composer N. Nabokov, Serge Lifar, V. S. Naryshkina, A. K. Glazunov, Countess Pastre (?), Konovalov, B. Poplavsky. Standing, from left to right: Aronsberg, Kuper, Prince Volkonskii, Galamian, Lev Konius, Iulii Konius, Perebinskii (V. F. Zeeler Collection, Bakhmeteff Archive, Rare Book and Manuscript Library, Columbia University

Ivan Bunin visiting the editorial office of Vozrozhdenie in Paris, 1939. From left to right: A. I. Kuprin, A. A. Pleshcheev, V. F. Khodasevich (standing), I. A. Bunin, A. I. Gukasov, Iu. F. Semenov, B. K. Zaitsev, P. S. Lukash, M. O. Bernatskii, A. O. Gukasov. (V. F. Zeeler Collection, Bakhmeteff Archive, Rare Book and Manuscript Library, Columbia University)

Staff of Russian Historical Archives Abroad in Prague, March 1931. Seated, from left to right: Prof. E. F. Shmurlo, V. A. Miakotin, N. I. Astrov, Prof. A. A. Kizevetter, Mr. Macha, Prof. Slavik. Standing, from left to right: L. F. Magerovskii, N. S. Nikolaev, Fal'chikov, Prof. A. Florovskij, Brusvit, S. N. Prokopovich, Arkhangel'skii, Suskhov, Mr. Zavasal, A. F. Iziumov, Krasnov. (S. Panina Collection, Bakhmeteff Archive, Rare Book and Manuscript Library, Columbia University)

5

To Keep and to Cherish:
What Is Russian Culture?

The Russian émigrés firmly believed that one of their primary tasks in exile was to preserve, carry on, and create Russian culture. What did they mean by Russian culture, the historical tradition that had to be preserved and continued? What literary, artistic, and intellectual traditions did the émigrés intend to preserve and continue? Of course, the émigrés themselves never specified a definition of Russian culture; we can only sort out the discrete elements that, together, were deemed to make up this tradition. Modern Russian culture, it seems, found its strongest expression, in its most individualized and characteristic form, in literature. Of course, literary media are easily transmitted and seem to be the most "exportable"; and language is the one feature that defines a unique national identity. Painting and music can also claim to represent Russian cultural achievements in unique ways, but such claims are contestable, since music and visual arts are seen rather as universal and are more easily assimilated into the Western or world cultural scene.

Since the late nineteenth century, there was a consensus in Russia about what constituted "classical" national literature. The early medieval chronicles and epics were included in good romantic tradition, but eighteenth-century literature was largely ignored—with some notable exceptions, to be sure. To most Russians, classical literature, therefore, meant nineteenth-century Russian writing. At its beginnings, and its very pinnacle, stood Pushkin. Ever since Dostoevsky's famous speech at the first celebration of Pushkin Day (1880), Pushkin had symbolized the highest level of Russian literary and intellectual achievement. He was not only read but also memorized by all educated, even semieducated, Russians. And since Pushkin's work was very difficult to translate, he was someone the Russians could claim as uniquely theirs. For exiles, far from their homeland, and wistfully recollecting every pleasant memory from the past, again, it was Pushkin who loomed large. His works not only were easily memorized, but they evoked myriad images of the homeland; moreover, his allegedly insightful depictions of other nations and cultures facilitated the émigrés' access to the world surrounding Russia Abroad. Through Pushkin, the new host countries, their literary personages, their ways of thinking and feeling, in short their mentalités, were "familiar" to the émigrés.

A veritable Pushkin cult developed in Russia Abroad. Of course, Pushkin had been recognized, studied, and celebrated in prerevolutionary Russia too; but not without reservations. The positivist generations of the intelligentsia had shared, to some extent, the dismissive nihilist criticism by D. Pisarev and N. Dobroliubov in the 1860s of Pushkin's lack of "social utility." The symbolists, although marking a return to the lyrical tradition, felt that their own poetry was more profound and philosophically sophisticated, and conveyed a metaphysical message in innovative form, engaging all human senses. To them Pushkin was respected as their teachers' teacher: he had shaped the language they were using, but they had moved away from him in form and contents. In emigration, however, the educated Russians rediscovered Pushkin as someone truly their own, the poet closest to them not only by language and form, but also by his stress on individual creative freedom, a freedom utterly destroyed in Bolshevik Russia.

Russia Abroad boasted the presence of the distinguished Pushkin scholar Modest Gofman, the energetic collector of Pushkiniana S. Lifar, and the poets V. Khodasevich and M. Tsvetaeva, for whom Pushkin was the perennial model of the formal excellence of Russian poetic language.[1] There was a lively émigré literature on Pushkin, and new documents on his life and oeuvre that were discovered in the diaspora served to underpin the cultlike celebrations of the poet. We have seen that his birthday was chosen as the Day of Russian Culture. Pushkin's political stance—his accommodation to the tsarist regime for fear of popular anarchy—his occasional praise of Russia's nationalism and imperialism, as well as his uncompromising individualism and spiritual libertarianism, were especially welcome to exiled intellectuals.[2] In the 1920s until the mid-1930s Soviet cultural propaganda neglected Pushkin in favor of other idols, such as the populist poet N. Nekrasov, or the socially committed novelists M. Saltykov-Shchedrin and V. Garshin. That neglect only strengthened the exiles' dedication to Pushkin as their main cultural hero.

Pushkin became the venerated figure of Russian classical literature, but he was not the only hero in the pantheon: also included were M. Lermontov, and F. Tiutchev, whose poetry had been much neglected in the second half of the nineteenth century, only to be revived with the symbolists. Tiutchev appealed to the émigrés because of his conservative political opinions, and his religious and pessimistic metaphysical views on life and the world. Many other secondary, though outstanding poets—I. Krylov, A. Koltsov, A. Fet— were much read in Russia Abroad and reprinted in anthologies or in individual volumes. The major precursor of Pushkin, G. Derzhavin, was the object of a very interesting and readable biography by the poet V. Khodasevich.

Of course, the nineteenth-century fiction was quintessentially Russian, for the émigrés and non-Russian alike. The major novels of Gogol, Turgenev, Goncharov, and the short stories of Chekhov, were all republished and much in demand in all libraries and reading rooms. Children read them in Russian schools and adults reread them. Gogol's baroque ambiguities and grotesqueries, to which the exiled scholars D. Tschiževskii and K. Mochulskii were calling attention, were not easily grasped by the rank-and-file émigré reader who, however, enjoyed Gogol's humor and brilliance. His comedies—*The Marriage* and *The Inspector General*—were on the repertoire of all émigré theater groups, along with the dramas of D. FonVizin, A. Ostrovskii, and Chekhov. Turgenev was popular for his poetically limpid style, as well as for his nostalgic descriptions of the Russian countryside, if not of the provincial noble life styles of the past century. Along the same line we can explain the ongoing popularity of Goncharov, Chekhov, and even of the biting satire of Saltykov-Shchedrin, as well as many writers of the naturalist school. This was the tradition that writers such as Bunin and B. Zaitsev were carrying on in emigration. When the Nobel Prize for literature was given to Ivan Bunin in 1933, this tradition received the accolades of the outside world.

But what about the two giants of the nineteenth-century novel, Leo Tolstoi and Fedor Dostoevsky? At the turn of the century, Merezhkovsky had begun a small revolution in the interpretation and understanding of both novelists from a philosophical, religious, moral, and metaphysical perspective. His book on Tolstoi and Dostoevsky marked the rediscovery and revalidation of Dostoevsky as prophet and psychologist—the Dostoevsky who until then had been condemned by the progressive intelligentsia for his morbid introspection and political conservation. Merezhkovsky stressed the religious and metaphysical dimensions of Dostoevsky, and pointed out that his prophetic social and political interpretations of the modern world as his great contributions not only to Russian but to world culture. Merezhkovsky's book no doubt triggered the popularity of Dostoevsky abroad, mainly in Germany where Moeller van den Bruck translated and popularized his major works. Dostoevsky's popularity did not wane in the Weimar Republic.[3]

Russia Abroad picked up this new direction in the interpretation of Dostoevsky but with some reservations. Those who had kept to their early progressive positivist traditions, and this included most left Kadets, Socialist Revolutionaries, and other socialists, continued to oppose a writer whom they still called the "sick genius." Many conservatives and philistines in émigré society did not like Dostoevsky either, partly because of his "unhealthy" probing into individual psychology, partly because they found him difficult, turgid, and not always irreproachably "proper" ("comme il faut'"). But there was another reason, I would suspect, for the émigrés' distrust of Dostoevsky's newfound fame. In the eyes of most non-Russians, the novelist evoked and represented the somber, unknowable Russian "soul"; exiles resented the way this image was used to dismiss Russia and its people as "mysterious" and "inscrutable." That same image could be used to rationalize what was going on in the Soviet Union: since the Russians are sick, incomprehensible, given to unaccountable *sauts d'humeur*, non-Russians argued, Bolshevism is something natural for them and their own fault.

On the other hand, some prominent religious and philosophic writers in Russia Abroad pleaded the case of Dostoevsky's prime importance as the mystical critic of the contemporary world, as someone who had suggested the true solution to the human predicament, based on his profound understanding of Orthodox Christianity. This was the argument set forth by N. Berdiaev and L. Shestov in philosophical terms and by S. Bulgakov and G. Florovsky in theological terms. The magisterial biography by K. Mochulskii, member of the Circle and *Novyi grad*, did much to popularize this interpretation.[4] On the whole, these writers dismissed the chauvinistic, anti-Semitic, anti-Polish, and generally xenophobic outbursts of Dostoevsky, or explained them away by the novelist's stress on true Christian charity toward all individuals.

Russia Abroad's attitude toward Leo Tolstoi was also marked by an uncomfortable ambivalence. Everyone acknowledged Tolstoi's literary achievement—his style, his absolutely true descriptions of the feelings and actions of the widest variety of Russian types and individuals. Nor was there disagreement about Tolstoi's philosophy of history, since it affirmed the decisive importance of chance and accidental factors. In contrast to Marxism (or historical materialism), Tolstoi denied the workings of so-called vast impersonal forces, or iron laws of history. Or so it seemed on the surface of things, and most émigré readers did not probe further. The popularity of Mark Aldanov's historical novels owed much to his writing in the manner of Tolstoi: Aldanov's simple and clear style was perhaps a trifle more Gallic than the master's, but his vivid portrayal of historic personages and his philosophy of history pointed out the unpredictable consequences of accident and individual decisions.

But there was another side to Tolstoi: his idolization of the peasant and his preaching of anarchism and nonviolence. This stand of Tolstoi's was unacceptable to exiles who had experienced at too close a range the effects of anarchy, the hate and violence of which the peasants was capable. Many exiles also believed that Tolstoi's ideological and religious opinions had contributed to the revolution. Indeed, the writer's rebellion against all institutions and authorities had done much to undermine the stability and social coherence of prerevolutionary Russia. It had warped the mind of many an intellectual, and compounded the intelligentsia's helplessness in the face of war, violence, and the Machiavellian power hunger of Lenin and the Bolsheviks. Characteristically, in marking the centennial of Tolstoi's birth in 1928, the émigrés stressed his literary genius as a novelist, while dismissing his socioreligious-political ideas with a condescending shrug as the unfortunate waywardness of a great man. For instance, the eloquent speech in the Tolstoi celebration that V. Maklakov delivered in Paris and Prague dealt with Tolstoi the man (whom he had known) and Tolstoi the writer; Maklakov only defensively and cursorily referred to Tolstoi's political and religious "aberrations."[5]

It is more difficult to say what was considered "classic" in Russian art (painting in particular, since by definition "Russian" architecture could not be practiced in Russia Abroad) and music. There were the neoclassical, academic paintings of the early nineteenth century and the realistic paintings with social messages by the *Peredvizhniki* (Wanderers) school. The Wanderers expressed national tradition and pride, so their canvases were reproduced for sale at charity fairs or various national celebrations (e.g., the Day of Russian Culture). This school of Russian painting was also related to the pseudomedievalism of popular art *à la russe* that swept Russia at the beginning of the twentieth century. It matched the image that foreigners had of genuine Russian art and was vulgarized in the decor of popular Russian cabarets, restaurants, knick-knacks, and the like. In a more sophisticated and imaginative form it constituted a basic ingredient of the sets for ballets, plays, or operas with Russian themes.

Music, as a language that knows no national barriers, was easily absorbed by and integrated into the host environments. Of course, the "classics" of nineteenth-century Russian music, the so-called powerful heap (*moguchaia kuchka*) and Tchaikovsky already had become indispensable to the international concert repertoire. Emigrés who were performing musicians (e.g., S. Rachmaninoff, F. Shaliapin, S. Koussevitsky, and other famous piano and violin soloists of Russian background) further popularized this music; however, they rapidly merged into the international musical world. Russian folk music and church choral singing were introduced to a broader international audience by Russia Abroad. Emigré Cossacks formed groups for the performance of folk songs and dances, and traveled to fairs, resorts, concert halls, and theaters. Their repertoire consisted of "popular" songs and dances, as well as religious music. The best-known Cossack choir, under the direction of S. Jaroff, toured all over the world throughout our period and after World War II. The best church choirs, for example that of the Cathedral Church on rue Daru in Paris, were invited to émigré centers and to concerts for foreign audiences as well. In this connection we may note that the study of Russian medieval church music was stimulated by such émigré specialists as Professor I. Gartner, and by the courses offered at the St. Serge Theological Institute in Paris. These courses were a notable contribution to Russian culture in view of Soviet Russia's ban on this subject throughout the 1920s and 1930s.

The medieval heritage of Russian culture occupied a special position, both in prerevolutionary Russia and in Russia Abroad. Interest in the music, painting, architecture, and decorative arts of the Middle Ages had experienced a renaissance at the end of the nineteenth century, and it had been a significant aspect of the cultural scene in the Silver Age. Its close association with religious life led the Bolshevik regime to discourage interest in it domestically, at least during our period. But the émigrés' renewed commitment to the church and to religion stimulated their interest in all cultural manifestations of Russian Orthodoxy. Since access to manuscript and archival collections in Russia was impossible, the scholarly study of Russian medieval literature was very much impeded, but comparative Slavic linguistics, folklore, and poetics could be fruitfully pursued in Russia Abroad—and their scope enlarged by methodological and documentary influences of Western scholarship. This task was brilliantly executed by N. Trubetskoi, and later by R. Jakobson, in the Cercle linguistique de Prague, which they founded and led until the outbreak of World War II. As noted, in an earlier chapter, the Seminarium Kondakovianum was the center of the study of the medieval heritage, especially in the graphic arts, and its work was carried on by individual scholars, such as A. Grabar and B. Lossky.

The émigré community's devotion to the church helped foster knowledge of the Russian icon and brought this artform international recognition. As a craft, icon painting was further developed in a number of ateliers and by many individual practitioners. They decorated the many new émigré churches (for example, St. Serge's at the Theological Seminary and Institute in Paris), and worked for a sizable market of individual purchasers. Icon painting was quite traditional, but thanks to the careful historical investigations that had been carried out by N. Kondakov and his pupils, and influenced by contemporary aesthetic values and techniques, exile craftsmen included original and innovative elements. Bolstered by the foreign traveling exhibit of icons organized by the Soviet government in the late 1920s, the émigré artisanal activity encouraged the popularity of icons among foreigners: private collections and public sales occurred in Europe (Recklingshausen) and in the United States (Hammer, Hahn, Davies collections). The heightened interest in medieval icons was closely related to a revival of spirituality and mysticism, a phenomenon that had already been observed in the Silver Age. The icons received spiritual interpretations that ignored the historical circumstances in which they were painted. This, in turn, led to their being seen as sentimental artifacts that were somehow uniquely and mystically Russian. And this view reinforced the belief, held by many in Russia Abroad, that they were the carriers of "true" Russian religious values, a belief propagated, for example, by Berdiaev, and readily absorbed by host milieus, especially in Germany. Unfortunately, this image served to perpetuate hoary myths of the peculiarities of the Russian "soul," with deleterious political consequences. It also led to a view of the Muscovite period of Russian history as a sad deflection from the "normal" or "true" Russian path, a deflection that almost "naturally" led to the Western Europe-inspired "perversions" of St. Petersburg.

It may seem arbitrary to single out, within Russia's cultural development, the "classical" tradition, but it is justified largely because the émigrés themselves defined their heritage in terms of a classical and a nonclassical element in their tradition. In fact, however, the exiles' true roots were in the period that they had experienced themselves in their youth and maturity, either directly, or vicariously through their parents and elders. This period was the Silver Age, so frequently mentioned in earlier pages. The Silver Age originally referred specifically to poetry, contrasting this era to the Golden Age of Pushkin's times, but later it came to designate all aspects of the extraordinary flowering of innovative, creative impulses in all domains of artistic and cultural even economic, life. The period lasted from the last decade of the nineteenth century—frequently associated with the revival of public and political activism following the great famine of 1891–1892—to the outbreak of the Great War in 1914. In some respects, the experimentation of the early years of the Soviet regime, to about 1925, was a direct continuation of the Silver Age; and so was the cultural activity of Russia Abroad in the 1920s and 1930s. It was typical of the primacy of the written word that the Silver Age was defined with reference to poetry; indeed, its significant first manifestations were in the realm of literature.

The Silver Age was at first synonymous with symbolism in poetry. It marked the renaissance of lyrical poetry, which the nihilists and positivists had scorned in favor of civic poetry and realistic fiction with a social message. From poetry, symbolism spread to other forms of art—painting (the Impressionists) and music (A. Skriabin), and renewed interest in spirituality, religion, and metaphysics. In the present context, we need not discuss the aesthetic and philosophical tenets of symbolism or evaluate the relative impact of French and German influences in shaping the Russian variant. French influences—Baudelaire, the Parnassians, later Verlaine, Rimbaud, Mallarmé—triggered the poetic renaissance, while German ideas proved more important in the realm of philosophy (Schopenhauer, Nietzsche, neo-Kantianism); Bergson's vitalism played a significant role, too. In any event, the influences from abroad converged with the almost febrile tempo of social, economic, and cultural transformation in Russia proper. The energies released by the Great Reforms in the 1860s—the emancipation of the serfs—even though stymied by government policy (or perhaps for that very reason), were transforming Russia at a pace unheard of since the time of Peter the Great two centuries earlier, and cutting broad and deep into the fabric of the Empire's society. The fact that this creative boom did not entail an optimistic outlook, accompanied as it was by forebodings of doom (also shared in the West) which stemmed from spreading technological and materialist concerns at the expense of traditional, spiritual values, in no way diminishes the seminal nature of the Silver Age. It could not fail to have a powerful impact on all those who were coming of age at the time. Whether in the expectation of ongoing positive progress, or in fear of a catastrophic, apocalyptic outcome, the Silver Age's creative drive was cut short by the outbreak of the First World War, and buried under the rubble of revolution and civil war.

Those who had matured in an atmosphere of intense creativity, and who had seen their expectations or fears acquire the anarchic and traumatic shapes of war, revolution, and civil war, were the very same men and women who, cast out of their homeland, set about to create the Russia Abroad. They hoped that in this new Russia they might be able to perpetuate the creative Silver Age while awaiting the fall of Bolshevism. But the cultural achievements of the Silver Age had not gone unnoticed in the West. As a matter of fact, the Silver Age was the first expression of modern Russian culture to have made an impact abroad: although the literature is not easily accessible to foreigners, even in translation, the works of D. Merezhkovsky, A. Blok, Dostoevsky and Tolstoi were widely known; R. M. Rilke tried to write Russian verse and popularized Russian poetry in Germany. More dramatic yet was the impact of the plastic arts and music, and to a lesser degree science and scholarship. During its Silver Age, Russia joined the stream of universal, Western-based, twentieth-century world culture.

To be sure, not everybody in Russia Abroad appreciated the poetic and literary production of the Silver Age. Ivan Bunin's dislike of the writings of A. Blok was notorious, for example. On the whole, however, the émigrés acknowledged the symbolist and acmeist poets (the heirs of symbolism) as belonging to the "classical" canon of Russian poetics. The continuity with the Silver Age was underscored by the ongoing poetic creativity of those who had moved to Russia Abroad—Z. Hippius, K. Bal'mont, V. Ivanov—and of the central role played in émigré literature by the heirs of symbolism, for example, V. Khodasevich, M. Tsvetaeva, and G. Ivanov. Literary critics and historians, G. Adamovich and K. Mochulskii, also focused on that glorious period of Russian poetry and helped make its creative impulses and accomplishments understood.

But positive appreciation was not without an admixture of serious doubts and questions. Had not symbolism opened the door, many asked, to destructive and anarchic notions which, from the realm of art, passed into the fabric of Russian life? Advocating a cleansing storm, as the Silver Age writers had done, came too close to wishing for revolution and chaos. This, in restrospect, seemed to have been the political message of A. Blok before 1917. And did not his deleterious impact find confirmation in his own acceptance of the Bolsheviks, an acceptance he seemed to proclaim in his admittedly ambiguous last great poem *The Twelve?* Might not the same also be said of V. Rozanov and his volatile mixture of avant-garde art, religious anarchism, and nationalist mystique?

Blok's and Merezhkovsky's pre-1917 writings had been a premonition and a warning of the coming apocalyptic end. This end, however, received enthusiastic applause from such modernist, postsymbolist writers as A. Belyi, and such poets as V. Mayakovsky. In their writings, in their public appearances abroad, they invited the exiles to return home and to accept wholeheartedly what had come to pass. Belyi's stand could be dismissed as belonging to the poet's own anarchic personality. But were not the anarchism and nihilism of extreme modernism legitimate heirs to symbolist experimentation? Their modernism was often associated with the political and moral destructiveness of the Silver Age, and this stood in the way of a full appreciation of, for example, the poetry of Marina Tsvetaeva (or of Boris Pasternak, while he lived abroad). Still more baneful, as far as the émigrés were concerned, was the work of those young poets who perverted the literary freedom gained by symbolism into anarchic license—V. Mayakovsky, S. Esenin, V. Khlebnikov. The shrill crudeness of Mayakovsky not only stood for everything that was loathsome, anarchic, and violent in Bolshevik Russia, but it also revealed, in the view of many, where the Silver Age had gone astray, namely, its excessive liberalism, its apocalyptic expectation of doom, and its rejection of traditional aesthetic norms and proven social values.

A similar ambivalence characterized émigré attitudes toward the art and music of the Silver Age. Because the visual arts and music are a translingual media, they could be readily integrated into the international artistic community. The experimentation in the arts that the Bolsheviks had permitted in their first years of rule meant that these media were known in the West, especially in Germany. Outstanding composers and artists—Kandinsky, Chagall, Stravinsky—rapidly became part of the German, French, and world scene. But their work, although it added a "Russian note" to contemporary art and music, did not, strictly speaking, belong to Russia Abroad, although émigrés certainly attended their exhibitions and concerts.

One artistic manifestation that specifically belonged to the Silver Age was continued, though in a less original manner, in Russia Abroad. This was the movement of *Mir iskusstva* (The World of Art), as its publication was called, combining the graphic arts and ballet. In a sense, *Mir iskusstva* was the Russian variant of Impressionism and symbolism, and it had had a powerful impact on the artistic tastes of the prerevolutionary generation. As a prewar Russian artistic movement, it had captivated the imagination of the Western world, mainly because of the decor and costumes for Diaghilev's ballets. The artists who had produced them emigrated and continued to work for the ballets and operas produced in the West in the twenties and thirties (and after World War II). In this way, A. Benois, M. Dobuzhinskii, N. Goncharova, L. Bakst—to name the best known—helped shape not only the artistic life of Russia Abroad by participating in its cultural events (e.g., the Pushkin celebrations), but also by continuing to display their heritage in foreign lands. They contributed greatly to the continued popularity of the successors of the Ballets russes that were a major force in transforming the world of ballet and art in the West. The Ballets russes de Monte Carlo carried on the traditions of Diaghilev, while Serge Lifar succeeded V. Nijinsky as prime dancer and choreographer in France, and G. Balanchine did so in the United States. The Russian ballet also gave an extra dimension to the music of I. Stravinsky, the only avant-garde composer in Russia Abroad who was easily absorbed into the Western, especially American, environment. On the other hand, the more traditional musicians, even if connected with *Mir iskusstva* before 1914, such as A. Glazunov, remained on the periphery of the international musical world; while S. Rachmaninoff made his mark abroad primarily as a virtuoso performer. It was the émigré conductor S. Koussevitsky, however, who popularized the modern, as well as "classical," repertoire of both Russias in the concert halls.

A distinguishing hallmark of the Silver Age—as it had been of the Golden Age in the 1830s and 1840s—was a keen interest in spiritual, religious, and philosophical issues. In opposition to the positivism of the late nineteenth century, the philosophical renaissance clearly emphasized idealism and metaphysics. Furthermore, we should note that philosophy became a genuinely autonomous scholarly discipline in the first decade and a half of the twentieth century. We shall deal with the revival of spirituality and religious concerns in the next chapter; here I shall say a few words about the philosophical rebirth.

It had its origin in the work of Vl. Soloviev whose reflections stimulated such thinkers as P. Novgorodtsev, S. Bulgakov, N. Lossky, N. Berdiaev, and, to a lesser degree perhaps, S. Frank. Most of these philosophers were expelled from Soviet Russia on Lenin's orders in 1922. Abroad they resumed their work, publishing articles and books in the émigré press. The philosophical renewal proceeded under the twofold headings of idealistic metaphysics and personalist psychology, or philosophical anthropology. At their root lay an ontology based on the recognition of the existential and historical autonomy of the human spirit as a creation of God and determined only by the freedom granted by God to his creatures. Not surprisingly, this philosophical orientation converged with the religious existentialism of Kierkegaard. It helped to relieve the Russian philosophical speculation of its exclusive preoccupation with concrete social or economic and political problems; yet all the while it prepared for the ultimate reconstruction or regeneration of society and institutions to give humanity the spiritual freedom to fulfill itself creatively, under God.

Berdiaev, the most widely read philosopher of Russia Abroad, whose works were translated into all major Western languages, gave an extremely libertarian interpretation to this basic position. His interpretation led him to reject bourgeois materialism as radically as Bolshevik atheism; at the same time he denounced the positivist intelligentsia whose neglect of means for the sake of worthy ends had led to the revolution. In acknowledging this guilt or shortcoming, the intelligentsia—including the émigrés—had to admit that the Bolsheviks were doing, albeit in violent and perverted form, the work of destroying bourgeois materialism, a task that they themselves had failed to accomplish. In the thirties and especially in the forties, Berdiaev's Russian nationalism made him quite tolerant of Stalin's Russia. This peculiar position did not make him very popular in some émigré milieus, but his influence did not suffer from it; he had the advantage of material security, and he enjoyed a forum in the publications he edited, as well as an international audience thanks to his many contacts in foreign circles. His friend and one-time colleague, Lev Shestov, was the main representative of a Kierkegaardian view of the existential predicament of Man, a predicament he felt was best exemplified by Pascal's anxiety over the existence of God; it brought Shestov to condemn human reliance on reason as not only limiting of our being, but as antispiritual in essence. Although his writings are repetitive and often vague, Shestov found a sympathetic audience among the intellectuals of Russia Abroad, and he even had an impact in Germany and France through his lectures and publications in foreign journals.

N. Lossky and S. Frank had less impact in Russia Abroad and in Western thinking before the Second World War. Frank concentrated on problems of social ethics—and indirectly on political philosophical anthropology—which he treated from a Christian and idealist point of view. Lossky pursued his investigation of epistemology and philosophical anthropology from a strict personalist perspective. Neither thinker was very influential, largely because they lived in relative isolation in Berlin and Prague. Lossky, moreover, was not a facile writer and devoted part of his energies to teaching in various Russian academic institutions in Prague.

Among the émigré philosophers of the Silver Age we may also mention L. Karsavin (strictly speaking, he was a historian but was particularly interested in the philosophy of history) and the two social philosophers, P. Novgorodtsev and B. Vysheslavtsev (who were concerned with issues of jurisprudence), and S. Hessen, best known for his work on pedagogy and political theory. This does not exhaust the list, but these were original thinkers whose words had some echo in the diaspora, and who greatly contributed to the development and popularization of existentialism and of a Christian approach to social and ethical problems, in opposition to the materialism and rationalism of radicals and Marxists of all stripes. They were broadening and deepening the social issues raised by the renaissance of critical idealism in the Silver Age, in the light of their own experiences in revolution and civil war.

Two younger thinkers, A. Kojève and A. Koyré, who had come to intellectual maturity in Russia Abroad, proved to have a lasting impact on Western philosophy after World War II. A. Kojève, who became a civil servant in the French Ministry of Foreign Affairs specializing in economic problems, organized a seminar on the philosophy of Hegel. This seminar, under the auspices of the Ecole des hautes études pratiques, played a dominant role in the revival of an interest in Hegel in France, a revival that was of importance for the development of Marxism and of a dialectical existentialism after the Second World War. A. Koyré made his debut with a thesis on the Russian idealist thinkers of the 1830s and 1840s, and from there moved to the study of the German mystical and *Naturphilosophie* traditions with works on Jakob Boehme and N. de Cusa. This in turn—following the direction suggested by the French historian of science P. Duhem—brought Koyré to the philosophy and history of science, areas to which he contributed seminal studies on Galileo and Descartes. But again, his recognition and influence came only after 1945, when he finally received a regular appointment at the University of Paris.

The émigré thinkers we have mentioned exemplified the Silver Age's new orientation in philosophy, but also its professionalization. Indeed, most had been members of university faculties, at least temporarily, and they considered philosophy to be not only their calling, but their profession as well. Obviously, philosophers were not the only profession to have acquired autonomous guild existence and recognition by the time of the Silver Age. All the liberal and technological professions had received full recognition, in law and by society, by the time of the outbreak of revolution in 1905. This imparted greater drive and gave fuller scope to the creative energies of the professionals, and also facilitated contact with their counterparts abroad. In the domains of science and scholarship, too, the Silver Age marks the entrance of Russia onto the international stage as a fully recognized and equal partner.

While those in law and the humanities were handicapped because of the language barrier—and the limited professional opportunities everywhere—Russian scholars in other fields, and those scientists who emigrated, found a niche for themselves in the host countries. Let us select a few instances that can stand for many more for which adequate documentation is lacking.

If the practicing lawyer had great difficulty in finding employment and a new secure base in foreign lands with a different legal system and tradition, this was not quite the case of the scholar in jurisprudence or the specialist in international commercial law. The leading practitioners of public and civil law in prerevolutionary Russia, B. Nolde and V. Eliashevich, gained high professional standing as jurists in France and recognition as leading scholars in the field through their writings in both Russian and foreign publications (and serving as expert advisors to courts and government offices). Jurists teaching at the Russian universities in Prague (N. Timasheff), Kharbin (G. Guins), and Helsinki (S. Korf) eventually found secure employment in the United States, but their contacts with Russia Abroad weakened, at any rate until the very last years before the outbreak of war. The younger jurist, G. Gurvich, however, whose broad interests spanned law, sociology, philosophy, and the history of ideas, made important and original contributions to all these fields which were rapidly integrated into the "state of the art" in the West. He remained a member of Russia Abroad until the late 1930s when his genuine integration into the French university began, an integration that was successfully completed after 1945, when he returned to France from the United States, where he had spent the war years. Gurvich was the most sophisticated advocate of social rights jurisprudence during his early years at the University of Dorpat (Iur'ev, Tallinn), and then later in Berlin and Paris. His critiques of Marxist socialism from the perspective of social rights, and his notions of a new system of property law in a liberal democracy, represènt a major contribution to social and political thought in the 1920s and 1930s that may still be studied with profit today. His interests had been stimulated by his teacher L. Petrażycki and the Russian school of psychological jurisprudence in the Silver Age. Later Gurvich moved on to sociology and developed theories that owed a great deal to the formalism and structuralism first developed in literary theory in the Silver Age.

As suggested earlier, scholars in the humanities did not have an easy time of it in continuing their creative work in a milieu foreign by language and historicocultural tradition. In this chapter I shall mention only one instance of a humanistic field related to philosophy: linguistics. Before emigrating in 1920, Prince N. Trubetskoi had been actively involved with new orientations in philosophy which argued that our use of language depended on a specific anthropological-spiritual context and on the role of symbols in a given society and culture. These structuralist preoccupations converged with the interests of a younger student and colleague of his, R. Jakobson, who had worked on the role of symbol systems and their relationship to sound patterns in the creation of poetic works. The works of symbolist and postsymbolist poets (e.g., Mayakovsky) served as his sources of illustration. Trubetskoi pioneered this new structuralist linguistics at the Cercle linguistique de Prague which he founded before accepting appointment to a chair in Vienna.

It was not altogether an accident that N. Trubetskoi was also a founding father of Eurasianism, the only truly novel (in spite of its syncretism) philosophy of history to emerge in Russia Abroad. The doctrine of Eurasianism stressed the cultural uniqueness of the territory lying between Central Europe and the Pacific Ocean, a uniqueness rooted in the common structural traits displayed by its climate, geography, languages, and, ultimately, what we call now the mentalité of its peoples. The Eurasians proclaimed the primacy of the spiritual elements in shaping history, elements that found their genuine expression in the linguistic framework of the people or culture. Eventually, R. Jakobson broke away from Eurasianism and focused his attention on the formal and structural elements at the root of both poetic and ordinary language—poetry reflecting the more "primitive" (or primary), in the genetic sense, aspects of a language's essence. Moving from Prague to Sweden, and then to the United States, Jakobson was the major theorist and practitioner of formalist literary criticism and structuralist linguistics in the West. Yet, he was very much—and remained so—a "citizen" of Russia Abroad, not only by his background, but also by his lifelong preoccupation with Russian poetics and the common Slavic heritage. He was active in various émigré institutions at which he lectured, and he wrote for Russian publications.

Literary scholars, as noted earlier, continued their work abroad, sometimes changing its main focus. For example, K. Mochulskii switched from Romance literatures to Russian. Despite limited access to foreign institutions, they contributed to spread the knowledge of Russian literature and culture in foreign lands, bolstering the sense of cultural identity of Russia Abroad. Such was, for example, the role of Th. von Braun and F. Stepun in Germany, K. Mochulskii in France, and D. Tschijewskij in Czechoslovakia (and later in Germany). For a while, D. S. Sviatopolk-Mirsky played a similar role in England where, after his return to Russia (where he met his death in the purges), his place was taken by Gleb Struve. In all these cases, prerevolutionary literary scholarship was carried on essentially without significant innovations, although inclusion of formalist criticism did mark a departure already initiated by the Silver Age. Thanks to their efforts, Russian literature, as a scholarly critical discipline not only flourished in Russia Abroad, but also enlightened the outside world, promoting unknown or neglected aspects of Russia's literary accomplishments and preparing for the rapid development of Western scholarship in this field after 1945.

In other humanistic disciplines—ancient history, paleography, Byzantine history—Russian émigré scholars made some major contributions when they were lucky enough to find the appropriate academic institutions and sponsorship. For example, M. Rostovtzev specialized in ancient economic and social history; his professorship at Yale University gave him the opportunity to broaden the field by his excavations at the Roman site of Dura-Europus in the Middle East. Far from breaking his ties to Russia Abroad, he was a lively contributor to several émigré journals, such as *Contemporary Annals* where he published accounts of his excavations and studies of ancient history (the economy of Ptolemaic Egypt) with pointed references to the present. A. Vasiliev, the historian of Byzantium, securely established at the University of Wisconsin, withdrew from the cultural horizon of Russia Abroad, while the younger G. Ostrogorski, trained at the Seminarium Kondakovianum and in Germany, may be considered part of the scholarly world of Russia Abroad as he published his early works in the émigré press. S. Dovgello, the wife of the novelist A. Remizov, was a highly regarded medieval paleographer. She trained many French scholars in the discipline at the École des hautes études pratiques. It should be stressed that in all these instances, the émigré scholars contributed a specifically Russian, prerevolutionary, methodological, factual, or conceptual innovation to their fields of endeavor. These ideas were fully absorbed in the progress of the various disciplines.

A few names will suffice to illustrate the scientific and technological work of Russia Abroad. If they were to continue their professional work, scientists and engineers had to be admitted to public institutions or business enterprises in the host countries. For the average engineer this was no easy matter: many had to accept lowly positions or even engage in manual labor. In Yugoslavia, some Border States, and in a few cases in Czechoslovakia, a Russian émigré engineer could also enter government service in a technical capacity. But this was practically impossible anywhere else in Western Europe. On occasion, especially during the height of cooperation between German industry and the Soviet Union, Russian engineers were hired, on a temporary basis, as consultants to firms that had contracts with the Soviets. But those who had already made a name for themselves in Russia were in a better position, of course. Russian science and technology had made tremendous strides in the last decades preceding the revolution, and their accomplishments had been duly acknowledged abroad. In some fields Russians had been pioneers in, for example, biology and aerodynamics. It is no wonder that the Institut Pasteur welcomed many émigré scholars who were pupils of the pioneering teacher I. Mechnikov. On the other hand, medical practitioners had a hard time in most cases. Host medical legislation and associations granted licenses very reluctantly—after difficult examinations. Most émigré doctors worked, semilegally, as associates of native physicians or in subaltern positions in hospitals and clinics.[6]

In chemistry, V. Ipat'ev's well-known early work assured him secure and prominent positions in laboratories and industry abroad; he settled in the United States in the late 1920s.[7] As a specialist on the resistance of materials, S. Timoshenko was recognized as a leader in the field. He moved to the

United States early on, and thus lost most of his ties to Russia Abroad, in spite of his abiding loyalty to his homeland and its past culture; the same was true of his brother, Vladimir, the agronomist. The pioneer in aeronautics, I. Sikorskii, made his mark in U.S. aircraft by developing the helicopter. Naval engineer V. Iurkevich was actively involved in the design and construction of the innovative ocean liner *Normandie*. The list could be extended. But I wish to stress in particular that all these men (there were no women among them, alas), and their less prominent or less lucky colleagues, had been trained and had taken their first independent steps in prerevolutionary Russia. The giddy, creative atmosphere of the Silver Age gave them new perspectives and the daring to work on the frontiers of knowledge. But we also should remember that many more scientists and engineers, both at the highest and at the routine levels, in sovietized Russia, either by choice or by circumstances, stayed and continued their creative life there.

Language was the fundamental element that not only defined the tradition of modern Russian culture, as reflected in its literature, but also provided the essential ingredient of consciousness and identity of Russia Abroad. It was the Russian language that tied the émigrés to their past and that helped them to transcend their dispersion. Quite naturally, literature was also their means of expressing their belonging and performing a cultural mission for both Russias. The émigrés were determined, however, to make sure that the language used was the appropriate one for the task. Essentially, this meant ensuring its purity. As mentioned in our discussion of émigré education, the first major symbolic issue in this connection arose over the adoption or rejection of the new orthography introduced by the Bolsheviks. The reform had been worked out under the auspices of the Academy of Sciences over many years before the revolution; its introduction had been postponed because of the war. In spite of some criticism, as might be expected, the reform had been endorsed by the leading academic authorities before 1917. Unfortunately, however, it was the Soviet government that promulgated and immediately implemented it in 1918. In emigration one's stand on the issue of orthography became symbolic of one's opinion of the Soviet system or to the revolution. We may recall that once before in Russian history, under Peter the Great, the introduction of orthographic and calendar reforms had provoked much resistance; their rejection served as banner to the opposition and their acceptance symbolized support of the Petrine efforts at modernizing and Europeanizing Russia. To most émigrés, refusal to adopt the new orthography represented their determination to preserve the genuine and pure Russian language; some émigré writers, Z. Hippius and I. Bunin for example, adamantly insisted that their works be printed only in the old orthography. It was argued that the new rules did not do justice to correct pronunciation, and introduced arbitrarily spelling norms, which were supported by neither etymological nor historical considerations. The disagreement was eventually resolved: the simplified rules found more and more acceptance by the young, and availability of books printed in Soviet Russia in the new orthography led more and more émigré publishers and editors to adopt it too. It was only after World War II that the process was completed, however.

The issue was one of "purity," not only of the language, but also of the tradition that had made of literature the main expression and carrier of modern Russian culture. The stand on language purity accounts for the energetic struggle waged by all émigré pedagogues and writers against neologisms, whether of Soviet or foreign origin, as well as against foreign words and turns of phrase. Soviet neologisms, particularly the excessive use of acronyms, provoked the ire and sarcasm of all émigré intellectuals. It gave rise to the ironic and negative label "Sovdepiia" given to the land of the Soviets in émigré publications throughout most of the twenties; only in the thirties was this label changed to the more neutral and acceptable Soviet Russia which, at least, contained the name Russia. The battle against the use of foreign words in ordinary spoken language, to which any group living abroad is particularly prone, was perhaps even more difficult. The poorly educated émigrés had little concern for the elegance of the language they used, or for its aesthetic adequacy to the thought expressed; ordinary people quickly turned to foreign words for objects of daily and routine usage. Foreign intrusions spread from vocabulary to grammatical forms and constructions, giving rise to mixtures resembling pidgin languages in which foreign words acquired a Russian inflective ending, or foreign expressions were transposed verbatim into their Russian equivalents. This tendency among the émigrés was ridiculed by such writers as Don Aminado and Teffi in their humorous commentaries in the daily press. Writers and grammarians regularly published articles defending good Russian usage, pointing out incorrect forms and pejorative uses in the Soviet Union, perpetrated by both ordinary citizens and writers. In contrast, Russia Abroad proudly claimed that it was perpetuating good usage and the best traditions of verbal expression. In truth, it should be said that most émigré parents and teachers did give solid grounding to the children in good Russian and, as a rule, high standards were maintained in exile publications.

Language was an instrument that had to be maintained and kept in good working order. But it was only an instrument, as much depended on how and for what purpose it was to be used. To evaluate the efficacy and results of the use of language was the task émigré writers and critics set themselves. Such a mission raised the question of whether Russia Abroad should create a new literature, distinct and different from the one published in the homeland. More generally, had not the revolution created the appearance of two Russian literatures instead of the single entity that had existed before? The interesting aspect of this question is that its character was constantly changing, and since this was only in part the result of external events, one had to assume that the flux was caused by the creative literary process itself. Even more striking was the difference, in this respect at least, between the evolution of poetry and prose. By and large we may distinguish two quite diverse chronological periods: the twenties and the thirties. The first decade was characterized by great experimentation in Soviet literature; the second was dominated by the imposition of socialist realism as a doctrine and practice for writers in the USSR. Consequently, the gulf widened between the literatures of the two Russias.

But first we should take note of a most significant event for the cultural, more particularly literary, life of Russia Abroad, which nearly coincided with the chronological division just mentioned. In 1933, Bunin was the first Russian to receive the Nobel Prize. Leaving aside the intrinsic aesthetic merit of the award (apparently Merezhkovsky and Gorky had been also candidates) it was clearly a political as well as a literary gesture. From the literary point of view, the Nobel Committee honored a representative of the realist school of Russian fiction, a school that had its roots, as well as heyday, in the pre-revolutionary period. The award also proclaimed the higher quality of the old literature compared to contemporary Soviet writing. Lastly, it was the public recognition of a literature in exile, of its artistic autonomy—this kind of recognition was not given again by the Nobel Committee until long after the end of World War II.

For the emigration, Bunin's Nobel Prize was a truly significant moment. It enabled Bunin to escape, temporarily as it turned out, poverty; and in a most honorable gesture, Bunin shared his good fortune with fellow writers in need. A committee was set up to distribute the amount of the prize that Bunin had set aside to this end. The distribution, perhaps inevitably, created some friction and wounded feelings, but it was the first substantial material help given publicly, by the outside world, to creative writers in Russia Abroad. But even more important was the moral significance of the Nobel award: it was public recognition not only of the existence of a Russian literature in exile, but also of the moral and cultural justification of a political emigration. The international cultural community acknowledged the creative power and moral aesthetic role of an exiled writer working far from his homeland. Indirectly, the prize also condemned the repression to which literature was subjected in Soviet Russia. The fact that Bunin was essentially a nonpolitical author—albeit an unforgiving hater of the revolution and everything Bolshevik—reinforced the message from Stockholm.[8] Bunin was feted by all of Russia Abroad; the celebration turned into the proud affirmation that in creating Russia Abroad the emigration had preserved their homeland's identity as a cultural and historical force. The award came just as Stalin was putting Soviet art and literature into the straitjacket of socialist realism; the timing reinforced the message and strengthened the emigration's self-assurance. Last, but not least, it served to distinguish émigré from the Soviet literature. This is what the award signified for contemporaries, but that this was not the whole story, and an oversimplified one at that, we shall see presently.

Nearly all of the well-established prose writers who went into exile belonged to the realist tradition of Russian fiction. (D. Merezhkovsky, like Bunin a poet on occasion, stands literarily apart.) An exception was A. Remizov, idiosyncratic, playful, baroque, fascinated by the supernatural (in the lineage of Gogol). Others, in particular Bunin, Zaitsev, Shmelev, and Aldanov, may be considered in the tradition of Turgenev, Tolstoi, Chekhov. Like their predecessors, however, they did not give accurate descriptions of life observed directly for their own sake, but to point out the general human meaning inherent in their heroes and the situations in which they find themselves. In their infrequent descriptions of émigré predicaments, too, they made statements about the human condition in general, though a significant part of their work in emigration was given over to personal reminiscences and nostalgic recapturing of the past. In any event, they shunned the didacticism that was characteristic of socialist realism, as well as deliberate prettifying and mythologizing.

These traits account, I think, for their ability to remain interesting in spite of their long isolation from life in the Soviet Union and in the land of refuge. Other writers, in a similar tradition, left us unforgettably humorous and poignant descriptions of émigré life: among them we should name Don Aminado, Teffi, and A. Damanskaia. To the extent that these prose writers had not participated in the innovative experimentation of the late Silver Age (Remizov was here, too, a partial exception), or the early twenties, they did not contribute anything new aesthetically, but their novels and stories were captivating and beautiful examples of the heights that Russian prose had attained in the past. They did not reflect in any noticeable manner the influence of foreign literatures or absorb the literary milieu that surrounded them in exile. The great figures of contemporary Western prose—Joyce, Proust, Mann, and others—produced no impact on them. This may explain why they were not as widely translated as might have been expected—even Bunin's Nobel Prize did not dramatically increase the translations and publications of his work in foreign languages.

The younger generation of writers in exile could not be expected merely to repeat and continue their elders' pattern. Theirs was not only a different experience of prerevolutionary Russia, of the revolution and civil war; but, willy-nilly, they were plunged deep into the atmosphere of the host countries. They were also more receptive to the works appearing in both the Soviet and Western literatures. As far as I can judge, the younger authors' specific contribution did not consist primarily in stylistic innovations or experiments, but rather in the selection and the way of handling their themes. Their language and style remained firmly rooted in the "classical" prose of nineteenth-century Russian fiction. However, they departed from a narrow naturalism by increasingly stressing individual psychological reactions to an alien and unnatural environment. Most important, perhaps, they also showed great interest for those manifestations of human psyche that were not accountable in strictly materialist, naturalist, and rationalist terms. They were influenced by Proust and Kafka, and felt, perhaps even more strongly, the spiritualistic yearnings of the avant-garde modernists in the 1910s and 1920s. Young prose authors—whose literary debut was in emigration—Sirin (V. Nabokov), Iu. Fel'sen, B. Poplavskii, and V. Yanovsky, for example—all embraced this orientation in more or less conspicuous and elaborate manner. Their reception was mixed; many became known and appreciated only after World War II; sometimes they were even first published in a foreign language. In conclusion, as far as prose was concerned, the older émigré writers continued in the traditional manner and, since socialist realism was proclaimed official Soviet doctrine in the 1930s, their work diverged more and more from the literary production in Soviet Russia. This was even more true for the younger generation of writers. But this circumstance also made it harder for the young to find their own path and obtain recognition of their work in either of the two Russias. At the same time, however, the innovative steps taken by the younger writers, their reception of contemporary foreign writing, while distancing them from their contemporary Soviet colleagues, appear to have had an influence on the post-Stalin generation of dissident and avant-garde authors in the Soviet Union.[9]

The situation of poetry was quite different and more difficult to describe. Poetry's relationship to the Soviet scene, too, was more complex than in the case of prose. The Silver Age had made a revolutionary impact on Russian poetry, as mentioned earlier. Its innovations had paved the way for even more experimental trends, such as futurism, that followed. Of the older generation of recognized symbolist leaders, the poets Viacheslav Ivanov, Z. Hippius, and K. Bal'mont went into exile. Although they continued to write poetry, their main preoccupation and interests lay elsewhere, or their inspiration dried up. The new verse that V. Ivanov wrote in the 1920s and 1930s in Italy was published only in the late thirties, and some of it even after World War II. On the whole, he withdrew from Russia Abroad, and his isolation was compounded by his conversion to Roman Catholicism.

The most important poetic school on the eve of the revolution and in the very first years of the Soviet regime had been acmeism. A few of its representatives eventually settled in Russia Abroad, for example, G. Ivanov, V. Khodasevich, I. Odoevtseva. The young Sirin may be counted among them also. Their output in exile was less voluminous and less innovative than it had been at home, but their presence played a significant role, and they appeared on the pages of most émigré publications—almanacs, reviews, newspapers. They provided a link to the ongoing modernism of the avant garde in sovietized Russia. Mayakovsky and Esenin may have turned too propagandistic, political, and shrill, but O. Mandelshtam, A. Akhmatova, N. Gumilev, and B. Pasternak were writing poetry that was well appreciated in Russia Abroad, even if not fully understood.[10]

The most significant poetic presence in Russia Abroad with strong affinities to modernism in the homeland was Marina Tsvetaeva. She never was unquestionably accepted by all readers in Russia Abroad, not even by all its literary critics, although she was widely published (in poetry and prose). She provided constant stimulus to the development of Russian poetry, which was encouraged by communication between poets on both sides of the border and by such émigré critics as M. Slonim, K. Mochulskii, and D. Mirsky, who treated the poetic work of both Russias as a single literature. The avant garde in the Soviet Union had close friends, if not outright followers, in Russia Abroad as well. In the realm of poetry, there was no point of speaking of two literatures: it was the effort of a single poetic tradition.

This situation could not but affect the generation of émigre poets too young to have published before exile. These poets began to make themselves heard in the late 1920s and early 1930s. Because of their geographic dispersion, one may detect a Prague, Berlin, and especially a Paris (and perhaps also a Kharbin) "note" in the poems of Russia Abroad. The Paris group was in fact the best known, thanks to their easier access to publication, and surely the most innovative. The Paris poets continued the effort of their elders in the post revolutionary period, both in Russia and abroad, at finding new ways to express their experiences. It is also important to point out that, unlike most of their compatriots in exile, they were quite aware of the literary and artistic cutting edges of the West, especially in France (Cubism, Dadaism, Surrealism). Theirs was the experience of a heretofore unknown spiritual desolation against the background of life in a foreign, alienating environment. They found models of form and technique—and on occasion also emotional inspiration—in the poetry of N. Gumilev, Mandelshtam, Pasternak, and fellow émigrés G. Ivanov, M. Tsvetaeva, and V. Khodasevich. The youthful émigrés of Paris contributed something totally new to Russian poetry, but were still solidly linked to the formal traditions of the national literature. It is for this contribution that the critic (also a minor poet) G. Adamovich praised destiny for having made them exiles in Paris.[11] The most promising of the young Paris poets was B. Poplavsky, who died very young without fulfilling all of his talents. The war thinned and scattered their ranks, too.[12]

The strong link between the two Russias, rooted in their common bond with the Silver Age, did not last. In Soviet Russia, distrust of experimentation and individual creativity, along with the authoritarian and arid environment of Stalinism, stifled the poetic creativity, at least in published form, as we know from the tragic lives of Mandelshtam, Pasternak, and Akhmatova. On the other hand, the younger generation of poets in Russia Abroad continued to work and to publish, while living in penury in a foreign land. Their creative efforts exacted a high emotional and physical price, and the scanty rewards did not always seem commensurate with it. The gap between the two Russias of literature was to be breached only long after the end of the war, much too late for the most émigré poets to have a direct impact on their dissident comrades in the Soviet Union.

The foregoing observations raise two complex issues. First, what was the relationship of the literature of Russia Abroad to the foreign literatures in whose midst it existed? Second, what "feedback" effect could writings of Russia Abroad have on the literary scene of Soviet Russia? In a provocative article that appeared in the *Contemporary Annals* in 1929, V. Weidlé (later a leading art and literary critic), who was most favorably disposed to the younger generation of émigré writers, pointed out that the Russians had always poorly understood foreign literatures, especially that of France. True, Weidlé added, they were believed to have been inspired by foreign models, most specially French ones, for example Pushkin was inspired by Parny, the symbolists by Baudelaire, and so on. But, argued Weidlé, it was a very superficial influence, and it went along with a genuinely poor understanding of the great French literary works. Characteristically, the Russians read Parny and Maeterlinck, but ignored Valéry, Claudel, and Proust, for example.

These harsh judgments should be qualified; there is no question that German and English writers did have an impact on Russian authors, including émigré ones (Tsvetaeva, for instance, had been under the spell of Rilke); younger émigré poets and writers had links with Dadaist circles in France (thanks to older writers and authors who had made contact with them before, or at the very beginning of, emigration, for example the Burliuk brothers and I. Zdanevich). Basically, Weidlé had a valid point. Life in Russia Abroad, however, was not very conducive to overcoming this deficiency, since the émigrés' energies were absorbed by the problems of daily survival while many foreign writers had at best only a patronizing and superficial interest in the Russians, especially the younger ones.[13]

Strange as it may seem at first glance, many émigré writers did not acquire an adequate command of the host's language to feel comfortable speaking it or reading its literature. There were outstanding exceptions, of course—most notably Sirin-Nabokov who was bilingual (in English) and Weidlé who became so in French. Yet Nabokov claims, though in his case it may have been a pose, that despite his decade-long residence in Berlin, he did not learn German or know its literature well. Some younger émigré authors switched to writing in another language. J. Kessel, H. Troyat, Z. Oldenburg, and Z. Shakhovskaia ended up writing exclusively in French. It is true, however, that the writers in exile did not reflect in any significant way the fact that they lived in a foreign land, with easy access to another, rich literary tradition that could offer an interesting and a novel element in their own writing. Russian literature in emigration remained as isolated from Western literatures as it had been in prerevolutionary Russia, perhaps even more so. The writers in exile were lonely and lost in a foreign milieu.

The other issue of a "feedback" to the USSR was addressed earlier. We have seen that during the twenties, especially in poetry, there was lively exchange between the two Russias. It would seem, though, that this communication was ovewhelmingly in one direction: from Soviet Russia to Russia Abroad. This was only natural, since Soviet Russia was experiencing the stimulation and novelty of forging a new society. The cultural impact of Bolshevik Russia was even greater on foreign writers and artists who watched these efforts with interest, nay fascination—whatever their attitudes about the Soviets' results and methods. Certainly the Soviet "experiment" (even present-day Soviet leaders seem to imply that it was indeed only an experiment with somewhat questionable results) elicited curiosity and a great deal of sympathy among Western intellectuals, a fact that also contributed to further isolating the writers of Russia Abroad from their milieu and affected their relations with foreign colleagues.

In the 1930s the contacts between émigrés and Soviet citizens decreased and they ceased for all intents and purposes after 1934. Soviet citizens were afraid to have links with the outside world, especially with émigrés. Intellectuals and writers in exile had no interest in the dull and stereotyped works produced in the homeland according to the rigid canons of socialist realism imposed from above. Under these circumstances, there was no chance for exile writings to have an impact on Soviet authors. First, the latter knew very little about these works and, second, the older generation had nothing to teach them. As for the younger, more innovative, exile authors, they could not expect to find much response to their works (even if accessible), with their underlying tones of alienation and despair, on the part of contemporaries whose experience had been so utterly different from their own. At any rate, official Soviet policy did not permit formal experimentation or innovation, the one area where Soviet authors might have been interested in learning from their émigré colleagues. The picture changed—and quite radically—with the thaw after Stalin's death, and it has been changing ever since, at a dizzying pace in the last few years. The Soviet public, first the younger generation and dissidents of all ages and tastes, discovered the culture of Russia Abroad, including its literary creations. Emigré writers of the older generation, Bunin, Tsvetaeva, Remizov, V. Ivanov, and V. Khodasevich, have again found their way into Soviet publications (including some works written in exile). Keen attention is paid to the writings of the thinkers, essayists, and critics of Russia Abroad. The émigré influence was long delayed, but it appears to be more effective and powerful for it.

For the arts and music, the situation was naturally quite different. Unlike literature, they were not organically bound by the linguistic medium—a medium not immediately accessible to the host world, and whose "purity" had to be jealously preserved. Let us also remember that in the first years of its existence, the Soviet government tolerated and even encouraged modernist trends and avant-garde aspirations (e.g., in architecture and decorative arts) as potentially useful instruments for the formation and dissemination of a new "proletarian" culture. Since no verbal expression that could carry explicit political messages was involved, the government could be more tolerant of artistic and musical expression. Of course, these arts can carry political messages, too, but in this particular instance their message was basically "revolutionary." As long as this Soviet policy lasted, there was no problem for both Russias in maintaining contact, even close ties, with Western artistic and musical life. But when Soviet policy changed and imposed the standards of what became known as socialist realism, the break occurred in music and art too. The division was reinforced by the integration of many artists in Russia Abroad into the Western artistic world and their subsequent common development with the latter.

We should also mention that modernist trends in Russian theater and staging, inaugurated by K. Stanislavski, V. Nemirovich-Danchenko, and Vs. Meierhold in the Silver Age, also had representatives in Russia abroad and attracted the interest of foreign theaters. Emigré directors and actors who managed to overcome the barrier of language in their art were absorbed into Western dramatic life. For example, G. and L. Pitoeff contributed to the modernization of German, and then French, drama production. They earned their greatest triumphs on the Parisian stage where they closely collaborated with the leading French actors and directors in the 1920s and 1930s. As long as films were silent, many Russian actors found a distinguished place in them (e.g., I. Mozzhukhin); the coming of the "talkies" ended this possibility.

Unfortunately, the legitimate theater was not as adaptable. The émigré actors of the Moscow Art Theater performed before Russian-speaking audiences almost exclusively. Eventually, émigré theater companies (e.g., the Prague "branch" of the Moscow Art Theater, and M. Chekhov's group) had to cut down on their tours and then disband as the population of the Russian diaspora declined and economic difficulties put guest appearances beyond their means. Even countries with a large Russian minority—such as Latvia—which had managed to support Russian theaters and operas in the 1920s, had to give up these efforts in the mid-1930s, under the impact of political restrictions and economic stress.

In conclusion, therefore, we can say that the diaspora made its most significant contributions to Western and world culture in the realms of literature, the arts, and music, to the extent that it continued the creative impulses of the Silver Age. This aspect is now proving to be the most significant heritage that the emigration left for both Soviet Russia and the West.

6

The Kingdom of God Is Within You: Church and Religion in the Diaspora

In the twentieth century we have alas become accustomed to the sight of thousands of people straggling from devastated lands to find refuge from the violence and horror of war, revolution, and civil war. We are struck not so much by their pitiful physical appearance, as by the forlorn hopelessness and despair in their eyes. It is the look of people who have lost everything: their material foundation and social status, to be sure, but even more devastating is the loss of psychological and spiritual guideposts. Their eyes mirror the death of all the ideals and hopes for which they had fought and suffered; their very bearing is witness to spiritual loneliness and the loss of a moral center. Both literally and figuratively this was also true of those who were escaping the Red Army's "reconquista" of the former Russian Empire. Inner emptiness dulled the eyes of those evacuated from the Crimea, of the civilian refugees in former prisoner of war camps, of children and students in temporary shelters, of the men, women, and children in transit barracks in Latvia, Bulgaria, Yugoslavia, or of those who eventually found themselves destitute on the pavements of Berlin, Paris, and other foreign cities.

Whatever their previous political ideas or social ideals, the émigrés had lost the stable signposts and meaning of their life. Few of the previously held social values remained intact in the crucible of revolution and civil war. The monarchy—except perhaps for evoking pity for the last emperor and his family—had lost its aura and displayed its inability to prevent chaos and to mobilize the people's loyalty. The liberal and democratic socialist programs had demonstrated their futility in taming the violence that had shaken Russia to its foundations. The upheaval had destroyed the moral values that had held Russian society together: it had revealed man's beastliness toward his fellow creatures. On the personal plane, too, Russia's "time of troubles" had left bleeding wounds and scars. Members of the same family had found themselves on opposite sides, and forgot their feelings for each other; close relatives were lost—killed in battle, dead from disease and hunger, executed, or disappeared without a trace in the rubble of a society in collapse. Many families were broken up, some members (usually the younger ones) in exile, and the remainder stranded or lost in the homeland: Marina Tsvetaeva left Russia to find her husband who had joined the White Armies; the future Harvard professor, M. Karpovich, had lost contact with his fiancee whom he found again only years later; a Nabokov sister was found by her fiance in a refugee camp, and so it went, on and on. Parents set out to locate their children who had been evacuated abroad, sometimes with bitter and ironic results, as in V. Nabokov's story "Mashen'ka." And as if this were not misery enough, material and physical hardships marked the first steps in emigration, compounded by the callous, if not hostile, treatment by former allies and foreign authorities and citizens.

For many émigrés, a renewal of faith proved to be a consolation and a source of the inner strength needed to confront the ordeal of exile, and to fill the vacuum left by the collapse of their idols. For the majority of the Russian exiles faith meant Russian Orthodoxy. But turning to Orthodoxy implied involvement in the church as the central pivot of daily life. It also meant, of course, renewing bonds with tradition, although the new circumstances of emigration would force them to abandon rigid old ways and to search for new forms of church life.

The heritage of the immediate past, however, was not particularly propitious for a new, active, forward-looking life in the church. Since the reign of Peter I, the Russian Orthodox Church had been a handmaiden of the state, and a rather meek and submissive one at that. It is true, as G. L. Freeze has persuasively argued, that in many respects, especially in internal discipline and family matters, the official church had preserved much of its authority, and effectively defended and implemented its interests and points of view.[1] But in matters intellectual and educational, as well as social and ethical, matters that were of primary significance for people of the twentieth century, the church's performance before 1917 left much to be desired. The close connection between state and church that prevailed in the latter decades of the imperial regime (e.g., the role of K. Pobedonostsev, the scandals surrounding Rasputin and other healers and "holy men" at the court of Nicholas II, and so on), had grievously undermined the prestige of the church as an institution, even among the devout members of the elites. It is also fair to say that the church had not effectively confronted the many urgent social and economic problems, including popular education, which Russian society faced at the dawn of the twentieth century. In short, under the old regime, the church had not exercised the influence that many educated members of the intellectual and professional elites believed it should.

Nor was it surprising under the circumstances that the church had provided no guidance to those educated individuals who were seeking answers to questions raised by modern philosophy, science, technology, and socioeconomic problems. The cruelties and mockeries inflicted on members of the clergy during the civil war, and at the behest of the Bolshevik government had outraged many believers; yet these outrages were not enough to rehabili-tate the church's past conduct. The more enlightened among the émigrés, especially the intellectuals, were well aware that the traditional character and role of the church had to be overcome if the spirit of religion were genuinely to permeate Russian life.

This somewhat bleak picture should be qualified. In the decade and a half preceding the outbreak of World War I—which put an end (believed to be temporary) to many constructive beginnings—some things had begun to change, both in the church itself and in its relationship with the state and society. This was particularly true of the years following the revolution of 1905, in spite of the so-called reaction under Peter Stolypin and his successors. In the first place, we can observe efforts to revive the parish. Parishioners were permitted, at times even encouraged, to play a more active role in the church, while parish priests became more involved in the social, educational, and economic problems of their flock. This trend was particularly noticeable in the growing importance assumed by parish and Sunday schools in spreading literacy among children of the peasantry. In the cities the parish, the clergy frequently provided for the social life of the peasants who had come to seek work in factories or households. Some parish clergy took a leading role in help-ing to alleviate the material conditions, as well as spiritual destitution, of these new urban dwellers and their children. True, as far as cultural and in-tellectual needs went, the church was not much help to the common people, for it was far behind the times with respect to the dominant scientific and artistic trends. This was a major reason for the clergy's attempt to keep their flock ignorant of advanced notions. But in so doing they were losing the chance of influencing the upcoming generation of educated and semieducated young people.

Besides the revival of parish life, the first decade of the twentieth century also brought about the realization of the need for extensive reform of the central organization of the church and its relationship to the state: clergy and laity demanded that a general council of the Russian Orthodox Church be convened to discuss this question. There was also a move to reestablish the Patriarchate, abolished by Peter I, as a means of freeing the church from the stifling embrace of the state. These reform efforts did not bear any significant fruit as long as the Empire lasted. But in 1917, under the Provisional Gov-ernment, a general council reestablished the Patriarchate in 1918. Thus church life was paradoxically reinvigorated at the very moment when a mili-tantly atheist government was taking power in the country. The "liberated," now independent church, involved itself more fully in the life of society, and during the civil war it shared the travails of the people.

Whatever the ambiguities of the reform drive, the first years of the twen-tieth century were a watershed in the relationship between the church and the educated elites of the empire. The Silver Age witnessed a dramatic renais-sance of interest in metaphysics, as well as idealistic and vitalistic philosophy in the mode popularized by symbolism, Bergson, Nietzsche, and neo-

Kantianism. This philosophical revival was directly related to similar trends in the West, although in Russia it found a much wider application in literature, the arts, scholarship, and sociopolitical ideas. A most characteristic feature of the Russian scene was the connection that the philosophical revival established with religious thought and scholarship. In addition, following the example set in the nineteenth century by the Slavophiles, the active lead was taken by laypeople, rather than by clergy or academics. As a matter of fact, since church authorities were at best lukewarm to this ferment, only a few rare individual clerics played an active role; although it might be noted that a few of the prominent laypeople involved in the spiritual renaissance eventually took holy orders, for example, S. Bulgakov, V. Zen'kovskii, A. Kartashev. An interesting experiment of cooperation between clergy and laity took place in those years: the Religious Philosophical Societies, founded in St. Petersburg and then opening branches in Moscow and Kiev, served as a forum where laymen and clergy came together to discuss problems of religion, philosophy, and politics. Eventually, the church authorities forbade the active participation of hierarchs (i.e., bishops and abbots), but individual priests and faculty from the theological academies and seminaries maintained an active exchange with lay thinkers and publicists. Thanks to this development, some members of the intelligentsia and leaders of the clergy could renew their contacts in emigration.

One more aspect of the Russian Orthodox Church in the 1920s should be mentioned at this point: the fate of the church after the Bolshevik seizure of power. The militantly atheistic and anticlerical position of the Soviet government needs no elaboration or comment. True, at first, the patriarch and the ecclesiastic authorities were left alone after Patriarch Tikhon had declared in 1919 that the church and clergy were not to engage in politics of any sort, especially not to promote one political regime or party over another. Yet the church and its clergy could hardly avoid controversy or confrontation with the Soviet authorities while dealing with the many difficulties that beset the population during the civil war. Eventually, Patriarch Tikhon and several bishops, for example Metropolitan Benjamin of Petrograd, were to die in defense of what they believed to be the higher interests of faith and church. Since religious education and proselytizing were prohibited, Russia was soon confronted with a lack of clergy, so that the young generation was not only growing up in ignorance of dogma and ritual, but was also enlisted in the antireligious campaigns. The very survival of Russia as a Christian nation or of the Russians as believers seemed to be at issue. These circumstances could not but color the attitudes and behavior of the émigrés, especially of those who wanted to keep alive the religious revival of the Silver Age, and to preserve the spirit of the pre-1914 social and political reformism.

The situation was complicated, raising moral problems for churchmen and believers, by the organization of the so-called Living Church (*Zhivaia tserkov'*). It was an attempt on the part of some hierarchs and parish clergy to find a modus vivendi under Bolshevik rule. In return for a pledge of complete loyalty to the political authorities, the parishes and episcopal sees of the Living Church were to be recognized by the government and allowed to continue their normal ecclesiastical activities. Experience, however, soon showed that the spirit of accommodation did not apply equally to both partners. It did not lead to a genuine "live and let live" relationship; appeasement resulted in the Living Church being more and more restricted, even though it was well used for the government's purposes. Once the Soviet government no longer saw any need to placate the church or its faithful, which became obvious after it declared war on the countryside, it unleashed a major campaign against known members of the clergy. In the late 1920s, show trials and sentences to hard labor, exile, and even death, decimated the ranks of the Living Church and the Patriarchate of Moscow. These events not only confirmed the émigrés in their uncompromising rejection of the Soviet regime, but raised anew the moral and practical issues of the relationship between church, secular society, and political authority. At the most basic level it questioned the church's ability to remain completely unconcerned about what political and socioeconomic system would be established. It provoked lively, even acrimonious, debates that agitated church authorities and religious circles in exile in the 1930s. It made it more difficult for the Russian church abroad to retain its traditional, prerevolutionary submissive and apolitical stance.

Quite clearly, both the fact of emigration and the situation of church and religion in the Soviet homeland, stimulated among the exiles great concern for religious issues and for the central role of the Orthodox Church in defining national and cultural identity. At the same time, these same circumstances made possible a number of new approaches and practices, not only for resolving problems of everyday life, but also for fruitfully discussing basic intellectual and spiritual questions. These same circumstances, too, allowed the Russian clergy in exile, and concerned émigré laity, to establish contact and engage in ecumenical dialogue with other Christian denominations.[2]

Before the revolution a number of Russian parishes had existed abroad; they were mainly attached to the imperial embassies in major states and to princely residences, some of whose members belonged to the Russian Orthodox Church (for example, Hessen-Darmstadt, Württemberg). These parishes and churches were under the jurisdiction of the Holy Synod that had governed the church affairs ever since Peter the Great. In 1918 the general Russian Church Council abolished the Holy Synod and elected a patriarch. Since this occurred after the seizure of power by Lenin, hierarchs and clergy in territories not controlled by the Bolsheviks refused to recognize the change. During the civil war, in the south, under the authority of the White Armies' command, the Temporary Ecclesiastical Administration, consisting of the metropolitans and bishops of the area, was set up. The end of the civil war brought about the emigration of practically all members of this Temporary Administration, which reconstituted itself in the Kingdom of Serbs, Croats, and Slovenes near the seat of the patriarch of Serbia, at Sremski Karlovci. The Bishops' Synod of Sremski Karlovci saw itself as the temporary lieutenant of the Holy Synod of the Empire, and it acquired prestige and authority thanks to the presence of Metropolitan Antonii (Khrapovitskii) the highly distinguished (intellectually as well as ecclesiastically) though controversial former metropolitan of Kiev. At first the majority of the parishes abroad, especially in the countries bordering on Russia, recognized the authority of this synod; but a minority accepted the newly elected Patriarch Tikhon as the head of the Russian Orthodox Church. The imprisonment of the patriarch (and his subsequent early death), and the emergence of the Living Church, led to much uncertainty about the real source of authority for the Russian churches abroad. The problem was compounded by attempts of Orthodox churches in the Balkans to take over responsibility for the Russian parishes in exile. For example, the metropolitan of Athens, and later the patriarch of Serbia, tried to have themselves recognized as the guardians of all parishes in exile and to appoint local bishops to supervise them at their own discretion. Nor could the patriarch of Constantinople remain unconcerned, though he was willing to recognize the Russian church in exile as an autocephalous entity.

The former archbishop of Volhynia, Evlogii, had been delegated by the Bishops' Synod of Sremski Karlovci to head the Russian church in Western Europe, with headquarters in Berlin, at the time when it was the center of the Russian emigration, since many former prisoner of war camps in Germany held a very large number of exiles. Soon after his arrival in Berlin, however, Evlogii was appointed by the patriarch of Moscow as the metropolitan of the Russian church in Western Europe, with jurisdiction over Germany, France, Belgium, Switzerland, Italy, Holland, and Scandinavia. Evlogii accepted and at the same time agreed to the patriarch's policy of renunciation, in the name of the church, of involvement in politics. At first this appointment and this policy stance were also accepted by the Bishops' Synod. When, however, the Bishops' Synod issued a statement (carried by the émigré press) endorsing the principle of monarchy for Russia, the patriarch of Moscow (Sergius, after Tikhon's death) reiterated the order to renounce political involvements in the name of the church. Evlogii accepted the order and publicly repudiated the Bishops' Synod endorsement of the monarchy (although personally he was, and remained, a monarchist). An attempt at reconciliation failed, and the Russian church abroad was split between those parishes and dioceses that recognized the Bishops' Synod of Sremski Karlovci and its pro-monarchist leanings and those that accepted Metropolitan Evlogii as their superior. In 1923 Evlogii moved his see to Paris where he remained until his death in 1946 as metropolitan of Western Europe, and accepted the jurisdiction of the patriarch of Constantinople in 1927, after the Soviets abolished the Moscow Patriarchate (they restored it during the Second World War). The split naturally gave rise to many conflicts—some ending before local courts—over property rights of individual parishes, and controversies within the ranks of the congregations that directly affected a number of church-affiliated activities, as we shall see. The division was exacerbated by theological disputes when the Bishops' Synod of Sremski Karlovci declared Father S. Bulgakov, dean of the Theological Seminary of St. Serge in Paris, a heretic and excommunicated him for his sophiological views. Since Bulgakov was a leading figure in the educational and intellectual life of the Russian church everywhere in Europe (except Yugoslavia), this act compounded the conflict, and disoriented many faithful. In any event, with respect to the cultural life of the emigration everywhere (with the exception of Belgrade and to some extent also Sofia), it was Metropolitan Evlogii and the institutions he patronized that were central and most creative. They will naturally be the focus of our account.

It should be noted that the split did not create particularly serious problems on the parish level, except in those few cases when a priest had a conflict with his parishioners, or when two persons claimed the same position. In most cases, however, such conflicts resulted in the creation in the same city or locality of both Karlovcian synodal and "Evlogian" metropolitan parishes—the congregation members selecting whichever was more appealing. Such a relatively peaceful solution was made possible by the "federalistic" tradition of Orthodoxy. In the absence of a single central authority, as was the papacy for the Catholic Church, multiple jurisdictions did not vitally affect individual parishes and their ability to minister effectively to the needs of their congregations. The impression one gains from the sources, especially the memoirs, is that the split was of consequence only to the hierarchy and to lay elites of the emigration. As for the latter, the personality of Metropolitan Evlogii made him the indispensable leader of Orthodoxy in exile. This remained the case even after the Nazi seizure of power when the extreme right-wing monarchists took control of the émigré organizations in Germany. During the war, under the Occupation, Evlogii preserved both the dignity of the church and his personal integrity, despite the efforts of Nazi appointees to have him confer his blessings on the doings of the German authorities. For all practical purposes, the influence and authority of Sremski Karlovci remained confined to Yugoslavia, the Balkans, and parishes (and clergy) directly affiliated with monarchist organizations (veterans' groups, nursing homes, cadet corps). Parenthetically it may be noted, although it is outside the framework of this study, that a major Russian religious center in the United States, the monastery at Jordanville, New York, remained affiliated with the Bishops' Synod, and the Russian church in America experienced the split when a number of displaced persons from Yugoslavia settled in the United States after 1945 along with some of the clergy from the Bishops' Synod.

Traditionally the Russian church was composed of relatively small parishes, which explains their large number in the Empire. This was even more characteristic of the church in Russia Abroad, as the émigrés were widely scattered in small groups in an alien environment. As a result, small émigré parishes were quite scattered too, often in makeshift quarters, and naturally quite poor. The demographic and sociological circumstances we have described earlier made many émigré parishes short-lived, and many more shifted their locale over the years. Only the central churches in the major capitals of Europe (and in Kharbin), which had served the diplomatic and resident colonies before 1914, had a continuous existence and encompassed a larger circle of the emigration. The best known among them was the Cathedral of St. Alexander Nevsky on rue Daru in Paris, the church of Metropolitan Evlogii. Not infrequently, especially in outlying places, congregations numbered only a few dozen parishioners, and services were held in converted rooms or stores. More likely than not, their priest had several such churches under his care and traveled from one to the other. Such was the typical situation of congregations of émigré workers in the coal-mining districts in northern France and Belgium, for example. This circumstance also explains how the émigré church managed to get along with a limited, and not easily replenished, clergy, for one priest had to serve several parishes for financial reasons as well.

The situation was quite different in the so-called Border States, the Baltic republics, Poland, Romania, where there was a sizable minority of "native" Russians. Their churches were well established, under the jurisdiction of local bishops. Their major problem, and not of concern to this study, was the discriminatory and oppressive administrative regime under which they had to live. Moreover, they practically played no role (except in some urban centers) in the life of the émigrés who were an almost alien element for them. But their plight was of interest to religious leaders of the diaspora who made efforts to assist them culturally. In some instances, in Estonia and Latvia for example, émigré church organizations, such as the Russian Christian Student Movement, were temporarily successful in this regard.

We should also remember that in addition to parishes (and episcopal churches) there existed émigré monastic groups for both men and women. In places that formerly had belonged to the Empire and that after 1918 became part of new (or enlarged) states, Russian Orthodox monasteries continued their earlier existence, though with little influx of new members—e.g., Valaam in Karelia and Pechory in Estonia. In some other instances, chased by war and civil upheaval, entire monasteries and convents moved to more peaceful environments—for example, the convent of the Mother of God in Lesna Yugoslavia (near Khopovo) was founded by nuns expelled from the convent in Chelm (Kholm) of the same name; and the monastery of Pochaevo, with its printing press, moved to Ladomirova in Slovakia. New monastic congregations arose in countries of exile, especially in the Balkans and in France. They, too, were small and on the whole condemned to slow death due to natural attrition of their membership. However, they often served as locales for émigré church conferences or summer camps. On the whole, monastic establishments played little part in the cultural life and everyday consciousness of the emigration. New vocations had to receive their first experiences and ordination in Russian Orthodox monasteries in Palestine or on Mt. Athos, Greece, as the life of Ioann (Shakhovskoi), later archbishop of San Francisco, illustrates.

Naturally, in the long run, the most critical problem confronting Russian émigré parishes was their staffing. The ranks of priests who had emigrated had to be renewed, not to mention the fact that the number of such émigré priests was insufficient to minister to all the widely scattered parishes and institutions. Nor could one count on replacements from Soviet Russia, even at a time when travel to and fro remained possible. Ecclesiastical seminaries and academies had been closed in Soviet Russia (some were reopened only during and after World War II), and in the few that remained students and faculty were constantly exposed to persecution and could not obtain permission to go abroad (and their presence was even more needed in the homeland if church life was to survive there). Training seminaries in Orthodox countries— Bulgaria and Yugoslavia in particular—could be of some help, but this did not always accommodate exiles living in Western Europe. Obviously, ways had to be found to train young priests abroad.

The problem was met by founding a specialized institution with a double purpose: to train new priests and to provide for scholarly study of the theology and history of the Orthodox Church. Theological scholarship had been a significant aspect of the growing professionalization, and of the widening of intellectual horizons, in Russia at the end of the nineteenth and in the first decade of the twentieth centuries. The deepening knowledge and the broadening methodology in the postreform era had affected all areas of science and scholarship, including religious, theological, and historical studies. The impetus for founding a specialized institution to meet the intellectual and professional needs of the Russian church in the diaspora came about under the following circumstances.

We have seen in an earlier context that the expulsion of more than a hundred prominent intellectual and academic personalities from Soviet Russia in 1922 had brought to Berlin, and later to Prague and Paris, the most active and leading figures in the religious life of prerevolutionary Russia. They joined such religious leaders as S. Bulgakov and A. Kartashev, who had emigrated earlier. Among the new exiles N. A. Berdiaev was the most forceful personality. Thanks to his energy and wide circle of acquaintances among Western intellectuals, he succeeded in organizing the Free Religious and Spiritual Society in Berlin. Financial backing was secured from leaders of the American YMCA. The society in turn founded an academy that sponsored series of lectures on cultural, historical, philosophical, and religious subjects. When Berdiaev moved to Paris, the two enterprises moved too, although some of their major active participants—e.g., S. Frank and F. Stepun—remained in Germany.

The existence of this academy prompted Russian exile personalities, concerned about the future of their church in the diaspora, to plan for the training of priests and to offer graduate level instruction for those already ordained. At first, Prague was considered for its location because it had the greatest concentration of students and academics, and the Russian Christian Student Movement was under way there too. The existence of a Russian library in Prague at the Methodist Center, and the generally favorable attitude of the Czech authorities toward émigré academic enterprises, were additional inducements. But there was also talk of locating the institution in the Kingdom of Serbs, Croats, and Slovenes where not only the Bishops' Synod at Sremski Karlovci served as an ecclesiastic rallying point (this was before the split with Metropolitan Evlogii), but where also the local Orthodox Church had extended a helping hand to the many Russian priests and parishes settled along with professionals by the fledgling state. Eventually, however, the opportunity to purchase a facility, and the presence of the most dynamic intellectual personalities in Paris, favored establishing the religious institution there.

The opportunity arose when the French government put on sale the buildings and grounds of a German Protestant church that had been sequestered at the outbreak of war in 1914. With the help of American and English funds secured by Dr. John R. Mott, Metropolitan Evlogii purchased the property for the Russian church in exile. The metropolitan, émigré scholars, and lay leaders, with the energetic backing of the YMCA, decided to use this property to establish an educational and scholarly center, with housing facilities for students to be recruited from among the diaspora all over the world, of course mainly from Europe. A special appeal to John D. Rockefeller secured additional funds to help defray the cost of instruction and fellowships for the prospective students.[3] Berdiaev's academy was first to recruit prospective faculty and plan the curriculum. The Russian émigré community responded quite enthusiastically and generously, at first at any rate, to Evlogii's appeal, and collected part of the money through a fund-raising campaign that reached to the Far East and the United States.

In 1925 the church and grounds were consecrated to St. Serge of Radonezh, the patron saint of Muscovy, and a seminary and a theological institute were opened the same year. The entire complex came to be known as *Sergeevskoe podvor'e*—it is still active, though its central role has been taken over by the St. Vladimir Seminary in the United States after World War II. Metropolitan Evlogii was the nominal head of the institution, but he always exercised an active supervisory role. His coadjutor, Bishop Benjamin was appointed rector and intellectual and spiritual leadership was given by the dean, Father S. Bulgakov. A distinguished faculty, both clerical and lay, was brought together: S. Bulgakov, I. Lagovskii, S. Bezobrazov, G. Florovsky, A. Kartashev, G. Fedotov, V. Il'in, N. Lossky, B. Vysheslavtsev, L. Zander, N. Kullman, P. Kovalevsky, and P. Chesnokov, and later K. Mochulskii and V. Weidlé (some, S. Bezobrazov for example, was later ordained as Father Kassian and became the dean after 1945).

The curriculum, patterned on that of prerevolutionary theological seminaries and academies, included the following major fields: Old and New Testament; dogmatic theology; patristics; general and Russian history of the church; history of the Western church; liturgics; philosophy; logic; Slavonic, Latin, and Greek languages; and theory of church chanting. The third year, 1926–1927, witnessed the graduation of the first class of the seminary: nineteen students graduated, twenty were in the second-year course, and twenty-three (and two auditors) were in the first-year course.[4] For both personal (mainly economic) and scholarly reasons, not all the students ended up by graduating, and not all pursued a strictly clerical career thereafter. Yet modest as the figures may appear today, in retrospect it is clear that St. Serge's did help to preserve and train the intellectual and spiritual backbone of the theological leadership of the Russian church abroad (we need only recall the names of such postwar personalities as Fathers A. Schmeman and J. Meyendorff). It also played a part in preserving Russian culture in the diaspora, overcoming great financial constraints through the generosity of the World Christian Student Federation, the YMCA, and the dedication of the émigrés themselves.[5]

The intellectual role of St. Serge's was not restricted to offering courses for future priests. It provided intellectuals and scholars with modest means to continue their own scholarly and pedagogic work, which benefited the émigré community at large, and helped to promote Russian culture in foreign circles as well. The seminary and institute also sponsored publications that were a contribution to Russian culture and scholarship. The major religious journal of the emigration, *Put'* (The Way), under the editorship of Berdiaev, was not an organ of St. Serge's, but the majority of its contributors were on the institute's staff, and it played a seminal role in the development of Russian theology and religious scholarship. The house organ of the St. Serge Institute was *Pravoslavnaia mysl'* (Orthodox Thought), which carried specialized studies on theology and questions directly related to the life of the church, i.e., liturgy and homiletics. For a wider public, St. Serge published the so-called *listki* (leaflets) of didactic and apologetic contents, in continuation of the example set by the brochures and pamphlets or broadsheets issued by the St. Serge Holy Trinity Monastery and others in prerevolutionary Russia.

Under St. Serge's auspices, though not under its imprint, the YMCA Press published books by members of its faculty and thus indirectly contributed to Russian historiography and religious scholarship. It is not possible to list here all these publications, especially because the boundaries are blurred between items resulting directly from the activities of St. Serge's and those that stemmed from émigré religious life in general.[6] Leaving aside the strictly theological works of S. Bulgakov on sophiology, I would like to mention the works of two faculty members, which were seminal in the West for what are now called Russian studies. The first, Father G. Florovsky, ordained after completing his historical studies in Prague, wrote many articles on Russian literary history and philosophy. In connection with his appointment to St. Serge's to teach patristics, he wrote two volumes of what he had originally planned as a comprehensive history, *Eastern Fathers of the Early Church* and *Byzantine Fathers of the Church*. They are classics in the field and, even though they were written in Russian, they had a significant impact on patristic scholarship and theology in the West. Florovsky's major work, however, was also directly related to his study of the Greek Fathers and to his teaching at St. Serge's: *Puti russkogo bogosloviia* (The ways of Russian theology), which appeared in late 1938, on the eve of the Second World War.

Its impact, therefore, came after the war, largely as a result of Florovsky's move to the United States where he had numerous students. Since we shall deal with the historiographic features of the book elsewhere, I note only that the book's contents encompassed much more than the title implies; in fact, it is an original, stimulating, as well as somewhat controversial, history of Russian thought, both religious and secular.[7]

The second scholar at St. Serge's, whose work also marked a new departure from prerevolutionary historiography, was G. Fedotov. Fedotov had made his scholarly debut in French medieval history by studying religious life and conceptions in Merovingian times. He had made use of well-known hagiographic sources in an original way that foreshadowed the sociology of religion and the "thick description" approach. He applied the same methodology and documentation to the study of Russian sainthood. Using hagiographical sources and, more important, the so-called spiritual verse that directly reflected the truly living aspects of Russian religiosity, Fedotov published the *Saints of Old Rus'*, in which he set forth the typology of Russian saintliness and described its peculiarities. This was followed by a short biography of Metropolitan St. Philip of Moscow, whose death on the orders of Ivan IV, had obvious contemporary relevance. Finally, Fedotov began a history of the Russian religious mind that was never completed, although the first volume came out after the war in English.[8] For this book, he brought to bear his analytical skill and his fine anthropological institution to paint a comprehensive picture of the development of Russian religious feeling and attitudes, from earliest times to the seventeenth century, and their intertwining with survivals of pagan and natural cults. His observations and conclusions had implications for the reform of modern society, particularly for a post-Soviet reconstruction of Russia, as had the allusions to contemporary events in his earlier works. Fedotov's writings served to restate and defend the notion of social commitment as a genuine native trait of the Russian Christian tradition and church practice. At the same time they helped redefine Russian national identity as rooted in this religious heritage—much needed by an emigration that had come to question the nature of its cultural heritage and identity.

Of course, St. Serge's was not the only institution that provided printed materials needed by clergy and faithful in the diaspora. Russia under Soviet rule could no longer be a source for such publications, at least until the late 1930s when, quite grudgingly, a limited amount of religious publications were again permitted. Nor did the Orthodox churches in the Balkans have the means, or perhaps the inclination, to step into the breach for the sake of the church in exile. Before 1914, liturgical and didactic materials had not been much needed abroad since there were few Russians in permanent residence outside the Empire; in any case, such literature could be easily ordered from the various ecclesiastical publishing houses in Russia. On the other hand, the majority of the most active, enterprising, and well-connected émigré intellectuals, who had been involved in publishing in Russia before the revolution, were little interested in religious literature. Theirs was primarily a secular orientation, and the majority also harbored a suspicious antichurch complex that had developed as a consequence of the alliance between the state and the church hierarchy under the Romanovs. There was thus a great need in the diaspora if religious life was to survive meaningfully in a foreign environment.

Fortunately for the diaspora, one of the most active presses of religious materials, connected, as was frequently the case in Russia, with a monastery, was located in territory ceded to Poland by the Treaty of Riga: the Monastery of St. Job in Pochaevo. Its abbot, Archimandrite Vitalii (Maksimenko), had established one of the most efficient and successful printing presses specializing in reading matter for the uneducated. Harassed by the Polish authorities, the monastery sold the printing press and moved to Vladimirovo (Ladimirova) in eastern Slovakia. With the money obtained from the sale of the original equipment, the abbot purchased more modern machines, and after some hard beginnings, the monastery again became the most active center producing liturgical books and, most important, the devotional brochures that were distributed throughout Russia Abroad. Rapidly Vladimirovo acquired what amounted to a monopoly on such publications in the West. Other religious publishers were only sporadically active, and had neither the facilities for distribution nor competitive prices to challenge Vladimirovo's hold on the market. The monastery's publishing activities lasted until the Second World War. Most of its personnel and activities have been taken over by the monastery at Jordanville, which now fulfills a similar function for the survivors of the first wave and the newcomers of the second wave of Russian refugees.[9]

Religious educational literature, as well as some devotional books, were published in other places, but on a small scale. Among the more important and permanent endeavors of this type were the leaflets prepared by the Russian Christian Student Movement in conjunction with their own publication, the *Messenger*, discussed later. Some parishes and schools brought out books and pamphlets for their young pupils—especially histories, grammars, readers. But their contents were not always strictly religious; moreover, these were only ad hoc publications to meet specific short-term needs.

This brings us to the topic of religious education in Russia Abroad. The parish was, of course, the natural framework for such instruction. But as we have noted, in emigration the parishes were quite scattered, small, and poor. Only a few could take on responsibility for religious instruction for their parishioners' children, even though there were few children because of the skewed demography of the Russian diaspora. Wherever the parish church took on the task of religious instruction, it pursued it only during the beginning years. Such instruction was complemented by classes in Russian language, grammar, history, and literature. These classes were usually taught by volunteer members of the congregation, mainly women. As far as can be ascertained, only in the large cities, with a sizable émigré population, did this instruction continue into the 1930s. In many instances the effort had to be abandoned by the late 1920s. Sunday schools, which had no strong tradition in prerevolutionary Russia, were organized in many places, but with mixed results. Essentially, instruction in the basic tenets of the faith and of the rudiments of the native language fell to the families. And here, as may be expected, situations varied a great deal; much depended on the degree to which the environment brought about what émigré educators called "denationalization," and in the United States was known as acculturation and "Americanization."

Where there were Russian elementary and secondary schools, primarily in the largest cities and in the unusual concentrations found in Yugoslavia, Czechoslovakia, and the Baltic states, religious instruction was part of the required curriculum. It was given by a local priest and closely tied to the other Russian subjects that were taught in the schools, along with the courses required locally. Language was an essential component of religious instruction since services were in a form of Russian (the so-called church slavonic in a modernized and Russified form). Eventually, the problem of using contemporary vernacular languages became acute, especially in the United States after World War II. The churchmen, and those laymen who believed that the ties between culture and religion were particularly meaningful, did not conceive of a Russian culture without a religious content. This attitude cut across political lines, but it was more prevalent among the conservatives and monarchists. This was at the root of the disagreement concerning what date should be selected to celebrate the Day of Russian Culture, discussed earlier. The intelligentsia had selected the birthday of Pushkin (8 June) as the date that most fittingly symbolized their cultural tradition, and in most places of the diaspora the church participated in the day's celebrations. The clergy officiated at the special services held in the local churches and actively took part in the various events that marked this day. But, as we have seen earlier, the conservative circles, with the support of the Bishops' Synod of Sremski Karlovci, decided to mark St. Vladimir's Day (28 July) as the Day of Russian National Consciousness to stress the religious component of the historical tradition. Unlike Pushkin Day, this celebration always had a strong political connotation, so that even many churchmen were opposed to it as recalling the less than desirable alliance between state and church that had prevailed before 1917, to the detriment of the latter's social and cultural role.

Yet, it must be admitted, the question of what constituted the essence of traditional Russian culture, which the emigration had a duty to preserve and transmit, was a justified one. Even those for whom religion was not a central concern could not ignore Russia's ecclesiastical past. Thus in 1938, the 950th anniversary of the baptism of Rus' was marked not only in the churches, but also in schools and secular organizations. The celebration was the occasion for the publication of several books, for example, the interesting *Vladimirskii sbornik*. As a consequence, the historiography of the emigration gave greater prominence and a more positive evaluation to the Kievan period of Russia's history, when the church had a truly autonomous role, and contrasting it with the Muscovite glorification of the state.

The scattered and frequently isolated groups of émigrés lacked most of the protection that public institutions of the host countries normally provided for their own citizens. Several countries had very little social legislation in the 1920s or even 1930s. Organizations of mutual help, funded by voluntary contributions of the émigrés themselves, or by philanthropic and individual donations, helped relieve the worst conditions somewhat. True to its tradition of charitable works, the church in exile endeavored to provide assistance to the poor and disabled. But unlike Protestant or Catholic churches, the Russian Orthodox Church had little experience in organized mass-scale charitable work. In prerevolutionary Russia, philanthropic activities were centered in monasteries and convents where, as in the Middle Ages in the West, the poor received food and one-time assistance. (There were many individual large-scale philanthropies by Old Believers in the late nineteenth century, but, with notable exceptions, they were restricted to fellow Old Believers and given in traditional forms.) When, almost on the eve of the world war and the revolution, the church in Russia began to show more institutional concern for the social and economic plight of the poor, its charitable activities were usually the work of individual parishes or priests. In emigration, too, the church was not prepared for charitable work on a large international scale. It was the individual parish, or the energetic individual—whether clerical or lay—who had to shoulder the burden. But we have noted that the parishes of Russia Abroad were small and poor. Perforce their social welfare activities had to be limited and they were quite inadequate to the task. Only in the big cities or large émigré settlements (for example, the self-administering colonies in Yugoslavia) could philanthropic and social work be set up on an interparish basis and benefit from public and private institutional assistance. There were some notable exceptions; for example in Asnières, a workers' suburb of Paris, a large congregation, under the energetic leadership of the priest and parishioners, succeeded in setting up not only a primary and Sunday school, but also a cluster of welfare programs for poor families, the unemployed, and the sick.

Material needs were only one facet of the émigré predicament. Unlike the poor or disabled citizens of the countries of asylum who were members of a "normal" society with personal, family, and institutional networks, the Russian exiles were cut off from such local ties, bereft of family, friends, or other meaningful associations. This was particularly true of people in the provinces, working in factories or mines, living in dormitories and eating in mess halls. Great as was their material plight, their spiritual hunger was most often still greater; and it could not be stilled by institutionalized charity that was far away in any case. Primarily in France (where it is better documented), there arose the Orthodox Work (*Pravoslavnoe delo*). It represented a revival of the tradition of voluntary lay communities of men and women (*obshchina*) who devoted their time and energy to assist the poor and the deprived, while continuing their own regular lives in society. They offered not only material relief but, most important, also spiritual and psychological help.

The leading personality of the Orthodox Work in France was Elizaveta Skobtsova, who eventually took monastic vows, under the name of Maria, but was allowed by Metropolitan Evlogii to continue her charitable work in the outside world. Mother Maria toured the industrial and mining centers of provincial France where there were Russian émigré workers. Unlike Simone Weil, to whom she has been compared, who tried to share the life of the worker for ideological reasons, Mother Maria was impelled by purely religious motives to bring comfort to the individual soul, rather than to try to change economic circumstances. She organized kitchens to feed unemployed Russians in Paris, and set up refuges for the homeless. An important dimension of her work was its close association with the church, although, unlike the Salvation Army, she did not require attendance at services or involvement with priests. During the war, she opened her refuge for the homeless poor to hide Jews from the German and Vichy authorities. Eventually this led to her arrest, along with her son and Father Dmitri Klepinin. She met her death in a Nazi camp.[10] She had enlisted the cooperation of intellectual personalities of Russia Abroad—K. Mochulskii, G. Fedotov, I. Fondaminskii—all members of the discussion circle Krug. In this way religious concerns were closely intertwined with both intellectual and charitable work; this encouraged a return to the church on the part of exile intellectuals, while the outreach to the émigré workers reactivated the latter's cultural interests, especially among the younger generation.[11]

Finally, we should mention that church and clergy were directly involved in the organization and administration of old-age and nursing homes, as well as orphanages. As noted earlier, such homes were established and supported by military and veterans' organizations. The close association of these institutions with the church was illustrated not only by the presence of a priest, acting as a kind of chaplain who ministered regularly to the needs of the inmates, but also by the fact that metropolitans and bishops provided financial assistance and administrative supervision.

Although the number of children among the émigrés was proportionately small, their physical and emotional needs were the first priorities of the refugees in the diaspora. Children received their introduction to Russian language, faith, and values in the family and the parishes. In view of the social isolation in which most émigrés lived it was relatively easy to raise the children with Russian as their main—or at any rate home—language. It was a little more difficult to inculcate a sense of belonging to a nation the child had never known firsthand. A major fear was denationalization, the loss of a commitment to Russia, to its past, and, hopefully, to its future. In prerevolutionary times, in the absence of a separation between church and state, there had been no need for special organizations to bring together religion and patriotic values, as had been the case in Protestant and Catholic countries. The notion of raising children with a conscious commitment to both religious and national values, and to develop fully their intellectual, moral, and physical potential in their service, was the origin of the Boy Scout movement founded by Lord Baden Powell in England and the *sokol* movement in what was to become Czechoslovakia. In a less nationalistic mode, the American YMCA aimed at the same goal, but it endeavored more self-consciously to relate the church and everyday life.

Before 1914 these movements had touched Russia only marginally. Scouting had some following among the Protestant, urban, educated populations of the Empire (mainly in the Baltic provinces), but it had been ignored by both the church and the Russian educated elites. The Czech *sokols* also found some imitators, but they were very few in number; after the revolution, coming into direct contact with these movements in the countries of their asylum, and recognizing the role they played in fostering patriotism and religious commitment among the young, the émigrés become interested. The example set by the YMCA in prisoner of war and refugee camps, and with young adults and children, stimulated further the Russians' curiosity, and prodded them into imitation. The outcome was the creation of a youth movement that was quite *sui generis,* while drawing inspiration from, and following the practices of, the Western organization. This was the Russian Christian Student Movement—hereafter referred to as RKS Movement.

The impulse for the organization of the movement came from two related, though distinct, developments. Students, whose educational career had been interrupted by their participation in the civil war, and who had managed to gain access to university facilities in the Kingdom of Serbs, Croats, and Slovenes, found themselves very much at sea, psychologically and spiritually. The hell they had gone through in war, their poverty and precarious situation, their loneliness—all combined to give primacy to the task of finding the vital core on which to rebuild their lives. Since circumstances made it difficult for them to become part of a congenial intellectual group of like-minded young people, they turned to their religious tradition and faith for inspiration and strength. Students of both sexes, with similar background and experiences, came together first in the émigré colonies in Yugoslavia, and then elsewhere. In the newly founded Russian educational institutions in Belgrade and Prague there arose circles dedicated to the study of religious literature, to praying together, and receiving the spiritual guidance of a priest. Some members of these circles, after completing their studies, entered the church, receiving priestly ordination; others became social activists and lay church leaders in the emigration, as did, for example, the several members of the Zernov family. The second development derived from émigré students' need to organize to find cheap housing and meals in a Europe left impoverished by war and unwilling to share its resources with the refugees. Collective housing and mess halls led to the establishment of libraries and reading rooms and to social and intellectual gatherings. This could be accomplished only under the sponsorship of the World Christian Student Movement. These groups and student organizations coordinated their efforts, to assist each other in overcoming their isolation as foreigners. With the help of the World Christian Student Movement they eventually called conferences and conventions of representatives of student groups from several lands of exile, in particular Yugoslavia, Czechoslovakia, Germany, and Bulgaria.

In 1923, in Přebov, Czechoslovakia, an all-European meeting of representatives of these émigré student groups and organizations attracted members of the informal circles for spiritual self-development mentioned earlier. It was at this conference in Přebov that the RKS Movement took shape. The YMCA and the World Christian Student Movement provided the means, and encouraged the movement's first steps. The principal aim in creating the movement was not so much to promote narrowly defined student interests, but rather to bring about a close interaction between the students' religious and practical needs. The connection between state and church in Imperial Russia had brought about a sharp separation between secular life and the life of the church, resulting in the spiritual impoverishment of the educated elites. The émigré students were now acutely experiencing this impoverishment. And they believed that the prime imperative was to establish (or recreate) a fruitful bond between the life of the soul and that of the mind and body. Such a bond was essential, they felt, not only to overcome their own desolate existence, but also to prepare for the eventual role they might have in the reconstruction of Russia on a spiritual, social, and political basis. Such a result would come about—and this was to be the movement's main goal—when all aspects of daily secular existence were permeated by Orthodox values and when the church, in turn, would inform the everyday existence of the faithful by displaying an active concern for its physical, economic, and emotional progress. The program of the RKS Movement thus called for the *otserkvlenie* (literally "churchification") of life and the *ozhivlenie* (enlivening) of the church. The double goal is best rendered in English as "Christianization of life."

Such a goal involved a close partnership with the Russian Orthodox Church, for from the very start the students rejected the interconfessionalism (interdenominationalism) that the YMCA was strongly urging on them, for they wanted to be a strictly Russian Orthodox movement. The European YMCA leadership agreed to this. On the other hand, the organizers did not want the movement to be an arm of the church, in the sense of a subordinate institution controlled by the hierarchy. They craved the church's guidance and patronage, but refused domination by bishops and metropolitans. The leading hierarchs, especially Metropolitan Evlogii, assented, and gave the movement their unstinting support. Not so the Bishops' Synod at Sremski Karlovci, which refused to recognize the organization because it did not accept direct church control. The bishops of the synod also claimed that the YMCA, which they were convinced was a notorious "Masonic" possibly even pro-Bolshevik, organization, would lead the movement into heresy. In spite of all the efforts on the part of the movement (and representatives of the YMCA and the World Christian Student Movement), the Sremski Karlovci Synod—and in its wake much of the monarchist emigration in Yugoslavia—

remained unalterably opposed. This affected the reactions of the most conservative, nay reactionary, monarchist student groupings everywhere. Consequently, the RKS Movement was to become "liberal" in social and political matters, and open to contacts and associations with other churches and denominations.

The movement grew rapidly, especially in Western Europe, where Paris became its main center. Its activities were manifold: its constituent element was a network of young people's circles (not all participants were students) where religious, intellectual, and day-to-day problems were discussed, and in which the spiritual dimension of the movement's members was enhanced. Some of these circles eventually constituted themselves into quasi-religious communities, *bratstva* (fellowships), which led an intense liturgical and spiritual life, committed to social activism in the diaspora. Inspired by the federative organization of the Orthodox Church, the movement, too, was a federation of circles and "fellowships" (admitting both sexes). In turn, the circles joined efforts in organizing common activities wherever possible: lectures, courses, groups for younger children (on the model of Scout dens).

At international conferences the movement's delegates from all European countries came together to discuss common problems, to listen to lectures by prominent clerical and lay personalities, and to receive communion. Frequently these conferences had a basic theme for their lectures and discussions; general conclusions served to orient subsequent activities of the movement.[12] Many of the conferences were held in conjunction with the summer camps organized by the movement for children. In these camps the youngsters not only had the opportunity of improving their health through sports, outdoor activities, and a good diet, but also of extending their knowledge of Russian historical and religious traditions. If we are to believe the accounts published by the movement and the reminiscences of the participants, the camps and conferences were inspirational and uplifting experiences that benefited the physical health as well as the spiritual growth of all participants. The intellectual and clerical leaders, too, found an opportunity to establish close contact with the young generation of the emigration and to influence their mental and spiritual development.

In addition to these activities, the RKS Movement served as framework for a number of other enterprises involving the emigration, particularly in Paris but also in other major capitals of Russia Abroad, including the Far East. The headquarters of the movement in Paris, at 10 boulevard Montparnasse, offered space for lecture series, Sunday classes, and after-school meetings for children. The youngsters received lessons in Russian grammar, literature, geography, and history; they put on plays and concerts, and were the main organizers and participants of the Days of Russian Culture and other festivities (for example, St. Tatiana Day, traditionally the day of the Russian university). The building at the boulevard Montparnasse also housed the Religious Pedagogic Bureau, where V. Zen'kovskii and his assistants studied questions of education, collected a specialized library and information about significant pedagogic developments everywhere in the world, not excluding the Soviet Union.

A central enterprise of the RKS Movement—and it is our major source of information on it—was the monthly publication of the *Messenger of the RKS Movement* (*Vestnik russkogo khristianskogo studencheskogo dvizheniia* (still published today, in modified form and contents). Starting as a mimeographed sheet with a circulation of only 75 copies, it had reached 1,500 copies per issue within a year, and on the eve of the war in 1939, about 5,000 copies were either subscribed to or distributed. Starting with half a dozen pages, the *Messenger* eventually printed twenty-four to thirty-six pages per issue. There were articles of didactic-homiletic nature dealing with major aspects of the Orthodox creed and its liturgic practice; an important section provided information and summary of the various activities of the movement in every country and town, and gave full accounts of the conferences and meetings organized by the movement, as well as descriptions of the yearly summer camps. The *Messenger* sponsored fund-raising campaigns and reported on them, describing in some detail the experiences of the solicitors. These accounts throw vivid light on the milieus and circumstances of Russia Abroad. Predictably, those who were less well-off were much more responsive to the solicitations than the few well-to-do among the émigrés (true, the latter were also the object of more frequent and insistent solicitations). In connection with the fund drives the *Messenger* published data on the movement's yearly budget which clearly show the importance of the contributions made by the YMCA and church organizations in England.[13] Occasionally the *Messenger* gave reports on the work and accomplishments of such institutions as the Religious Pedagogic Bureau and St. Serge's, and information on religious movements, ideas, and debates in French, German, and English intellectual circles. Throughout the 1920s and early 1930s, the *Messenger* was the more "popular" and "democratic" (intellectually speaking) version of the major religious-philosophical journal, *Put'*.

As time went on, a key aspect of the RKS Movement's activities (and taking an ever larger space in the *Messenger*) were the encounters—meetings, discussions, conferences—between Orthodox émigré clergy, intellectuals, and youth leaders and their counterparts in England, and to some extent in Germany. They were only a particular aspect of the wider ecumenical movement into which the Russian church in Western Europe was drawn in the 1920s. This involvement was sanctioned by Metropolitan Evlogii (but denounced by the bishops at Sremski Karlovci), and received the active participation of the St. Serge faculty.[14]

In 1927, in St. Albans, leaders of the Anglican Church, more specifically its Anglo-Catholic wing, organized the first encounter between the Russian Christian Student Movement and interested English student groups. The meeting was a great success and initiated a series of conferences between émigré Orthodox personalities (lay and clerical) and Anglicans. Eventually, a fellowship—St. Sergius–St. Albans—was established under the directorship of N. Zernov (an early participant in the spiritually interested student circles mentioned previously), who was also appointed to lecture on Eastern Christianity at Oxford. The fellowship sponsored exchanges of students, mainly Russians coming to study in England, as well as conferences where liturgical questions of mutual interest were discussed. Metropolitan Evlogii and his Anglican counterparts eventually recognized each other church's communion. Yet, at no point was there any question of an interconfessional unification, in the sense of reaching a compromise position on basic dogmatic and liturgic issues. The relationship remained that of a fellowship, a fraternity, with each partner acknowledging the identity of the other, and respecting its sacraments, while agreeing to work out common positions on ecclesiastic as well as social questions.[15]

The Anglo-Russian exchanges did a great deal to acquaint each side with the other, and they were a great moral boost to the Russian Orthodox youth, helping them to overcome their sense of isolation and deprivation, by recognizing the value of their traditions for the Western world. In this way a few of the leading members of the movement, and their intellectual mentors, for example G. Florovsky and G. Fedotov, established close intellectual and religious ties with England; the conferences stimulated the Russians' awareness of the intellectual and social currents in the West, and made them feel that they were members of a community of nations and cultures in which they represented an "absent Russia." Groups of English students and youngsters also attended the summer camps of the RKS Movement. It is difficult to say what the long-term impact of the experience might have been, since the descriptions in the *Messenger* are a little too euphoric to be taken at face value.

As the statement of purpose of the movement repeated in every issue of the *Messenger,* the goal was to "Christianize the life" of the emigration, in the hope and expectation that it would eventually be brought home to a free Russia.[16] The patriotic as well as Orthodox intent of the movement cannot be gainsaid. But at the same time the *Messenger* expressed the young emigration's awareness of the social, political, and economic problems confronting the world, in particular Europe, in the early 1930s. In reporting on select facets of the intellectual scene in France, Germany, and England, the *Messenger* contributed to a reflection on contemporary issues that eschewed the usual narrow, ghettolike émigré perspective. We should, therefore, turn our attention to the intellectual activities of the religiously committed circles of the diaspora. But before doing so I should perhaps warn again that it is difficult to separate trends, events, and individuals belonging to the religious circles from the wider intellectual scene of Russia Abroad. For many individual exile thinkers and writers, the separation between secular and religious intellectual life grew less and less sharp with time. Of course, some individuals and milieus remained quite impermeable to this development—this was as true of the secular, anticlerical groups (socialists and traditional liberals and positivists) as it was of the extreme conservative ecclesiastic side (Bishops' Synod). In the pages that follow, therefore, when speaking of intelligentsia, unless otherwise qualified, I have in mind only those who openly, publicly, committed themselves to Orthodoxy and religion as the principal feature of their Weltanschauung and inner life.

As might be expected, the intellectual roots of the religiously minded and pious émigré intelligentsia lay also in the Silver Age, the decades when its members had reached maturity and taken their first independently creative steps. Nor had they been spared the harrowing experiences of war, revolution, and especially civil war; and they were not immune, of course, to the material deprivations of life in exile, although in some rare lucky instances (e.g., Berdiaev and, perhaps, Shestov), they escaped the worst of it. Circles, discussion groups, public lectures and debates, active participation in publications—all of these features of the Silver Age, were recreated in the same pattern in Russia Abroad. For those actively concerned with spiritual and religious questions, and an important share of whose life was taken by the church (as parish members, contributors to ecclesiastic publications, members of religious-philosophic groups and societies), there was an additional institutional manifestation that we should note.

In the late nineteenth century, based on similar earlier models, a number of "brotherhoods" had sprung up in Russia. These *bratstva* were informal communities of laymen, mostly academics with similar religious and intellectual concerns, and an active participation in church life. The members came together as regularly and as frequently as possible to study and discuss scholarly and philosophic problems of common interest, but also to pray together, to assist each other spiritually, and to promote moral values. They also obligated themselves to follow a strictly defined pattern of religious rituals (e.g., regular and frequent communion), and to practice in their lives all the basic precepts and values of Christianity. Such was, for instance, the Priiutino Brotherhood, which included among its members such prominent intellectuals and scholars as A. A. Kornilov and V. I. Vernadsky.

Once they had settled down in exile, the religious-minded intelligentsia endeavored to renew the old ties. The need to recreate the association of brotherhoods, and to be actively engaged in promoting their values and ways, appeared particularly critical; for it was necessary to counteract the nihilism and despair of the émigré condition, and to resist the threats to individual integrity and national identity that life in exile constantly posed. But since such brotherhoods were a very private affair, their membership and activities are not easily documented. Only the chance mention in private correspondence informs us of their existence. Such was the case of the bratstvo Sviatoi Sofii (Brotherhood of St. Sophia) whose members pledged to pray and commune at specified times, wherever they might be, so as to maintain a spiritual connection in spite of distance and political frontiers. There was a direct connection of this group with that of prerevolutionary Priiutino Brotherhood by virtue of the membership in both of G. Vernadsky and P. Struve.[17] The brotherhood formed an informal network—similar to Masonic lodges—which, on occasion, might have been of some help in securing employment or publi-

cation facilities for individual members. These were no doubt, consciously or
not, the model for the religious circles and fraternities of émigré students mentioned earlier.

A similar, but in this case fully public, role was played by the Free Spiritual and Philosophic Society founded by Berdiaev in Berlin in 1922, which
was the origin of the academy of the same name, and involved, as we have
seen, in the founding of St. Serge's Seminary and Institute. The same might
be said of the Orthodox Work and of its Circle (Krug), for they combined
spiritual-intellectual fellowship with socially responsive activism. Other more
secular groups or circles, should be mentioned in this connection. Although
their purpose was not strictly ecclesiastic, a heightened concern for religious
and spiritual problems pervaded them. We may mention as illustration the
periodic gatherings at private homes—e.g., chez Madame Lot-Borodina, the
Merezhkovskys, and the public meetings of the Green Lamp circle. Another
such group met every week at the house of N. Berdiaev in Clamart, a suburb
of Paris. Here gathered French and Russian intellectuals interested in the
Orthodox Church and in personalist philosophy, most notably Jacques Maritain and Father d'Hérbigny. Very similar to Berdiaev's circle was the weekly
gathering at the house of Jacques and Raissa Maritain in Meudon, which also
involved such an influential publicist as Emmanuel Mounier (editor of the
journal *Esprit*). Berdiaev himself, as well as some other Russian émigrés (e.g.,
A. Koyré, V. Weidlé), were invited to the Colloques de Pontigny, a significant manifestation of French (and European) intellectual life in the 1920s
and 1930s.[18] Berdiaev was also the driving force in organizing several col-
loquia with French intellectuals associated with the *Cahiers de la Quinzaine*,
where spiritual concerns, but also historical and sociopolitical issues, were
raised and opinions exchanged. In this case, however, it seems that the Russians were merely asked to provide information, rather than contribute actively to a dialogue.[19]

This brings up the larger question of the émigrés' contacts with the intellectual scene of the host countries, and of the latter's influence on the Russian intelligentsia in exile. We shall confine ourselves here to the religious-
spiritual trends that manifested themselves in Western Europe in the 1920s
and especially in the 1930s. Only moral and social issues were of immediate
mutual interest, bringing about a degree of understanding between the Orthodox émigrés and the Catholic or Protestant world of their asylum. It is
worth noting that in the Catholic West, ever since the turn of the century
(more precisely since Leo XIII's *Rerum Novarum* encyclical and its rein-
forcement in 1931 by Pius XI's *Quadrogesimo Anno*), there was much ferment in the minds of laity and clergy about the problems that had been
created by industrialization, and the threats to peace and the destruction of
war. In France the ferment had begun before 1914 with the literary efforts
of Léon Bloy and Charles Péguy. The social consciousness of Catholic intellectuals had been awakened, and it found expression in a populist and proto-
socialist manner by Marc Sangnier in his publication *Le Sillon*. Under the im-

pacts of the Great War and the Depression, greater political intensity was imparted to the debate by Emmanuel Mounier's *Esprit*. Closely related to the latter orientation, but even more militantly political, were the groups that published the *Ordre Nouveau* and the *Troisième Force,* among whom we should mention Denis de Rougemont, the Protestant socialist activist André Philip, and the dynamic Georges Izard.

All these individuals and their journals were seeking to formulate a practical socioeconomic program, within the framework of a democratic political order, which would relieve the misery and overcome the economic crisis with which the Western world had been struggling since the end of the Great War of 1914. In international affairs they took a stand against war and worried about the increasing aggressiveness of nationalism and its fascist and Nazi proponents. Toward the Soviet system they were somewhat ambivalent: in it they hoped to find practical suggestions for a constructive economic policy (state planning was an inviting suggestion), but they were also aware of the Soviet dictatorship's threat to freedom of expression and opinion, and to the individual's security. They had a heightened curiosity about the present and past of Russia, and the émigrés in their midst could help them satisfy this curiosity. Moreover, and it was an essential ingredient of their Weltanschauung, these French publicists were attracted by Berdiaev's philosophy, especially his stress on individual freedom. The personalism at the basis of the philosophy of the Russian Silver Age, as espoused with many variations by Lossky, Frank, Stepun and, of course, Berdiaev, was close to the personalism professed by Mounier (and one of whose roots was Bergson's vitalism). On the other hand, Leo Shestov was close to the religiously inspired existentialism of Jean Wahl, who also had ties to *Esprit.* The cerebral neo-Thomism of Jacques Maritain was not very attractive to the Russians, but his liberal humanism in social and political questions, and his anti-Fascist stand, made him particularly interesting to the émigrés, especially when contrasted with the positions of the official Catholic establishment (and Raissa Maritain's Russian-Jewish background provided a common language).

The Protestant world, especially in Germany, had also been much shaken by the effects of industrialism, and even more so by the First World War and its psychological and sociopolitical consequences. The relative social and political calm in France (at least until the early 1930s), and its more disciplined Catholicism, did not create as great a need for the reexamination of the basic assumptions of the political and social system, as was the case of Lutheran circles in Germany. After 1918 the connection between the old Prussian state and the conservative Lutheran establishment was perceived as a moral burden, a burden that had to be atoned for, since the state had been ignominiously defeated. The economic misery and social disruptions accompanying defeat and inflation, and the resentment and anger at the peace terms, combined to bring many German intellectuals to a reconsideration of their previous beliefs and positions. Thus Paul Tillich came to advocate a socially committed Lutheranism, whose main task was to find an alternative to the dehumanizing and unjust capitalist order. He went so far as to see in Bolshevik Russia a possible model for his own plans for a reform of the economy and society. He called his socialism "religious socialism," not wishing to preserve the adjective Christian, so as to make for a broader appeal. He also desired total independence from any kind of established church.

Other intellectual movements in postwar Germany fostered nationalist plans of restoring the country to a major role in Europe and the world. They were not as sharply critical of the prevailing socioeconomic system; rather they expected improvements as the result of new attitudes and institutional reorganization, not from fundamental revolutionary transformations. The Youth Movement (Jugendbewegung), initiated before 1914, combined a strong religious, broadly Christian, commitment with concern for a healthy, natural way of life that would liberate the individual psychologically and physically from the artificial, noxious aspects of modern industrialized society. After 1918, the Jugendbewegung also stressed the necessity for a sane patriotism to overcome the effects of defeat and as a basis for the reform of German society. There are echoes of this project in today's ecological and "Green" movements in West Germany.

The starting point of the conservative intellectual critical trends was not just an intense nationalism, but also a romantic notion of the communal predisposition of the German *Volk*, race or nation, in its past cultural and religious traditions, in contrast to the "possessive individualism" and materialism of the Anglo-French West. In contrast to the Jugendbewegung, they criticized contemporary capitalism, especially its nefarious role as a parasitic finance capitalism, while accepting industrial and technological productivity. They exalted the heroism of workers, as well as their individual creative energy and power, as did for example Ernst Jünger, who was also the bard of war and military heroism. Bolshevism attracted them by its success in rebuilding the state power of Russia, and for honoring the "heroes of productive labor." These somewhat contradictory and inchoate notions, some of which turned up as ingredients in the Nazi brew, also reflected the Wagnerian and Nietzschean heritage of the late nineteenth century—a heritage that was not unknown to the Russians of the Silver Age. The spokesmen of these conservative, nationalist, and romantic trends gathered around the publisher Eugen Diederichs. His journal, *Die Tat* (The Deed), gave these ideas a more systematic and socioeconomically oriented expression. There were also close affinities to the corporatism of some conservative Catholic circles that had a following in Germany and Austria, not to speak of its modified form in Portugal and in Fascist Italy (especially Othmar Spann—France was not much touched by corporatism, but the historian E. Lousse and some monarchists were advocating some form of it). The German scene was perceptively illuminated by Russian émigré publicists and thinkers, for example, F. Stepun and B. Izhboldin, who maintained contact with Berdiaev and the faculty of St. Serge and their publications.

Anglo-American Protestantism was the source of ideas and practices that also influenced émigré religious intellectual circles. Its main impact was in the practical sphere, as we had occasion to observe in our frequent references to the role played by the YMCA. The nondenominational, but clearly Christian and Protestant, activist orientation of the YMCA and of the World Christian Student Federation had given concrete form to the drive for the "Christianization of life," and in bringing the Orthodox Church closer to the realities and needs of Russia Abroad. Neither the YMCA nor the various Anglican organizations with whom the Russians had contact were basically critical of, or opposed to the existing social and political order in the West. But their acute awareness of the social and economic plight experienced by many, and of the need to become actively involved to find remedies, especially where they would be most fruitful for the future, inspired many émigré social activists and thinkers.

We have mentioned the efforts made by the Orthodox and Anglicans to come closer. They were only a particular instance of the broader ecumenical movement that acquired dynamic force in the twenties. The movement had been started by the Protestants, and it found its strongest echo in countries where they were predominant; but it aimed at encompassing all Christian denominations, and hoped to engage the great Oriental religions. The Roman Catholic Church refused to participate in the interconfessional efforts, claiming that they undermined and diluted the essential dogmas of Christianity. The Russian Orthodox Church in exile, humbled by its own national experience and closer to, also more dependent on, the Western world (unlike its sister churches of Bulgaria, Greece, and Yugoslavia) decided to participate. In fact, only the West European Metropolia under Evlogii became actively involved, as for all practical purposes the Sremski Karlovci Synod stayed away, and the Patriarchate of Moscow was prevented from participation by the Soviet government.

Russian émigré hierarchs and clergymen took part in the ecumenical congresses of Lausanne and Stockholm, and became members of the commission that was entrusted with the practical implementation of the concluding act of the Lausanne conference. In this way intellectuals of Russia Abroad, S. Bulgakov, G. Florovsky, N. Zernov, A. Kartashev, and N. Vladislavtsev, to name the most prominent, became actively involved in the ecumenical movement (and renewed their participation with even greater enthusiasm after World War II). This involvement had, of course, also practical advantage of giving émigré leaders direct access to influential church leaders, who could have a crucial influence in decisions affecting the material and legal support of the Russian emigration (e.g., the League of Nations and the Nansen Committee), and who could assist in raising funds for Russian Orthodox activities abroad. These contacts also brought about a widening of the intellectual and experiential horizons of the exile intellectual community. The Russians participating in the ecumenical conferences reported in journals accessible to wider circles of the émigré community—there were rather extensive accounts in the exile daily press, too (*Vozrozhdenie, Poslednie novosti,*

Segodnia). This allowed émigré intellectuals to travel widely, something that visa requirements and shortages of funds would have normally prevented. Within the specific framework and milieu of Protestantism and ecumenism, the Russian emigration obtained an active role, and was able to contribute, albeit modestly, to the cultural and religious scene of the West in the interwar years.

The trends and events described in this chapter reverberated in the cultural life of Russia Abroad thanks to the printed word that reached émigrés scattered over the globe. The impact of the printed word was much more condensed and effective than that of personal meetings and institutional activities that normally reached only the few directly involved in them. Let us turn, therefore, to an examination of the two major émigré journals that were primarily devoted to religious spiritual and cultural concerns.

More than once we have noted that the YMCA stood at the origin of many an émigré enterprise, and also that Berdiaev was one of the most influential exile personalities in carrying to successful conclusion intellectual plans and activities. This was precisely also the case with *Put'*, the most significant religious journal of Russia Abroad. From the start *The Way* was the mouthpiece of the Free Spiritual Religious Society and of its academy, both initiated and headed by Berdiaev. The name was a deliberate reference to the influential religious philosophical journal of pre-1914 years, *Novyi put'* (The New Way). The purpose of the journal was defined as showing the "way" to Russia's regeneration and reconstruction. Berdiaev persuaded the YMCA officers in Berlin to finance the journal and to keep up the subsidy after the move to Paris. Even at the height of the Depression, prodded by Berdiaev, Paul B. Anderson, the YMCA representative to Russia Abroad, managed to convince his superiors in the United States and their associates in England of the central importance of *The Way* for the intellectual and religious life of the emigration; and of its potential significance for a philosophical-religious revival in Soviet Russia in the future.[20] It would seem, on the evidence of the illegal Berdiaevite group in Leningrad in the 1960s, and the keen interest shown by some circles of the dissident Soviet intelligentsia that this hope was not quite in vain.[21]

The Way was published from 1925 until just before the German occupation of France. Berdiaev remained its editor in chief throughout, and it was he who shaped the journal's contents. Like most émigré publications the beginnings were more impressive than the later phase; as a matter of fact, in its last years it appeared less frequently, with fewer pages and fewer contributions—reflecting both the financial straits and the gradual exhaustion, physical and intellectual, of the émigré intelligentsia in war's shadow. There are no precise figures on the print runs and sales, although they must have been in the neighborhood of 1,000 or 1,200. The subscription price in 1925 was $2.25 per year (for four issues), a single issue costing 70 cents, compared to 90 cents for a single issue of the major émigré "thick journal," *Contemporary Annals*. The editorial board consisted of Berdiaev with the collaboration of B. Vysheslavtsev (also on the faculty of St. Serge's) and the representative of the YMCA, G. G. Kullmann. The list of contributors, on the other hand, was large and varied, and included practically all the prominent scholars and thinkers of Russia Abroad. Neither belles lettres nor literary criticism were represented in the *Put'*; it was strictly a journal of religious, philosophical and social thought on a high level of erudition and intellectual sophistication. It represented what was best in the intellectual life of Russia Abroad.[22]

The first issue carried a lengthy editorial statement, obviously written by Berdiaev, reflecting his own ideas and the journal's editorial policy. The editorial declaration made the following points: Despite its dispersal and material deprivation, the emigration had a positive task to perform. Even though they were free, the intellectuals in Russia Abroad were no better off than those in the Soviet land, and they should not feel superior to those opppressed by the Godless Bolshevik state. The exiles' economic deprivation was a blessing in disguise, for the revolution made clear the bankruptcy of the old regime, which was not only political but also socioeconomic bankruptcy; most specifically it spelled the end of the corruption brought about by the petty, philistine, bourgeois materialist consequences of modern capitalism and culture. Moreover, the revolution had the positive effect of putting an end to the unholy alliance between state and church; it thus freed spiritual life, permitted the revival of genuine Orthodoxy and of a religious life untainted by false association with the state. In short, the revolution could not be denied and should not be rejected; in spite of the suffering that it visited on the people, the intelligentsia in particular, there was no way of going back—quite the contrary, it assigned a new role to the emigration. The exiles, who enjoyed the freedom of expression denied their compatriots in Russia, must make use of this favorable circumstance to work hard for their people's spiritual regeneration, and for a new Russian culture firmly anchored in Orthodoxy.

All this, the editorial argued, implied a double-faceted approach to the situation that history had created: on the one hand, rejection of the capitalist and prerevolutionary order of things and, on the other, an effort at formulating a postrevolutionary sociophilosophical perspective and program. One must avoid looking back wistfully to all that had been the cause of the emigration's predicament, for the revolution was the punishment visited on the Russian intelligentsia and elites for their sins of omission and commission. The postrevolutionary order would have to be based on a purified Orthodox Church and a creative spirit. To this end, principles and programs must go beyond mere political expediency to provide the firm foundation necessary for spiritually constructive intellectual work. Finally, since fate had willed that the émigrés would find themselves in alien lands and amidst foreign peoples, they should also learn from the latter, especially what pertains to religious life and practice. But clearly, they should not give up or dilute their own historical tradition and national cultural heritage—quite the contrary, for the threat of denationalization had to be exorcised constantly and energetically. The future Orthodox Church should be rebuilt in a spirit of friendship and cooperation

with the Western churches, and with a willingness to learn from foreign religious experience. It would not be enough to know one's own past and cogi-
tate on the lessons of one's own history; one should take advantage of one's
enforced residence abroad to absorb what the outside world had to offer, and
to incorporate it meaningfully into a future Russian culture that will have a
cosmopolitan worth and mission. The critique of the capitalist, materialist
past should help bring about an acceptance of progressive social policies and
a socialist restructuring of society; even though the emigration should remain
adamantly opposed to all tyrannical and dehumanizing features that characterize not only the Bolshevik, but all dictatorships, whether of the right or of
the left.

Early on, *The Way* was opposed to Italian Fascism and German Nazism
on both libertarian and humanistic grounds, and was equally firm in refusing
to listen to the siren song of a Bolshevik nationalism, whether Russian or foreign. This last comment should be qualified as far as Berdiaev himself was
concerned, for he aproved of Stalin's restoration of Russia's role as an international power, and Berdiaev advocated defending the motherland against
German aggression, even thouhg this meant legitimizing, at least temporarily,
the Soviet regime.[23]

In view of *Put'*'s criticism of the prerevolutionary interdependence between church and state, its negative view of any effort at perpetuating or re-
constituting this situation is not surprising. Thus *The Way* denied the claims
of the Bishops' Synod at Sremski Karlovci to be the only representative of the
Russian church in exile, and still more adamantly rejected the synod's advocacy of a monarchic restoration and active involvement with pretenders to
the Russian throne. On intellectual and theological grounds, too, *The Way*
criticized the Bishops' Synod for their refusal to modernize church life and
to acknowledge the Orthodoxy and worth of such spiritual organizations as
the RSK Movement. *Put'* was unequivocal in supporting the metropolitan of
Western Europe, who stood for creative freedom and the émigré intelligentsia's modernizing reformism, as well as in support of Evlogii's recognition of
the authority of the patriarch of Moscow, as long as this did not entail a political commitment to the Soviet regime. The conflict with Sremski Karlovci
deepened and acquired a theological dimension when the Bishops' Synod condemned S. Bulgakov's sophiology. Without taking a clear position on the
theological merits of Bulgakov's doctrine, *The Way* kept its pages open to
his writings, and defended his right of free expression as long as he did not
reject the basic dogmas of Orthodoxy. In a future free Russia, *Put'* consistently maintained, the church should be free of control by the state, and
should regain (for the first time since the sixteenth century) its spiritual autonomy to resume its creative role in Russian culture.

In the same spirit of rejection of the prerevolutionary world, the contributors to *Put'* were most critical of the capitalist, bourgeois social and ethical
norms that had prevailed in Russia before 1914. In so doing they carried on
and broadened the critique by former Marxists such as Struve, Bulgakov,

and Berdiaev himself, and by symbolist philosophers and publicists such as D. Merezhkovsky. Their critique had a double target: one was the philosophical and ethical materialism bolstered by the false doctrines of positivism; the other, the tastelessness of bourgeois, philistine cultural values, fostered by capitalist economic development. Seen from this perspective, the Bolshevik system only validated the shoddy materialist culture, and merely made it more accessible to wider circles of the population. The most significant and pernicious consequence of the wrong turn taken in the value system of modern man, claimed *Put'* writers, was the relegation to second rank of the religious, spiritual, and creative dimensions of the individual. It was, as we know, a major concern of prerevolutionary philosophical and psychological speculation to conceive of the individual personality, the creator of all true cultural values, as the symbiosis of the material and the spiritual, within the framework of a transcendent religious commitment.

These philosophical premises also account for *The Way*'s interest in the dignity of labor—in the dignity of the individual worker's existence as a person. No doubt, this concern became more pressing as many émigrés, including former intellectuals, were forced to earn their living as factory workers or, unskilled manual laborers. The collaborators of *Put'*, for the most part, advocated a genuine humanistic socialism whose ultimate philosophical justification and validation would be found not only in the simplistic materialist positivism of the nineteenth-century radical intelligentsia, but in a recognition of the spiritual and religious potential of the full personality. A socialism rooted in, and combined with, Orthodox religious values was the goal that most writers in *The Way* were advocating. To counter the polemic identification of socialism with Bolshevism, *Put'* reminded its readers not only of the "communist" features of early Christian communities, but also argued that any system of social organization had only instrumental value. As long as it promoted the free personality, a socialist system was compatible with the church. Consequently, contributors to *The Way* were much interested in the developments taking place in Western socialism, and in those religious thinkers who endeavored to come to grips with the so-called social question, a question that essentially dealt with the function and place of labor in modern society and economic organization. It also accounts for *Put'*'s favorable attitude to the doctrines of corporatism, especially where the latter was to be firmly anchored in a nation's religious and cultural traditions. One gains the impression that, while rejecting specific Catholic and Protestant antecedents of medieval corporatism in the West, because of their legalism and materialism, *The Way*—especially Berdiaev—was very keen on introducing "genuinely" corporative values into a Russian Orthodox framework.

In this connection we may note that *Put'* did not shun political issues, although it eschewed narrow partisan politics and the squabbles that punctuated émigré political life. In deplored, as we have seen, the close connection of church and state in prerevolutionary Russia, for it had resulted in the church's avoiding social and political questions, and thus its loss of genuine influence on the life and thought of Russian society, particularly its elites. The emigration's heightened awareness of social, economic, and political problems would, *Put'* believed, provide the right foundation for reviving the church's commitment and involvement in society. It would not be a threat to freedom, since only the individual personality, as a believer, would introduce the problems and values of concern to society into his or her own life in the church. Agreeing with the RSK Movement, Berdiaev and his friends thought that if the church were to be brought into life and life into the church, the church's correct involvement in social and political problems would automatically follow. An essential element in *The Way*'s revulsion against Nazism, and to a lesser extent its dislike of Fascism and Francoism, was precisely the subordination of (Protestant) church life to Nazi ideology. The Catholic Church offered greater resistance in this respect, and could be a model for the role of church and religion in a future Russia.

In international affairs, *Put'* condemned the aggressive policies of the Fascist and Nazi powers. Nazi Germany was particularly iniquitous, first because of its suppression of all free voices and its racism (Berdiaev was quite outspoken in his condemnation of anti-Semitism), and also because it clearly represented a direct threat to Russia. Evil and horrible as it was, war could be ineluctable, as the events of 1936 and especially those of 1938 and 1939 made clear. *Put'* argued for the resistance to Hitler's expansion as a threat both to Russia and the Western democracies where the émigrés had found refuge. But in all fairness, *Put'* was not very much involved in foreign policy issues, and in retrospect its opinions on these matters are of little interest.

With eyes focused on the future revival of Russia's culture under genuinely Russian, as well as universal values, the writers of *Put'* endeavored to define the essence of Russian culture. As for most émigré intellectuals, *The Way*'s symbol of modern Russian culture was Pushkin, but a Pushkin who, by exemplifying all the facets of Russian culture, also had a genuine religious dimension. S. Frank's little study of Pushkin's religiosity, and S. Bulgakov's *laudatio* in the same spirit, offered a new perspective on the traditional and Soviet portrayal of a Pushkin reflecting eighteenth-century skepticism, secularism, and *marivaudage*. Bulgakov even went so far as to argue that Pushkin deliberately sought death, in the knowledge that it alone could atone for the hybris of his poetic genius—a Christian death was the necessary concomitant to the artistic task he fulfilled so brilliantly.

Other figures of modern Russian culture did not elicit the same degree of admiration. But *Put'* had numerous articles on the history of Russian monasticism, saintliness, and ecclesiastical past, as well as reports on the situation of the church in Soviet Russia. Representing something of an innovation over pre-1914 journals, *The Way* carried a number of articles illuminating Byzantine and old Russian religious life and thought. To my knowledge, it was the first secular Russian journal to set forth serious information and discussion of theological and ecclesiastic issues and history. Before 1917 only church publications, and occasionally specialized scholarly journals, appearing under the auspices of theological academies or the Ministry of Education, carried such material. There no longer was any excuse for an émigré intellectual to remain ignorant of the past and traditions of church and religion, as had been the case for most of Russia's intelligentsia throughout the nineteenth century (the Slavophiles were an exception, as *Put'* took pains to point out).

In Russia Abroad, the only interesting new set of ideas concerning Russian culture and history had been formulated by the Eurasians in the twenties. As a movement, however, Eurasianism "degenerated" rapidly as it fell under the influence of *smenovekhovtsy* and eventually it disintegrated in political and partisan squabbles.[24] Originally Eurasianism was rooted in an unqualified recognition of Russian Orthodoxy as an essential aspect of the culture that had developed in Eurasia. The leading thinkers of Eurasianism, especially N. Trubetskoi, L. Karsavin, and P. Savitskii, always had stressed their commitment to Orthodoxy. Nevertheless, Berdiaev and most of the *Put'* writers were extremely critical, if not outright negative, toward the Eurasian creed, for primarily philosophical reasons. They could not accept the naturalism and historical determinism, based on climatic and geographic factors, that were at the core of the Eurasian conception of Russia's historical development. To them it smacked too much of a variation on positivism and biological determinism. The latter in particular was unacceptable to Berdiaev, who believed that only the free individual personality could be a valid and secure foundation for building a people's culture. The libertarian personalism that informed *Put'*, as well as the pious émigré intellectuals, could not be accommodated to the determinism, rooted in natural physical factors, of the Eurasians.

Last, but not least, *The Way* played a significant part in acquainting Russia Abroad with select intellectual trends of the contemporary West. It was an important role, for we should not forget that the émigrés, as a group, lived in isolation from the host societies. First, they were preoccupied by the difficulties of daily existence. Second, many had matured mentally at a time when Russia was cut off from the West, as the prewar cosmopolitan connections of the intelligentsia were interrupted by political events. Moreover, the professionals, who had risen in the last decade of the imperial regime, were much more narrowly educated and parochial in their outlook than the free intelligentsia and best-educated noble dilettantes in the nineteenth century. Finally, reflecting their insecure and deprived circumstances, the exiles harbored deep resentment and felt very inferior vis à vis their Western confrères. Naturally, the émigré press of wide circulation was more concerned with disseminating information directly relevant to the daily life of the diaspora than with providing adequate coverage of Western intellectual happenings. *The Way* attempted to fill the gap left by the daily and weekly press. True, it too was quite selective, paying attention only to those developments that were relevant to its overall religious and spiritual concerns. It did so, moreover, primarily in form of book reviews. Whatever separate articles there were on the West, they tended to inform the reader of institutional developments in the

Western, primarily Anglican, churches. But the book reviews give us an idea of the main interests of *Put'* and of what kind of information they wanted their readers to have. All in all, *The Way* reviewed about 160 foreign titles (including some works of Russians in a foreign tongue) as against only about 75 Russian titles. We can easily see the didactic purpose of the *The Way's* book review policy, which also testifies to the ecumenical bias of the journal, and is witness to the high intellectual level expected of the readers. Closely related to this purpose was the regular and comprehensive reporting of inter-denominational conferences.[25]

If the main orientation of *Put'* was religious and philosophical, then that of *Novyi grad* (New City), the other journal dedicated to a spiritualist religious position, was self-consciously social, economic, and political. The need for a journal focused on contemporary issues as they affected the Russian diaspora—and might affect the Russia of the future—became more pressing as the Great Depression engulfed Europe and the United States, bringing in its wake serious threats to freedom and democracy. The initiative for the new journal came from three leading émigré intellectuals, deeply committed to a revival of Orthodoxy and of its role in solving social, political, and personal problems of Westerners and Russians: G. P. Fedotov, to become its most influential and active contributor, taught hagiography and Russian history at St. Serge's; I. I. Bunakov-Fondaminskii, one of the editors of *Sovremennye zapiski,* a former member of the Socialist Revolutionary party's combat organization, and active promoter of philanthropic and educational enterprises in the emigration; F. A. Stepun, an academic sociologist-philosopher and member of the Technological Institute of Dresden. All three had past ties to some form of populism, and they continued to harbor strong sympathies for it. Both Fedotov and Stepun had emigrated later than most other intellectual leaders of the diaspora, arriving in the West after witnessing the profound transformations that had begun to take place in Russia under the New Economic Policy. Since Stepun resided in Germany, he was also a firsthand witness of the turmoil that led to the demise of the Weimar Republic and the seizure of power by Hitler. Funds were secured, largely with the assistance of the YMCA, and the journal's first issue appeared in late 1931. It was to survive until the outbreak of the war in 1939, although it did not manage to appear regularly—only fourteen issues were published, some at a year's interval.[26]

The opening editorial (written by Fedotov) stated that the "old city" was becoming more and more unlivable. This was in part due to the insecurity that was mounting, but even more was it so because of the danger of spiritual emptiness that stemmed from the chaotic economic, social, and political conditions. The journal's task was to prepare and elaborate the fundamental elements of a "new city"—the City on the Hill—resting on Christian faith and universally valid spiritual norms. The journal was to be an open forum in which to debate the major ideas that could serve as building blocks for the new city. At first, the articles in *Novyi grad* emphasized the social and economic conditions in the West (and Soviet Russia), that were creating the ethical problems that needed resolution. This was only too natural, since the Depression had just demonstrated the incapacity, or so it seemed, of capitalism to improve conditions, to guarantee material security, and to reform itself in such a way as to cure the disease and prevent its recurrence. *Novyi grad* was, therefore, alert to, and curious about, the experimentations in matters social and economic that were taking place in several countries, and the many diverse plans put forward to rescue the world from the Depression and its social ills.

But as the thirties progressed, the center of attention of *Novyi grad's* contributors, especially of its main editorial voice G. Fedotov, shifted to international affairs; for it was becoming evident that the peace of Europe, if not of the world, was sorely threatened. The Spanish civil war was the crucial event: it constituted a danger to peace and also illustrated the aggressive and vile goals of Fascist Italy and Nazi Germany. Since the aggression would eventually be aimed at the Western democracies, where the émigrés had found refuge and where they could express themselves freely, it was a danger that the exile elite could not ignore. The international security of Russia was jeopardized as well. How should Russia Abroad react in case of an invasion of the Soviet Union by an expansionist and brutal power, such as Nazi Germany? The question produced a crisis of conscience among the émigrés. Early on the *New City* took a firm stand in favor of supporting the Soviet Union in a conflict with Nazi expansionism and racism, and it opposed appeasement as only postponing the ultimate reckoning.

A detailed analysis of *Novyi grad's* reactions to the crucial sociopolitical events of the day would yield fascinating insights, but would also lead us too far afield. Let me briefly summarize the journal's responses to the major events that dominated the 1930s: the Depression and its socioeconomic problems in Germany and Hitler's seizure of power; the crisis of democracy in France and the coming to power of Léon Blum's Popular Front government; developments in the Soviet Union; and the Spanish civil war. In regard to the last, *Novyi grad* was clearly on the side of the Republic, even though it deplored the mistakes and excesses committed by its various governments. The *New City* was indignant about the brutality of Franco's troops, and outraged by the hypocrisy of a "crusade," conducted in the name of Christianity and the preservation of the church, that resorted to the most ferocious, cynical, and brutal repression.[27] *Novyi grad* was more outspoken on this than even the liberal émigré dailies such as *Poslednie novosti*. As to developments in the Soviet Union, the *New City* shared the shock expressed by all exiles at the news of the famine of 1932 and the later purge trials. Its reaction, shared by all in the diaspora, of course, was one of utter horror and unqualified condemnation of the brutality of Stalin's policies. True, some of the indignation was a bit more muted when the threat to peace became a paramount concern; many leading émigrés, including the editors of the *New City*, came to wish for a Soviet Russia that was militarily and diplomatically strong, to effectively support the Western anti-German coalition.

Novyi grad followed closely the situation in the last years of the Weimar Republic and the first measures taken by Hitler upon his appointment as chancellor in January 1933. The journal (well informed by Stepun and B. Izhboldin) showed interest in the various schemes for solving the social and economic ills of the Weimar Republic, especially those that drew their inspiration from the corporatist arguments for an organic society structured along professional lines. It responded on the whole favorably to the proposals to reform the German economy by restricting the role of the banks and by introducing some planning to achieve a better balance between production and distribution (or consumption)—since the main cause of the Depression was thought to have been overproduction. At first, the *New City* did not view the economic legislation of the Nazi government negatively, especially with regard to the measure creating a *Reichsnährstand* to improve the situation in agriculture. But from the very start, and increasingly so as time went on, *Novyi grad* remained adamantly opposed to the political, and especially the racial, practices of the Nazis. Stepun's outright condemnation of Nazi brutality and antidemocratic rule forced him to resign his teaching position in Dresden (but he stayed in Germany where he died after living through the whole war there): and his name had to be removed from the masthead of *Novyi grad,* although he continued to contribute to the journal under his own name.

The "American experiment" of Franklin D. Roosevelt's New Deal met with the approval of *Novyi grad.* The ability of the United States to carry out a far-reaching social transformation and economic reform in a democratic way, without destroying the basic political and social institutions, was much praised by *Novyi grad* as a model worthy of emulation in Europe. The preservation of capitalism, however, especially of the role of banks, did not appeal to the journal; but it felt that the other gains easily outweighed this drawback which, perhaps, could be corrected in the future. The positive results brought about by the New Deal (especially in its first legislative period) led *Novyi grad* to give full support to the Front Populaire and Léon Blum's legislation, which seemed to be largely inspired by the American example.

The events of February 1934 had frightened the liberal Russian emigration by revealing the moral degeneration of the political system of the Third Republic, and by raising the specter of a France falling into the hands of the Fascist leagues. The apprehension was understandable, even if it proved to have been exaggerated, for the status of the Russian exiles was particularly vulnerable, both for economic and political reasons. Russian workers had more to fear than their French comrades from the effects of the Great Depression and unemployment; politically, an authoritarian or dictatorial regime might limit still further the legal guarantees, small as they were, that permitted so many Russian exiles to reside in France. *Novyi grad* showed less fear of the Popular Front's collaboration with the Communist party than did other left and liberal organs of the Russian diaspora. As for Blum's social legislation, it was greeted enthusiastically as long overdue in securing for the first time the human dignity of the French worker. The only criticism that *Novyi grad* had of Blum's experiment was that it did not go far enough, that it accommodated itself to a continuation of the role played by finance capital. The writers of the *New City* firmly believed in the parasitic character of finance capital, a feature that prevented it from working for the industrial recovery and for an efficient policy of economic planning. We can easily detect here the influence of economic analysis, as practiced by the German and Austrian social-democratic leaders (O. Bauer, F. Adler, R. Hilferding). As mentioned earlier, after the outbreak of the Spanish civil war and the headlong rush into war after 1938, international affairs were to take precedence over plans of economic reform.[28]

The editors of *Novyi grad* shared with the RSK Movement, with whose leaders they were intimately connected, a social activism imbued with a specific Christian Orthodox outlook and practical contents. The Orthodox Work of Mother Maria found active participants among the contributors to the *New City*, and the meetings of the Circle associated with the Orthodox Work were reported in the journal. But if one reads the articles of the editors, one gains the impression that the journal had a more socialist orientation than the movement. As a matter of fact, the movement was neutral and noncommittal on specific social and political issues, except for its broad advocacy of a spiritual and Christian respect of the personality of the worker, and of active efforts to improve the worker's material lot. *Novyi grad,* on the other hand, took clear stands on contemporary political and economic issues, as we have seen, and believed that a planned economy was the only solution for the Depression and for securing the workers' material welfare and social dignity. Sharing the same personalist philosophy as *Put'* and the French writers in *Esprit, Novyi grad* also had much sympathy for the *Die Tat* circle, with its corporatist and nationalist ideas.

Social activism in a Christian socialist spirit, such was the basic intellectual goal of the *New City*. It was taken for granted that a realization of this principle would have a positive effect on the further development of culture. Naturally, it was hoped that with the assistance (not guidance or leadership) of the émigré elite, inspired by *Novyi grad,* a future free Russia would find its own voice and social constitution. Like Berdiaev, Fedotov and his friends judged the Russian revolution to have been a positive—and under the circumstances unavoidable—event. True, the price had been too high, but this was laid at the doorstep of the old regime. In any case, there was no way of undoing the revolution; one must sift out its positive results and incorporate them into any planning for the future Russia. Both Stepun and Fedotov never tired of repeating that Russia had undergone—perhaps it was still undergoing—a profound social revolution; collectivization and the Five Year Plans were still consolidating and extending the results.[29] All this gave them hope that the New City, which would eventually emerge in Russia, might serve as a model and inspiration to the West, for it would combine the spiritual values of Orthodoxy with the social, economic, and cultural benefits of a Christian socialism rooted in a personalist, spiritualist metaphysics.

There is no question that significant segments of the emigration, especially among its intellectual leadership, experienced a revival of interest in, and commitment to, religion and the church. Religious institutions were looked to for both material and spiritual assistance. Many exiles returned to the Russian Orthodox Church for worship and for the preservation of their cultural traditions and ways. They began to regard the church with greater respect than before, and were willing to assist it in expanding its social, material, and cultural (particularly educational) roles. Many began to advocate bringing the church into daily life and bringing life—concerns of the secular world—into the church. The goal was the "Christianization of life." These notions encountered some resistance, to be sure. And we have seen that it contributed to a split within the church in exile, a split due as much to jurisdictional disputes as to different conceptions of the church's place in Russia Abroad.

In spite of this rift among the émigré church hierarchy, the role of religion and of church-oriented thinking increased dramatically in the emigration. While in Soviet Russia the church was pushed into the background, and its intellectual influence appeared to have declined to almost zero, intellectuals in Russia Abroad placed Orthodoxy at the very center of their intellectual and cultural concerns. The St. Serge Theological Seminary and Institute became a lively and innovative scholarly center, whose publications served to give Russian ecclesiastical studies a new resonance in foreign milieus. Much of what was created and published before 1939 under the aegis of St. Serge's and of the West European Metropolia fertilized scholarship on Russia Abroad, and it is now also beginning to have a direct impact on the cultural scene of the Russian homeland. The formation of the RSK Movement, with its ancillary educational, social, and publishing activities, drew many educated émigrés back into the church, and imparted an Orthodox "note" to their social and political thinking. The church in Russia Abroad thus was able to take an active part in émigré intellectual life, and to help preserve cultural and national traditions. It formulated programs for social, economic, and cultural betterment that could be of value for the world at large, as well as for Russia in the future. By its participation in the efforts made by English Protestantism in favor of a rapprochement between the Christian churches, and of an ecumenical understanding, the West European Metropolia of the Russian church in exile asserted its presence and importance to Christendom. As a result, the Russian church was no longer, in the eyes of its Western brethren, the somewhat primitive, ultraconservative, self-centered, and tradition-bound body. This new image has no doubt facilitated the recent ecumenical efforts of the Moscow Patriarchate as well.

Similarly, a socialism firmly anchored in Christianity was defined and developed, both as an ideal and as a practice, by members of the Russian émigré church, and it has played a significant part in the success of Christian social-ism on the public stage after World War II. At the very least, it has brought committed Orthodox laypeople into intellectual exchange with Western Chris-tians. The great help of the YMCA and other Anglo-American Protestant organizations goes far in explaining the survival of the Russian church and its influence on the cultural productivity of Russia Abroad.

It may be a common impulse for a group in exile to retain and reinforce the traditional role of its church. But it has not been common for émigrés to modernize the social role and to activate the intellectual life of their church, as happened in Russia Abroad. It remains to be seen whether this accomplish-ment can be brought back to the homeland. Some signs point to this very possibility. If so, it may have striking consequences for the development of Russian culture, and perhaps for Russian public life as well. It would be a major legacy of Russia Abroad to the future Russia at home.

7

Remembrance of Things Past:
Historians and History in Russia Abroad

War, revolution, and civil war shattered Russian society. They not only dramatically transformed the accustomed ways of public life, but they also revealed depths of cruelty, savagery, depravity, misery, and sheer horror that had not seemed possible. Whatever the idea or picture of a harmonious, idyllic, and cooperative society many may have held on the eves of 1914 and 1917, it was destroyed by the behavior of all classes. True, one also had witnessed instances of heroism, self-abnegation, devotion, and love—but these acts seemed exceptional and isolated islands in the midst of the swirling sea of human suffering and misery. The Horsemen of the Apocalypse had not spared anything that educated society had known before 1914. At the end of the years of horror, a regime had imposed itself which was brutally contemptuous of everything held dear and sacred in the past, and which stopped at nothing to retain its grip on the country and its inhabitants. The Bolsheviks, so it seemed, were bent upon implanting what was most ugly and despicable, and doing so in a most offensive and beastly manner.

For the many who had fled across the border, the old Russia was gone. But even that was not the most painful change: everything good and beautiful appeared to have been smashed; the accumulation of riches, memories, and traditions was irremediably lost as well. It seemed to them that something ugly, coarse, and inhuman had taken over, and it was in the process of transforming the very nature and soul of the Russian people. Even without answering the questions of how it could have happened, who was to be blamed, and what could be done, every thinking and educated person in emigration had to shape a new, acceptable image of Russia's past. How could one face life in exile with only the images of death, destruction, and vicious dictatorship in one's consciousness? It was natural to turn to the past and cling to anything that seemed to suggest how things might have gone differently. Emigrés wanted to recall selectively those trends and manifestations of Russia's past that would help them overcome the recent horrors; they sought things that represented the perennially valuable aspects of Russia's true identity. And since the exiles had been raised in the post-Romantic era of modern nationalism, they expected to pinpoint in the past those features that always characterized the Russian nation, its culture, and explained its historical process.

It was an all too human reaction. As individual memory selects the pleasant and useful in its own past, so does the group's, especially if its members are educated and can give literary expression to their perception of this past. We find the most dramatic—and effective—example of this in the Great Polish Emigration of 1831. Not only did it nurture the greatest national poets, A. Michiewicz and J. Słowacki, but also its most influential historian, J. Lelewel. They built their image of Poland from selected periods and events—either the glories of the most remote past or the sufferings of the more recent centuries—and endowed it with a meaning that pointed to their own role in preparing for a great national revival.

Nor did the émigrés from Germany in the 1930s remain content with tracing the roots of the evil, which had triumphed in their homeland, to the entire course of German history. They felt that some aspects of that history offered an alternative course, and held out the promise, however dim at the time, of the possibility of change and a better future. Rejecting a deterministic reading of the baneful legacies of Luther and Frederician Prussia, émigré intellectuals turned to the literary and philosophic achievements of Goethe's Weimar, to Germany's contributions to science and scholarship, to the traditions of individual freedom and local autonomy in the Holy Roman Empire.[1]

How did the Russian historians in emigration rise to the challenge of an appropriate and meaningful reading of the Russian past?[2] Let us first turn to their organizations and activities in exile to help us find an answer.

In 1922, after the expulsion on Lenin's orders of more than 100 intellectuals, it was estimated that there were about 500 active scholars and scientists in emigration.[3] As was true of the entire "Great Emigration" from Russia, these professional scholars were dispersed all over Europe and the Far East; but their centers were in Berlin, Prague, Kharbin, and Belgrade and, to a lesser extent, in Riga, Warsaw, and Sofia. As a result of the course taken by the civil war, a proportionately larger number of professors and scholars had been associated with the universities in the Ukraine and Siberia, although many had also been connected with Moscow and St. Petersburg at some time in their careers. Of course, not everyone who might have wished to leave was able to do so, as the recently discovered diary of the Moscow historian Iu. Got'e illustrates.[4]

The scholars who found themselves in emigration took immediate steps to secure their material and professional existence. The opportunities of the Duma period, and the experiences of the civil war, had taught a number of intellectuals how to coordinate their efforts for a common purpose. As we have seen in an earlier chapter, the scholars and intellectuals, who had been politically active in Paris since 1917–1918, took the initiative in setting up so-called academic groups. With the encouragement and modest material help of English academic circles and of the YMCA in Berlin, a number of such academic groups sprung up in the European centers of the Russian emigration.[5]

The academic groups of Russian scholars set themselves the following tasks. First, they wanted to find material assistance for émigré scholars; second, they hoped to enable them to pursue their professional and scholarly-scientific activities; and, third, they intended to spread knowledge of Russian science, scholarship, and culture among the host societies. A fourth purpose came to be added later, coordinating and cooperating with those organizations that endeavored to give the younger émigrés (and their children) a Russian education, so as to prepare them for an eventual professional role in the motherland.

As we have noted, the most elaborate effort to attain the goals of the Russian academic groups abroad took place in Czechoslovakia. The so-called Action russe involved the establishment of the Russian University in Prague, as well as a series of scholarly institutions. Among the Russian historians prominently active in Prague we should mention A. Kizevetter, E. Shmurlo, V. Frantsev, G. Vernadsky (until his move to the United States in the late 1920s), and the somewhat younger M. Shakhmatov and A. Soloviev. The Russian University also helped train a few "younger" historians—S. Pushkarev, G. Florovsky, N. Andreyev, and (on a temporary visiting basis) M. Karpovich.

The struggle for mere survival all too often absorbed the lion's share of the émigrés' energies. This largely explains why most were in no position to produce large-scale studies and monographs—or did so only when they had some economic security, as was the case of the "successful" lawyers V. Eliashevich and B. Nolde, or P. Miliukov during World War II. A few, e.g., N. Berdiaev, lived on "retainers" provided by sympathizers, usually American, and friends.

But even shorter studies were published with difficulty, for a simple reason: the dearth of sources. There were no adequate collections of Russian materials at the leading European universities. Even printed materials had to be garnered in many places; and under the prevailing technological, legal, and economic conditions, duplication and travel were practically unavailable to émigré scholars. Because of the ethnocentric historiographical tradition of the time, most émigré scholars could not turn to foreign archival sources on the history of Russia. There were notable exceptions: for instance, Shmurlo continued his researches on Italo-Russian contacts, but he added almost nothing to the sources from the Vatican archives he had identified and partially published before 1917; A. V. Florovskij devoted most of his time, from the mid-1920s on, to a monumental two-volume study of Czech-Russian relations in medieval and early modern times. To my knowledge, however, no other émigré scholar tried to plumb the archival holdings for their *Russica* contents in Paris, Berlin, or elsewhere. Partly, perhaps, because access to official archives was not easy for foreigners to use in those days; but also, I suspect, because prerevolutionary Russian historians had focused almost exclusively on the internal history of their country, and they did not realize the potential that the view of an outsider, *altérité*, offered for an understandnng of oneself.

An important concomitant of the émigrés' parlous economic and professional situation everywhere, except perhaps in Prague, was the difficulty of finding a venue for the publication of their works. Most scholars abroad were not in a position to write directly in a foreign language—even though some had an excellent passive command of a major Western tongue. The few who could do so found interest only in popular books (*ouvrages de vulgarisation*, as the French call them) on contemporary themes and periods. Translations were expensive and not always easy to arrange. Thus the émigré historians were restricted to the limited forum of publication in Russian. Naturally, such a situation did not encourage them to make material sacrifices for the sake of research.

In Prague, the historians organized their own professional society (Russkoe istorichesko obshchestvo v Prage) first under the chairmanship of Shmurlo and later of Frantsev. It sponsored meetings, seminar discussions, and published its own irregular serial (*Zapiski russkogo istoricheskogo obshchestva v Prage*, 1927–1930). The faculty of history of the Russian University in Prague also participated in the "learned notes" of the university and in the notes of the evening school affiliated with it, the so-called Narodnyi russkii universitet (*Uchenye zapiski osnovannye russkoi uchebnoi kollegii v Prage*, 1924–).[6] But as the bibliographic record of these publications makes amply clear, their appearance was neither regular nor very frequent. Since the claims on their space was great, any sizable publication had to be arranged separately. This entailed scraping together money for the printing with much effort and great investment of time. Benefactors were hard to find in the twenties or early thirties, especially after the onset of the Great Depression; besides, most of them had their own preferred causes. The correspondence preserved in émigré archives gives a vivid picture of the many appeals, and the few successful responses, that were launched on both sides of the Atlantic. Even the most faithful and dedicated supporter, the YMCA, was not so forthcoming with its funds, especially after the failure of its effort at mass production and mass distribution of Russian textbooks.[7]

I have mentioned that scholars had difficulty in finding an outlet for the publication of their writings. As we have seen, there existed, attached to the several institutions of advanced learning and the academic groups in the major émigré centers, scholarly serials. They appeared more or less regularly and opened their pages to articles in the humanities, law, sociology—and, in some cases, to the natural and physical sciences as well. These serial publications offered interesting, original contributions to various aspects of Russian history. By and large, however, they were based on materials the authors had previously found and worked upon in Russia before emigrating. In a few rare cases archives in foreign locations came into play. Because of limitations of space these articles have a narrow focus and deal with a single discrete event or a limited problem.[8] But given the erudition and high technical level, practically all of the articles in these "learned notes" are worthy of the professional historian's attention and should be consulted in every case in which they deal with a topic of relevance to the contemporary searcher. Unfortunately, few libraries have full runs of these serials, and they are only partly, and not very satisfactorily, registered in bibliographies. It should also be stressed that these contributions were written in the manner and style of prerevolutionary professional articles, which had little appeal to the educated lay reader. Their impact, therefore, was quite limited and, given the slight interest displayed by foreign scholars in Russian history (and wide ignorance of the language), they were largely ignored by non-Russian historians, with the exception of the rare specialists. The summaries in French or German appended to some of the serial publications did little to widen their audience. Only articles summarizing significant new findings or interpretations that touched on broad topics of European import were sometimes translated and published in a foreign professional journal.

One last general issue remains to be mentioned in setting forth the material and psychological conditions under which the émigré historian had to work. It is the question of the emigration's "receptivity" to historical knowledge and interpretations, in short, its interest in and attitude to history. The émigrés who settled in Europe and the Far East (and in small scattered numbers all over the globe) had just experienced one of the most upsetting, dramatic, and harrowing series of "historical events." Their world had crumbled before their very eyes; a completely new political, social, and cultural order had taken over after years of bloody fratricidal war. All of this occurred just after the First World War, which most of them had also experienced more or less directly. Is it surprising that the émigrés were "tired of history"? They felt, even more so than did the literary critic M. Gershenzon in his letters to Viacheslav Ivanov, the "burden" of history and civilization.[9] They could not work up much interest in remotely past events, in the kind of issues and sources that excited and fascinated the historian.

To be sure, the émigrés had a natural curiosity about the experiences of fellow participants. The memoirs of leading prerevolutionary personalities, as well as those of both prominent and humble participants in the war and civil war, found an eager audience. They were readily published in books or serialized in journals and newspapers. The interest in memoirs was akin to nostalgia, a desire to relive the past, not necessarily a better, but at any rate a memorable past.

Not surprisingly, the émigrés asked themselves how it had been possible for the revolution and the civil war to engulf Russia. How had Russia departed from some "normal" path, be it a Russian, or a European, or a universal one? But such questions were better treated, better "digested" in reflective or polemical essays, not in scholarly treatises. And such essays, raising the perennial "accursed question" of Russia's relationship to the West, to Europe, of the peculiar makeup of the Russian national character and experience, were constantly appearing on the pages of émigré journals and newspapers. But these ruminations were far from being an analysis of causes and effects, a kind of analysis that, if undertaken at all, appeared lifeless, dehumanized to those who had only recently experienced historical events in all their inconclusiveness.

This kind of experience was better conveyed by historical fiction (or memoirs) than by scholarly studies. This goes a long way, to my mind, to explain the popularity enjoyed by the prolific Mark Aldanov's novels and historical sketches. Indeed, Aldanov "relativized," so to speak, the Russian experience by writing about the prehistory and history of the French revolution, and by setting the later prodromes to the Russian revolution in an all-European framework. In second place, he described and explained events as the result of unpredictable consequences of the concatenation of actions taken by individuals. These individuals intended one thing, but, most frequently, what resulted was not what they expected. Consequently, there are no laws of history, no predictability—everything is chance and flux. History is the stage for our activities, nothing more, nothing less. Aldanov's skepticism, detachment—as well as great narrative skill—were like a soothing balm on the raw wounds of his émigré readers. He provided the kind of historical reading that appealed to them, and unintentionally foreclosed their interest in scholarly, "scientific," or "objective" history.

The foreigners among whom the Russian émigrés lived did not evince much interest in the past of their guests' homeland. Most were at best attuned only to recent events—in part to understand how the tragic collapse of Russia could happen, in part to bring the Soviet regime and its policies into some kind of framework. By and large the feelings toward Russia were unfriendly, either because of the belief that Russia had "betrayed" the Allies in 1917–1918 or for having allegedly contributed to the instability of the postwar world. Since there was much ignorance about Russia and its past, the foreigners dismissed the subject in anger or with a contemptuous reference to the incomprehensible "Slavic soul" and Russian "barbarism." On the other hand, the so-called progressive public opinion—pacifists, socialists, fellow travelers, committed Communists—considered the Bolshevik revolution to have been a positive and necessary event, and did not want to hear about the evil past of tsarist Russia from the pen (or mouth) of those whom history had deservedly condemned to exile. Given the increasingly pro-Soviet mood of the European intellectuals in the 1930s, the historian of Russia, especially of émigré background, had a dwindling foreign audience.

This was surely in contrast to the role played by Adam Mickiewicz, for example, of the Great Polish Emigration in pioneering the study of Slavic languages and literatures at the College de France in the 1840s. But it was also very different from the German historians who emigrated to England and the United States after Hitler's accession to power.[10] They were relatively easily and rapidly integrated into the academic establishments of their asylum. In the case of the United States, the German refugee scholar played a most influential role in both war and peace, contributing to raising the professional level of universities and colleges. As a glance at the development of historical studies in the United States (and to a lesser degree in England, too) shows, they also made for important historiographical changes, introducing, for example, the history of ideas, a new understanding and expansion of Renaissance history, revolutionizing art history, not to mention their contribution to the study of Germany and in training specialists in that field. One may well ask what caused this difference with the Russian historians among whom there were equally distinguished scholars. There may have been a difference in numbers, but that was hardly the crucial factor. The most important single factor was that the Russians were and remained émigrés, always hoping to return to the homeland, and therefore unwilling—and unable in the Europe of the time—to integrate. The Germans, on the other hand, came to the United States (and England) having made a clear break with the country of their birth; they were committed (with some exceptions, to be sure) to making their permanent home in the new land. In the second place, we should also remember that graduate studies in the United States had developed on the German pattern. Although most Russian scholars before 1914 had also studied in Germany, and their university system was similar to the German, this did not lead to as much interdependence. Anyway, most Russian historians did not settle in Germany but in France and other countries that had different practices and traditions, or that aimed at developing their own academic ways. Finally, Russian history—unlike the German—was more "exotic," more remote for the European academic community. For most Westerners the break in 1917 seemed radical enough to encourage them to ignore what had preceded it. This was far from being the case with Germany— especially after the outbreak of the war, soon after the arrival of the refugees from there.

What about the young generation of émigrés? The children of those who had actively fought in war and civil war spoke Russian and had received an introduction to Russian literature and history. But few were truly interested in deepening this knowledge. There was the predictable negative reaction to their parents' unfortunate past, reinforced by their position as outsiders in the schools and country of asylum by virtue of this very past. The prospects of economic survival, and of securing a socially satisfactory status in the foreign land (once a return to the homeland became virtually impossible), were not furthered by a professional commitment to the study of Russia's past. Of course, some émigré children were interested in history and later pursued that interest in the university; but in this case, too, they turned rather to the history of foreign countries where they could at least do archival work and enlist the guidance and support of established academics.[11]

As a result, the émigré professional historian (with the qualified exception of a few instances in Prague) had no successor, no *relève*, to train, to supervise, and to promote. The Russian University in Prague did grant a few advanced degrees; but they were obtained by scholars who had already reached the last stage of their professional training in Russia, e.g., S. Pushkarev and

G. Florovsky. Only N. Andreyev, who had been educated in Estonia, received all his graduate training in Prague. Marc Szeftel, who had studied with A. Eck in Brussels, first received a law degree in his native Poland.

At first glance it may appear surprising that the professional historians of the emigration did not turn their immediate attention to chronicling the revolutions of 1917 and the civil war. As a matter of fact I know of only one serious and comprehensive history of the revolution by an émigré (before 1939). It was written by the indefatigable P. Miliukov, and it partakes as much of the genre of memoir and brief *pro domo sua* as it does of academic history.[12] I think that the reason for this is obvious: the events were too painful and too close to allow dispassionate treatment. Equally important, of course, was the fact that the official archives were not accessible, while the documents of the White Armies, which had been evacuated along with the officers and troops, were dispersed and in a chaotic state; it would take years for the archives in Prague and at the Hoover Institution to be constituted as research instruments, and it would have taken many years more to work up and analyze the material—the Second World War cut short any effort in that direction.[13] Perhaps it was neither unnatural nor accidental that the first comprehensive account of the revolution and civil war was written by an American journalist, William H. Chamberlin, and it is still the best overall chronicle.[14]

This certainly does not mean that the émigré historians were not interested in the causes and course of events that preceded and followed upon the collapse of the imperial government in February 1917. But their energies went into the writing of memoirs, collecting them and other relevant materials for future scholarly treatment. The memoirs were primarily personal statements, or special pleadings, by all those who had been directly involved in any of the major events of the last decades of the Empire, as well as of the "time of troubles" that followed.[15] But they also try to account for the causes that brought about the end of the old regime, although from a personal perspective. Several serial publications were specially founded to provide a vehicle for this memoir output: the best and most comprehensive was the *Archive of the Russian Revolution* (*Arkhiv russkoi revoliutsii*); in addition we have the short-lived *The Historian and the Contemporary* (*Istorik i sovremennik*), and *On Foreign Soil* (*Na chuzhoi storone*).[16] In addition, as I have already pointed out, the journals of general interest and the better newspapers serialized memoirs of participants and witnesses to the revolution and civil war. As the archival collections abroad show, almost as many memoirs were never published. Quite clearly, in the twenties and thirties the émigrés were still too much in a state of shock to face the task of critical analysis, synthesis, and "objective" reconstruction of events.

Naturally, the broader question of the origins and causes of the revolution could not fail to be of great concern for the émigré historians. Theirs and their fellow exiles' memoir efforts aimed at suggesting answers. Basically, there were two types of answers: the first consisted in seeing the revolution as an accident that had disturbed the more or less natural, harmonious, and progressive developments of the last decades of the imperial regime (or since 1861), and prevented them from coming to fruition. The "accident" may have been the result of an unexpected series of events, for example, the First World War, or a conspiracy by evil men bent upon destroying the greatness of Russia and of its culture—whether to further the interests of Germany or to promote nihilism. The second answer, given by all "liberal-minded" historians among the émigrés, was that the trends operating in the Russian Empire since 1861, or the accession of Alexander III, had created problems of such magnitude that they could not be addressed by a conservative bureaucracy and an obscurantist emperor; society had to be integrated with the government and failing this, the collapse of the imperial regime became inevitable, although the specific events that set off and accompanied the collapse were not predetermined by the long-range trends. Except for S. S. Oldenburg's defense of the last tsar as an individual and ruler, there was no one to argue seriously in favor of the ways in which the old regime had responded to the critical issues confronting Russian society. This, however, did not preclude the publication of a large volume of popular, sentimental, and patriotic literature that grieved for the tragic end of the imperial family; it reflected a retrospectively emotional rehabilitation of the last tsar and his wife, which had arisen and grown in the course of the civil war.

The preceding remarks bring me to the crucial aspect of émigré historiography which, in my opinion, goes a long way in explaining its relatively unoriginal and uncreative character. Emigré historians had received their professional training in the last decade or two of the nineteenth or in the very first decade of the twentieth centuries. This was the period of the dominance of positivism, both in Western Europe and in Russia. The positivist orientation in historiography had two sides to it. For one, the belief that the historian's main task was to accumulate all possible facts, preferably those based on archival documentation (for the modern period—for earlier times manuscript sources were used), and dealing with the political and public socioeconomic facets of the past. The mere accumulation of all documented facts, which were critically assessed as reliable, was the ideal toward which the historian should strive, because the interpretation of these facts would follow almost automatically. This is, obviously, an oversimplification of the "fact"-oriented bent of this historical school, but it points to the reason for the lack of popular success of history written in this mode. There is an absence of color, drama, and personalities. And indeed, with the exception of Kliuchevskii, who was an exception in most respects, at least in his lectures and his university course based on those lectures, Russian historians wrote turgidly and displayed no interest in biography, so that their readership was largely restricted to the profession and a few aficinados.[17]

As we all know, however, the mere accumulation of facts does not create a meaningful synthesis; besides it is impossible to obtain all the facts. Facts are selected, and the choice is determined by certain assumptions. Moreover, the selection and interpretation of facts must be based on some underlying intellectual scheme if they are to have any meaning. The other side of the positivist historiography, therefore (and its tenets were first formulated by Auguste Comte, founder of positivism), was the belief that the facts will reveal the specific forms in which the laws of social development manifest themselves. The laws of development are universal, though varying in their specifics and chronological sequence from case to case. However, if one posits the existence of laws of social and historical development, one at once enters the realm of determinism—a determinism that can only partially and inadequately be tempered by individual actions and accidental events.

The scheme of development proposed by positivism has a teleological character in that it presupposes, or sets forth, the next state, or the ultimate goal, of this development. Positivist historians believe that we normally know what the next stage will be, because all humanity has to pass through a similar set of stages in a prescribed order—a belief inherited from the Enlightenment. We, therefore, must know what the immediate goals of development should be in the case of a certain society and historical period, for other societies (or nations) that have reached a subsequent stage provide both a model and a standard. Such a scheme can be associated with geographic, ethnic, racial, or other factors as determining the evolution of a given society. Thus Russia, its positivist historians concluded, would pass through the stages that Western and Central Europe had passed or entered, since it, too, belonged to Europe. The peculiarities of Russia's development stemmed from a chronological discrepancy that was largely due to geography and its past evolution. It meant that Russia, too, one day soon—once the artificial barriers had been removed— would become a member of the European social, economic, and political civilization *à part entière*.

I have dwelt at some length on this scheme because it was the scheme adopted by the most influential and significant émigré historian, P. N. Miliukov. It was the leitmotif of his *Ocherki*, more particularly in the "jubilee" edition. And the scheme also underlay the writings of more narrowly focused historians, such as A. Kizevetter, D. Odinets, P. Bitsilli. It was the conception that was at the basis of the organization, and the few general interpretations, to be found in the three-volume history of Russia published in Paris, in French, and edited by Miliukov, who also wrote a good part of it. His collaborators were V. Miakotin, A. Kizevetter, and several other specialists who wrote the short sections dealing with prehistory, geography, and diplomacy. The history's intellectual sponsor was the French "high priest of positivistic historiography," Charles Seignobos.[18] Their philosophy aside, the three volumes offer a still useful compendium of the essential political and socioeconomic events of Russian history. But they are short on interpretation, and whatever explanations they do offer are mere repetition of the nineteenth-century liberal clichés. Nor is their style very engaging, and if we also mention that there are few, if any, suggestive portraits of leading personalities, it becomes understandable why they are not terribly readable.

The positivist approach, regardless of its philosophical and epistemological problems, presented the émigré historian with a major difficulty in connection with the revolution. Indeed, however one evaluated the "backwardness" of Russia in comparison to the West and Central European (or North American) pacesetters, the anticipation was that Russia would become a modern society with all the attendant critical issues. The revolution was, therefore, the culmination of Russia's moving in the direction of modernization, and of the old regime's inadequacy in solving the attendant difficulties. This evolution, however, could also be explained as an almost natural, or organic, result of the special path taken by Russia in its earlier historical development (whose determining roots go back still further, ad infinitum). The conclusion imposes itself, therefore, that the revolution had been inevitable and in the natural order of things, given the special circumstances of Russia's history, geography, society, culture, and so on. But was this a palatable, nay possible, conclusion to face for émigrés who had suffered so much as a result of this revolution, and who were still deprived of their homeland because of it?

The alternative to such an interpretative approach was to see the revolution as resulting from the sudden and capricious impact of a historical accident, of a catastrophe along the lines of a meteorological or geological upheaval, which could neither have been foreseen nor prevented. This was not much of an explanation, but in accepting it, one could dispense with any investigation of the past in search for reasonable causes. Many, especially among the uneducated and prejudiced monarchists, were inclined to accept such a view of the recent past and it explains their impatience with historical literature in general. The unpleasant conclusions about one's own past offered by these alternative schemes were the major barrier to the emigration's enjoyment of history. Similar reactions could be observed among the German liberal professionals who emigrated after 1933, bewildered by the failure of the Weimar Republic. They began coming to terms with the past only after the Second World War had run its course. The delayed reaction to the Holocaust is another instance of men's preferring to forget the unpleasant immediate past.

The positivist methodology and interpretative scheme dominated almost all émigré historical scholarship in the interwar period. Was there no alternative to them? At one point it seemed that an alternative did emerge. As has been well shown by Nicholas V. Riasanovsky, this alternative, too, had some of its roots in the prerevolutionary cultural atmosphere. It was the so-called Eurasianism. Its tenets, as they pertained to history, may be summarized as follows. The unit for the historical study of Russia is Eurasia—not a combination of Europe and Asia, but a separate entity with basic characteristics of its own. It is defined, first of all, by its geographic location, which also determines its climate, resources, and modes of economic organization. Eurasia is the geographic area of steppes and forests, land-locked, devoid of mountainous massifs (except on its southern and southeastern borders). Its continental climate has stamped its agricultural development.[19] By defining Russia's geographic identity in this way, the Eurasians were in fact equating Eurasia with the boundaries of the Russian Empire on the eve of 1914, or of Soviet Russia—

though the latter had been deprived of the Western fringes (Baltic states, Bessarabia, eastern Poland). The social and political development of this Eurasian entity was marked by the struggle between steppe and forest, with the latter eventually subduing the former. But the struggle underscores the importance of the steppe nomads in shaping the civilization—political, material, spiritual—which evolved organically in the territory of Eurasia. Hence, to understand Russia's past one has to pay proper attention to its steppe heritage, and not forget that for many centuries it was facing Asia rather than Europe. From Europe, however, it has received a major element of its identity, Christianity; but characteristically it was the Christianity of the East. This explains why the Western elements of modern Russian culture are so alien to it—they were mechanically imposed on Russia (by Peter the Great and his successors). The Bolshevik revolution, among other things, was a revolt of Eurasia against this alien intrusion. It proved, once again, that Russia's cultural specificity is anti-Western, even if modern science and technology are compatible with it. Here we need not take up the question of the political consequences the Eurasians drew from this interpretation—it belongs to another book.

On closer examination, however, the Eurasians did not offer an adequate alternative to the positivist scheme either. Their interpretation, too, led to a deterministic view of Russian history, a determinism based on geographic and climatic factors. Any determinism, however, implied the inevitability of the Bolshevik revolution, and the Soviet regime's "legitimate" and lasting character.[20] This was a conclusion that few émigrés were prepared to accept. Nor did it make for an interesting history, because its teleological nature deprived epochs, events, and actors of their singularity and individuality and—consequently—of their fascination for both student and reader. For all these reasons Eurasianism did not have the impact on historical writing that one might have expected at first. The only professional historian to be, and to remain, "converted" to Eurasianism was G. Vernadsky. In fact, however, except for acknowledging the importance of the Mongol invasion and domination, something that Russian historiography had indeed tended to downplay or to ignore (e.g., the curious omission in Kliuchevskii's course), Vernadsky's account of the process of Russian history was hardly different from the one found in earlier general surveys of Russian history (or from the three-volume history in French, for that matter). To be sure, specific issues of the prehistory and the early Kievan period were given by Vernadsky new interpretations, based on hypotheses rooted in philological considerations that argued for the unity of the Slavic (Russian) and "Turanic" (Eastern) cultures. But these hypotheses (and his arguments in their favor) have been contested and, on the whole, rejected by both historians and linguists. (In all honesty, it should also be acknowledged that Vernadsky lacked the ability to organize his material effectively, and even in Russian his prose did not inspire.) His most significant contribution, five volumes on pre-Petrine Russia, were written and published after World War II and, except for the chapters on the Mongols, they owe more to traditional positivism than to Eurasianism. In spite of the stimulation it provided, for a brief period, to émigré discussions on the nature of Russia, its past, its culture, and the revolution, Eurasianism had no significant impact on Russian historiography.

Both the positivist scheme—with its standards of interpretation derived from the Western and Central European experiences—and the Eurasian theory, in its fascination with the steppe and nomadic elements of Russia's past, confronted a crucial problem of definition: what was subsumed under the rubric "history of Russia"? In other words, what was Russia? The political unit known since Peter the Great as the All Russian Empire? But what was its relationship to Muscovy, the appanages, Kiev? And what about all those areas, the Ukraine, Byelorussia, the Baltic and the Caucasus or Central Asia, which became part of the Empire; how was their history to be treated and fitted into the evolution of the Empire? Since by common consent neither geography nor the political events of state building were an adequate base for the study of the past, and more specifically for its transmission to the young after the revolutionary upheaval, what methods should one use? To be sure, the process of state and empire building was an important aspect of Russia's past. But this was a very ambiguous heritage; could it also be considered a permanent element in defining the national identity of the Russians (not to speak of Ukrainians, Caucasians, Jews, and others who were also part of the emigration)? After all, had not the events of 1917 and the aftermath revealed the brittleness of the imperial establishment and brought it to a permanent end? There was no going home again, the past was a closed chapter. Finally, stressing the political aspects would only run up against the political divisions of the emigration, become the source of bitter disputes and fragment still further the émigré community. And this at a time when the stress should be on what united the exiles and what was valuable in their heritage and could be passed on to the generation of children born abroad.

Not only the political but also the traditional social structures of Russia had disintegrated in the course of 1917–1921, and new ones had been fashioned by the Bolsheviks. It was, therefore, difficult to speak of Russia in the usual, primarily political, terms. True, with the introduction of the New Economic Policy, and even more so after Stalin had restored some of the nationalist and historical heritage of the past, it seemed that the Soviet government had re-created a politically powerful state—another "imperial" Russia. This development elated chauvinists in exile; even liberals, including Miliukov, could think again in the traditional terms of a Russian state in a historical continuum from Kiev, by way of Moscow and St. Petersburg, to the Red Kremlin. But this return to politically determined historical continuity in approaching Russian history came late, on the eve of the Second World War, when most émigré historians had passed their active, creative period.

It can be readily observed that whenever a traditional political or sociopolitical unit suffers a major catastrophe, or collapses altogether, the tendency is to look for those manifestations of public life that seems to provide a longer perspective, and a more permanent foundation for a sense of historical continuity and identity.[21] For example, the collapse of the Weimar Republic, or of Germany after 1945, led scholars in exile (and not only there) to view their country's past not in customary political terms, but to search for another coherence-giving concept. In the case of the Germans it was the "humanistic" heritage of the classical period of Schiller and Goethe. After 1945, for many, it was the notion of Western Christendom. For the Poles of their Great Emigration it was the idea of Poland as the bulwark of Christendom, home of political freedom, and martyr destined to be the future savior of Western civilization. What concept could replace the political idea of the All Russian Empire? One possible suggestion was to define Russia as the society of Orthodox Christianity and of the institutions that issued from Prince Vladimir's conversion of Rus' in 988. The suggestion was taken up by some émigré scholars, especially those of a conservative bent who settled in Yugoslavia. They contributed to and published a few books of essays, and supported an effort to have the feast day of St. Vladimir (28 July) celebrated as a symbol of the unity and purpose of the emigration.[22]

But they had no appreciable impact on the scholarly writing of the emigration's historians. Indeed, for most the approach was too closely connected with the failings and, in their opinion, reactionary role of the Russian Orthodox Church in its subservience to the Muscovite and imperial state establishments. Moreover, most of the émigré historians were positivists of mildly liberal persuasion, and, consequently, also profoundly secularist. Whatever their personal religious feelings and faith, and some were pious church-going individuals, they advocated the separation of church and state. Firm believers in the Enlightenment ideas of progress and human rights, they scorned the "obscurantism" and "barbarism" of Muscovy, let alone Kiev and the so-called appanage period that preceded it. We should also remember that although all émigré scholars possessed Russian language, culture, and education, not all were ethnic Russians or Orthodox Christians.

Something that clearly united all émigré scholars, as well as their audience, and tied them to the past, was language, language in the wider sense of the aesthetic, spiritual, and moral values that the Russian word, through its great literature, had created. The Great Polish Emigration had been the cradle of modern Polish literature—and its greatest achievements came about because of the exile writers Mickiewicz and Słowacki. It also was contemporary of the romantic period when art and nationalism combined to create the very notion of a distinct national culture. The Russian emigration, for its part, could draw on a great literature, with its own traditions and seminal role in defining the cultural values and national consciousness of Russians of all persuasions and classes. (Soviet successes in education showed how this great literary tradition could help cement the entire population.) It was natural, therefore, for the émigrés to adopt as their unit of discourse modern Russian literature—the creation of the St. Petersburg period. The poet Alexander Pushkin was its most glorious symbol, as had been publicly acknowledged ever since the famous celebration of 1880.

The notion of culture was not precisely defined; it was a somewhat hazy concept tinged with sentimentality and nostalgia. Culture, in the usage of émigré historians, essentially referred to the great works of Russian literature and their moral and spiritual message, as interpreted by the intelligentsia. The function of literature as the almost exclusive element in defining both culture and national historical identity was given additional prominence because many historians were also active as literary scholars, lecturers, and critics. This was the case of Kizevetter, as well as Miliukov, while Bitsilli, Florovsky, and Fedotov devoted almost as much attention to literary themes as they did to historical topics. This was also true of philosophers and theologians such as Berdiaev, Shestov, Frank, and Zen'kovskii. "Russianness" was thus seen and defined in terms of the accomplishments of the greatest figures of Russian letters, from M. V. Lomonosov and G. R. Derzhavin to the great novelists of the nineteenth century.

The émigrés perceived Russian history as characterized by a series of profound and radical breaks—particularly noticeable in aspects of culture—each of which defined and determined a new period. The perception of the deep and irrevocable character of these breaks was much more intense in the case of Russian historians, before the revolution and after, than in any other historiography. Be that as it may, Russian history was traditionally seen as a succession of very distinct periods whose relationship to one another gave rise to a great deal of acrimonious debate. The Kievan period was sharply contrasted to the era of the appanages and of the Mongols, both assessed very negatively; fifteenth- to seventeenth-century Muscovy, with its several great crises, was marked off by the Petrine "revolution" from the St. Petersburg period which, in turn, ended in the brutal revolution and civil war that the emigration had experienced. It may be a generalization, but not an overly rash one, I think, to say that every Russian historian not only preferred one or the other of these major periods in his country's history, but tended to dismiss or ignore those he did not like. The most striking instances of this selectivity were the appanage and Mongol periods—they were downplayed, deplored, or even ignored. The prerevolutionary historiography, under Romantic and Hegelian inspiration, had concentrated on the process of state building, of the formation of the centralized state of Moscow and St. Petersburg. It had paid little attention to Kiev, and generally ignored the scattering of political sovereignty and the cultural poverty of the appanage and Mongol centuries. In contrast, it had extolled the grand princes of Moscow for their "gathering of Russian lands," for patronizing church culture. It also had praised the Petersburg era that had issued from the Europeanizing efforts of Peter the Great. The Slavophiles, like the Eurasians in emigration, had little use for the Petersburg era and the turn to Europe that it had signified, but they had few representatives in the historical guild; and anyway, they could not help but praise the imperial and cultural accomplishments of Peter and his successors.

The majority of the recognized émigré historians also had distinct preferences when it came to the Russian past. With the exception of mainly ecclesiastical writers, Kiev was treated cursorily; even Vernadsky before 1945 wrote about it only as an instance of Eurasia's steppe connection. Miliukov, in the posthumously published volume of his *Ocherki* dealt at length with the pre-history and the migrations of the Slavs, but evinced little interest in the Kievan "state." The appanage and Mongol periods remained neglected or ignored, as had been the case of most prerevolutionary treatises. On the other hand, the émigré scholars displayed a distinct lack of sympathy for the Muscovy of 1400–1600, although they acknowledged its positive contribution in "gathering the Russian lands."[23] Even when the amateur historian I. Bunakov (Fondaminskii) branded Muscovy an "Asiatic," centralized state, a negative label for most intellectuals, the rebuttal merely consisted in pointing out that not everything in Muscovy was the result of the tsar's (and his court's) auto-cratic direction but that, as a matter of fact, it was the autonomous organiza-tions of Russian society on the local level that had been responsible for what-ever positive accomplishments occurred in that period.[24]

The tsardom of Muscovy was excoriated by émigré historians (and their liberal predecessors before the revolution) because it was identified with the church's domination over all culture and the origin of entrenched autocracy. The allegedly absolute power of the tsar, as displayed in the brutal conquest of the free cities of Novgorod and Pskov, and in the capricious and barbaric tyranny of Ivan IV's *oprichnina*—so reminiscent of the Bolsheviks—stood irre-mediably condemned in their eyes. To make matters worse, the autocracy proved so powerful that its stamp was indelible on all following centuries, down to 1917. As Miliukov had proven in his first scholarly monograph (and as Kliuchevskii had also stressed), Peter the Great's manner of rule was in-conceivable without the background of Muscovy. Autocracy was the handy tool Peter seized to carry out his policies, and this is what gave a warped twist to his reforms and transformations, and split Russia into two nations.

There was a distinct ambivalence about the St. Petersburg period. Its major accomplishments had been to serve as the matrix and taproots of mod-ern Russian culture, especially its glorious literature. It also deserved praise for having set Russia on the path of modernization and intensive European-ization—a path that was so abruptly disrupted by war and revolution. On the other side of the ledger, however, was the fact that Imperial Russia's autocracy had been the major stumbling block in the liberalization and modernization of public life. It withheld freedom of expression from the intelligentsia. The revolution had thus been largely prepared by the Romanovs on the Neva—by their stubborn clinging to bureaucratic autocracy and their perverted and limited cultural outlook.

What conclusions can we draw regarding the focus of interest and themes of émigré historians, as compared to those of their prerevolutionary predeces-sors? In reaction to the dominant influence of the so-called statist school in Russian historiography, beginning in the 1890s, there had been a marked shift to the study of the social and economic aspects of Russia's past—Kliuchev-skii's university course was a dramatic and popular instance of the new trend.

This shift of focus encouraged scholars to find new fields of investigation (on the basis of new materials, of course), e.g., the fate of the peasantry, not only in its relationship to the state, but primarily with respect to the serf system as an all-encompassing socioeconomic phenomenon, and to its subsequent impact on the agrarian problems. The role of the bureaucratic apparatus was displaced from the center of attention it had occupied to the benefit of the "root processes" on the local level. This line of thought continued to be pursued to the extent possible in emigration. Those who had managed to bring along their research notes were able to write monographs of which the magisterial study of V. Miakotin on the transformation of the Ukrainian peasantry in the late seventeenth and early eighteenth centuries is the best illustration. Another instance was the set of articles by A. Florovskij that complemented his major monograph on the elections to the Great Commission of 1767, which he had published in Russia before the revolution.[25] In exile, the peasantry continued to hold the attention of historians, although it became more difficult to study the subject abroad. If archives were out of reach, a fresh reading of the published documentation might yield new insights. Such was the approach taken by the "younger" historian S. Pushkarev, who completed his degree work and became active in Prague, and published a suggestive thesis on the repartitional commune. In the same vein, the jurist V. El'iashevich took advantage of his enforced leisure under the German occupation of France to complete a two-volume juridical investigation of the principles and practices of land tenure rights from the sixteenth to the eighteenth centuries. A few articles dealing with the peasantry and serfdom were published in the festschrift in honor of P. B. Struve, and Struve himself worked in his last years on an economic history of Russia, concentrating on agrarian issues.[26]

The experience of the civil war had brought many émigrés into closer contact with the Russian provinces. Some scholars had been active in various provincial universities (Saratov, Tomsk, Irkuts, Odessa, Rostov), or local public organizations. They had had occasion to witness not only anarchy and disintegration, but also impressive displays of local initiatives and resourceful energy, once St. Petersburg's (or Moscow's) grip had loosened or disappeared altogether. It reinforced a historiographic trend that had been noticeable since before 1914, the discovery and recovery of the elements of local and regional autonomy and initiative that the previous historiographic perspective had neglected. Thus a greater interest in and familiarity with the border areas of the old Empire resulted in several monographic studies by historians in emigration. Fulfilling an assignment of the Cossack émigré establishment, S. Svatikov wrote a comprehensive general history of the Don Cossack Host, stressing the autonomous and independent development of the territory it occupied, all the while strongly emphasizing the Russian character and orientation of Cossack society. On the basis of his research in the 1920s and 1930s, B. Nolde, during World War II, undertook the writing of a comprehensive history of the acquisition and incorporation of the border territories into the Muscovite and St. Petersburg Empire. His work remained incomplete, and only a fragment of it was published posthumously in French after the war. But it is a seminal and magisterial monument of émigré historiography, which bears witness to the transformation of the emigration wrought by the 1940s, and to the de facto integration of émigré scholarship into their lands of asylum. We should also mention the studies of V. Riasanovsky on Mongol law, to some extent a product of his Siberian experience during the civil war, and association with the Chinese and Manchurian milieu of Kharbin.[27]

On the preceding pages, I alluded to the "younger historians" or the "younger generation." It is time we turn to them. First, we should clarify that "younger generation" had two separate connotations in our context, chronological and professional. In the chronological sense, "younger" or "next generation" referred to the children of the émigrés who had grown up abroad (though some were born in Russia). But as suggested earlier, before 1939 there were practically no successors to émigré scholars in the humanities and history in particular. The generation of children of émigrés, especially those who came to adulthood only in the late thirties or the war years, had given up any intention of going back to Russia. (A few did go back after 1945. Some fought on the side of the Western Allies in France and were fully integrated into French society after the conflict.) They had grown up, and had been educated, in the expectation of integrating into the country of their asylum. The fact that some of them had to emigrate again because of the advances of the Red Army did not affect their prewar situation. True, in Yugoslavia and Czechoslovakia many lived still steeped in a Russian linguistic and cultural milieu, but they were on the road to integration, which would have been completed had the military operations at the end of the war resulted in another map of Europe. What I am suggesting here, in short, is that this generation of children, although they spoke Russian and were acquainted with the culture of their parent's motherland, no longer belonged to "Russia Abroad."

In another sense, "younger generation" denotes those who had begun their graduate studies in Russia, but completed them only in exile. It was for them that the educational institutions and Russian universities had been set up in the centers of the diaspora. Among them we find several historians; *sensu stricto,* these attained a scholarly or academic position only during World War II and in its aftermath. Their scholarly output thus occurred after the terminal date of our study, but their professional formation did take place within it. They may be briefly considered here. As already noted, S. Pushkarev completed his training in Prague, and made his major scholarly contribution with studies on the peasant repartitional commune; he also took up teaching and related activities in Prague. After the war, in the United States, he published several general surveys, as well as a few notable articles in which, following in the footsteps of his teacher A. Kizevetter, he stressed the role of local administration and institutions. M. Karpovich, who did some advanced postgraduate work in Prague, propounded in his teaching at Harvard the historiographical orientation of the liberal émigrés Miliukov, Kizevetter, and Maklakov. The two "younger" medievalists, M. Szeftel (a student of A. Eck in Brussels) and N. Andreyev (a graduate of the Seminarium Kondakovianum) also stressed in their work the importance of local and social initiatives and their juridical framework, both in the Middle Ages and in the so-called Duma period. It was to this younger professional generation that fell the task of training historians of Russia in the West after 1945. Belonging to this group by their origin, but trained and active in the United States, were A. Mazour, G. Lantzeff, and M. Florinsky (partly trained in England). They did not belong to "Russia Abroad," for they managed to be professionally active within the American academic community right away. V. Leontovitch, also active after 1945, was a product of German universities.

At this point a few brief remarks on the relationship between émigré historians and the study of Russian history in the West after World War II are in order. It should be clear from what has been said so far that the emigration had but tenuous contacts and associations with the societies and academic establishments of the European countries of asylum (the same was even more true of Kharbin in relation to its Manchurian and Chinese environment). Emigrés were of interest to their hosts only when, and to the extent that, there was concern about Soviet power in international affairs. (The interest that Communists and fellow travelers had for the Soviet "experiment" never involved the émigré community; on the contrary, it only contributed to the latter's sense of isolation from the host environment.)

In the early 1920s, when there was still some hope for the émigrés' return to another Russia, or the possibility of beneficial relations with a nondogmatic Communist regime, the émigrés were seen as a potential source of expert information on their country. Thus one of the several motives that brought about the Action russe was the belief that, by granting asylum and academic facilities to émigré students, the Czechoslovak government was helping to prepare the future cadres of Russia. As this expectation faded, support of the émigré institutions faded as well. In Germany, too, with the onset of active economic and military contacts with the Soviet Union after the Treaty of Rapallo (and later when Hitler started preparing for conflict with Bolshevik Russia), there was an inclination to use émigré expertise, though naturally, historians ranked low in priority in this respect. (One should mention that the Germans had another pool of Russian expertise at their disposal: the Baltic Germans who had fled the USSR and the new Baltic states, and the so-called German Russians whose families had settled in Russia in the eighteenth or nineteenth centuries but maintained a German cultural and political loyalty.) The fact that there was much less interest or need for émigré expertise in France and elsewhere helps to account for the isolation experienced by scholars of the emigration there. (This did not exclude occasional personal ties; for example, through the agency of a Russian-born wife as illustrated by Ferdinand Lot's receiving M. Lot-Borodine's émigré acquaintances, but not after a period of reserved distance.)

This isolation was true in the United States before 1941, as the inferior academic status "enjoyed" by Vernadsky at Yale and Karpovich at Harvard shows. The situation changed radically during World War II, when knowledge about the Soviet Union was sought by the Allied governments, and after 1945 when a clear public interest in that country became manifest. Of course, the ease with which foreigners were integrated into the academic establishments in the United States was in stark contrast to the aloofness, even hostility, of European countries before 1939. In a sense, the precedent of the integration of German scholars who had fled Hitler helped pave the way for those Russian émigrés who came to the United States just before or during the war in greater numbers. The latter did establish associations with American government and university institutions, and helped to train the next generation of historians of Russia in the West.

So far I have pointed out some of the factors that prevented the émigré historians from striking out in significantly new directions, either thematically or methodologically. But this is not the whole picture, although it dominated the landscape. In one area in particular the emigration did innovate in several respects—and it is to this aspect that we turn now.

As noted, the years before the outbreak of the First World War had seen an extraordinary intellectual ferment and spurt of creative energy in Russia. The inadequacies of nineteenth-century traditional positivism were felt more and more acutely; Kliuchevskii himself, while holding on to its methodological assumptions, was in fact breaking out of their straitjacket in his lecture course by the way in which he let his literary gifts shape the material. Kliuchevskii's course became the historian's counterpart to Impressionist painting and symbolist poetry. Also, Kliuchevskii publicly called attention to the role that psychological factors, and political and cultural symbols, played in shaping the nation's history.

Not surprisingly, therefore, the work of the younger historians, whatever their political or philosophical preferences, was revisionist, critical of many traditional interpretations and methods. This was particularly noticeable in the domain of medieval history, but other periods did not remain untouched. For example, A. Presniakov and S. Veselovskii were revolutionizing the traditional perspective on the formation of the Muscovite centralized state, while Marxist historians were questioning the current interpretations of the social and economic aspects of modern Russia. Moreover, archaeology on the one hand, and fascination with the non-Russian world on the other, were gradually having their impact on historical scholarship. The philosopher-poet V. Soloviev and the poet A. Blok (later imitated by A. Belyi in his novels) had taken up and popularized the notion of a "yellow peril," and of an apocalyptic end of the modern world coming from Asia. This had sparked renewed interest in Russia's Central Asiatic and Caucasian territories, and in the period of Mongol domination. These were the harbingers of themes that would be developed further in the historiosophy of the Eurasians. But we should emphasize that, on the eve of the revolution, the "revisionism" in historical scholarship had neither reached the broader public nor had it affected the outlook of the mature professional historians. This explains why the scholars in exile did not pursue the innovative lines taken by Presniakov and Veselovskii, or N. P. Pavlov-Sil'vanskii for that matter. Of course, lack of access to the necessary archival documentation also stymied efforts in that direction.

Yet another aspect of the Silver Age's culture scene needs to be mentioned, although its main influence on the émigrés has been touched upon in chapter 6. The Silver Age was also a period of great spiritual-religious renaissance among the educated classes of Russian society. The laity was becoming increasingly concerned about the moral and metaphysical dimensions of religious life, while the clergy (at least some influential members) had recognized the official church's need to be more involved in the socioeconomic circumstances of the people's life and to establish closer ties with the intelligentsia. The discussions in the religious-philosophical societies of St. Petersburg, Moscow, and elsewhere, and the social activism of individual clergymen, such as Ioann of Kronstad (not to speak of G. Gapon) will have to stand for the many instances that cannot be listed here. The religious interest and spiritual revival also affected scholarship—and not only in theology—by creating a broader audience interested in books and studies dealing with the church and its past and present sociocultural role. This development was brusquely halted in Russia when the Bolsheviks seized power and pursued an aggressive anti-religious policy. It was little wonder that all those who had religious commitments endeavored to emigrate after the defeat of the White Armies. Furthermore, as mentioned earlier, in 1922 the Soviet government expelled a number of personalities that had been actively involved in the philosophical-religious renaissance of the prewar years, chief among them Berdiaev, Frank, Novgorodtsev, Karsavin, and others.[28]

The renewed and heightened concern for religion brought about new interest in church history and reassessment of the religious dimensions in Russian intellectual and cultural life. The historians, and their work, effected this reorientation of historical scholarship in emigration, for Soviet Russia could no longer provide either facilities or support for such a concern. It is true that neither of the two magisterial books in the field had a direct impact on Russia Abroad before its end in 1939. One was published on the eve of the war and most of the copies perished in a bombing. The other, though matured throughout the thirties, was published after 1945, and in a foreign language. Strictly speaking, therefore, neither book is part of the cultural history of the emigration, yet neither can be omitted from this history, for both are the product of the intellectual experience of emigration. It also should be noted that both authors, G. Florovsky and G. Fedotov, came to Russian history from the outside, so to speak. They also belonged to the "younger generation" who completed their professional formation after the revolution.

George Florovsky, the younger of the two (born 1893), left Russia after the first years of university training. On the solid base he had acquired in Russia he built on his own. Early in his intellectual development he decided to devote himself to the study of the patristic heritage of the Russian church.

His interest in patristics led to an invitation to join the faculy of the St. Serge Theological Institute in Paris in 1926. He remained on the faculty of the Institute until the outbreak of the war, when he found himself stranded in Switzerland, and later in Belgrade. After much difficulty, traveling by way of Prague, Florovsky managed to return to St. Serge Institute after the war's end. In 1948 he was appointed dean of the St. Vladimir Theological Seminary in New York, and in 1955, largely as a result of policy disagreements with both his superiors and his colleagues, Florovsky accepted appointment to the faculty of the Divinity School at Harvard; upon his retirement he moved to Princeton University, where he taught Russian intellectual history until his death in 1980. In the United States he was also very active in the ecumenical movement, as well as a prolific writer in English on theological issues.

After a brief flirtation with Eurasianism, Florovsky concentrated on both patristics and the intellectual history of Russia. It is the latter that will concern us here.[29] To understand Florovsky's contribution in this field it is necessary to recall the ways in which Russian thought had been studied before 1917 by liberal historians. Traditionally, Russian intellectual history meant the history of *obshchestvennoi mysli*, that is, of all those social and political ideas that were critical of the existing Muscovite and imperial order and establishments. Disregarding the rare antecedants in Muscovite times, it meant the study of those ideas, based on Western intellectual and ideological trends, which, on the basis of a critique of the ways and conditions of tsarist society and government, advocated reforms and transformation. In the final analysis, such a history merged with the history of revolutionary movements and ideas, and of their effect on Russian public life up to the revolution. In the period immediately preceding 1914 this kind of history was based on materialist, positivist philosophical assumptions. It was teleological in its main thrust, for it aimed to show that ideas and movements had served to develop those revolutionary or radical ideologies that would prepare the ground for the upheaval, which in turn would renovate Russian social, economic, and political life. A trenchent critique of this radical-progressive tradition had been made by the contributors to the collection *Signposts* (*Vekhi*) in 1909, and had generated lively and acrimonious debate. The debate was naturally resumed under the impact of the revolutionary events of 1917–1918, but the collection *De profundis*, which contained the main statements, remained unknown to the public at large.[30] The main criticism was directed at the traditional historiography's materialistic and teleological (deterministic) bias, but also at its ignoring the metaphysical and spiritual seekings of Russian intellectuals throughout the eighteenth and nineteenth centuries.

This was the challenge that Florovsky took up. His predecessor, M. Gershenzon, a contributor to *Vekhi*, had written sympathetically on the Slavophiles and the generation of 1810–1820, paying particularly attention to their spiritual yearnings. But Gershenzon had steered clear of specifically religious issues, and he had not been interested in uncovering the patristic and Russian spiritualist sources of inspiration for his heroes. Nor had he been fully aware of the potential implications of their philosophical assumptions. In addition to Gershenzon, Florovsky drew inspiration from the writings of Soloviev, C. Renouvier, H. Bergson, and the American pragmatists C. S. Peirce and William James. Combined with his own historical experience of revolution and civil war, this extensive and solid philosophical background enabled Florovsky to reinterpret the traditional (and Gershenzon's) view of Russian intellectual history. In several essays dealing with F. Tiutchev, V. Soloviev, N. Fedorov, and L. Tolstoi, Florovsky laid bare the metaphysical assumptions contained in their ideas. He concluded that their major "mistake" consisted in accepting an evolutionary framework and, more important still, in following the lure of utopia as the end product of the historical process.

Florovsky illustrated the consequences of these two guiding presuppositions in an essay on the "metaphysical presuppositions of utopianism." In an article on A. Herzen he showed how the lures of *Naturphilosophie,* utopianism, and spiritual-religious seekings outside the Christian framework affected Herzen and made for his basically negative and historically tragic Weltanschauung. Florovsky presented his study on the nature of Herzen's religious seekings as a dissertation to the Russian University in Prague. It was accepted, but it did stir a lively, and not always friendly, discussion at the public defense in which such luminaries as Miliukov took part. Florovsky's thesis did not have the impact it deserved, for it was not published—except for a brief summary article—by the émigré periodical press dominated by traditionalist positivist and "liberationist" views.

Florovsky's major innovative contribution to historiography came in the *Puti russkogo bogosloviia* (The ways of Russian theology). It appeared in 1938, but was printed and distributed in Belgrade. It received practically no notice—except for a polemically critical review by Berdiaev in the religious journal *Put'*, which Berdiaev edited in Paris. The *Puti* had to await the revitalization of interest in Russian history in the United States after World War II to become the classic in the field. It was only in 1982 that a second edition in Russian appeared (the destruction of the publisher's stock in the bombing of Belgrade had made it a bibliographic rarity); an English translation, after many false starts, is only now in the process of publication.

The *Puti* marks a radical departure from the traditional way of writing Russian intellectual history. In the first place, Florovsky firmly believed that ideas are the product of an individual, of a creative and living personality. To understand this personality's ideas, one has to know as fully as possible everything that has contributed to the formulation of specific concepts and presuppositions. The living, seeking personality is embedded in his or her world, for one "does not build, does not give birth to, and does not posit one's world—one finds it." Each person is thus engaged in a creative process of discovering the world, as well as reacting to it. Such a process is an act of "ascetic creation" (*podvizhennicheskoe delanie*), and only in understanding this process in the unique context of the thinker's time and place can one truly comprehend the ideas that result from this act of "ascetic creation"; it is then that one can also assess the ideas' dynamic impact and consequences. To this kind of investigation Florovsky brought a thorough knowledge of and a profound empathy for the metaphysical and theological presuppositions that undergirded all of Russian (nay, Christian European) intellectual creativity and speculation. By bringing together individual historical factors and the underlying religious (in the broadest sense) presuppositions, Florovsky shed new light on the intellectual history of Russia in its series of "enticements" and "rifts." He explained—in a way that had not been done previously—the immanent elements of the vicissitudes of Russia's recent cultural history; he also suggested the alternatives that existed in the past, which had not been taken but which may contain lessons for the future, if past intellectual errors ("enticements") and failings ("rifts") are properly understood.

The seminal nature of Florovsky's book renewed interest in many areas of Russian history and deeply influenced the approach to them (church, clergy, theology, Slavophilism, 18th-century Europeanization, Silver Age). Its significance requires that we attempt to characterize its main features. The book's chronological limits are specific and circumscribed: the Kiev and appanage periods are omitted. The *Puti* starts with the neo-Byzantine influences at the end of the fifteenth century, during the spiritual crisis that coincided with the triumph of Moscow over all its competitors. The book ends abruptly in 1917, even though some of the trends and figures had significant impact in emigration. Thematically, too, the book is selective: it deals less with the history of theological ideas per se, which, admittedly, played practically no role in Russia, and concentrates on the history of modern Russian thought. Even here Florovsky picks and chooses, for he eschews discussing all strictly social, economic, and political ideas, unless they directly reflect some basic philosophic conception and religious or spiritual inclination.

Finally, the book discusses the particular features of the systems of clerical and lay education that produced the leading intellectual personalities and also explains the specific philosophic predilections and basic mental sets that were imparted to these thinkers. Florovsky argued that every thinker and every generation had a set of basic psychic traits and shared philosophic assumptions that gave coherence and significance to their Weltanschauung. This enabled him to point out the inner fault lines, that is, those elements that introduce disharmony and account for the ultimate failure (rifts) of the adopted world view. Florovsky drew the intellectual group portrait of each significant generation—for example, the educated Russian eiltes of the eighteenth century in their efforts at creating a new cultural synthesis with Western secular and religious ideas, the spiritual seekings of the reign of Alexander I, the nihilistic positivism of the 1860s with its lure of materialist utopia, and the apocalyptic mood of the first years of the twentieth century.

It is important to stress that Florovsky was interested only in the "high culture" of Russian religious life and thought. Only very occasionally did he refer to the people's religious attitudes or beliefs. As we shall see, this gap was to be filled, in part at least, by the other innovative émigré historian, Fedotov. Emphasizing the history of Russian philosophy and religious ideas, Florovsky had to grant several Western influences: Graeco-Byzantinism; Latinism of the sixteenth century, which reached a high point—in neo-scolastic protestant form—in the seventeenth century and thereby affected the entire eighteenth century; and Protestant inner religiosity and Leibnizian metaphysics in the early eighteenth century, which prepared the way for the reception of idealism and Romanticism with their lure of *Naturphilosophie* and utopianism. The latter received a materialist interpretation under the impact of Western positivism and scientism on the generation of the 1860s; and finally neo-Kantian philosophy and symbolist aesthetics went a long way in accounting for the ideas of the Silver Age, although they marked a return to native traditions in culture and spirituality. Florovsky's understanding of "influences" was a radical turning away from the notion of a mechanical transfer of ideas, which had been the explanatory scheme in Russian positivist intellectual history; it directly affected subsequent work on the history of ideas in Russia by Western scholars. Similarity, wrote Florovsky,

> should not be taken for influence, of course. Generally speaking, the question of the genesis of a system or a world view cannot be substituted by the question of influences. Not every influence means dependence, and dependence does not mean direct borrowing—an influence can be a push and a stimulus (*pobuzhdenie*), an influence may also stem from the contrary. . . . One should not cover up the initiative of the thinker by reference to influence. The question of influence can be raised correctly and solved reliably only . . . when the genetic process can be reconstructed in its entirety and followed through the sequence of all its stages. At the same time, of course, it is most important to identify (*razpoznat'*) and seize upon the basic intuition, to find the starting point of the development—otherwise it will be difficult to speak of influences.[31]

Florovsky was not interested in merely listing the foreign elements, but in accounting for the way the Russians chose, and then transformed in the new environment, specific elements from the body of ideas available to them. This kind of approach to intellectual history was universally adopted after the war; it also bears a strong resemblance to the contextualist method now dominant in the field of the history of political ideas. Florovsky was particularly effective and suggestive in using this approach to account for the "enticements" of Romanticism and *Naturphilosophie* which he traced to an unrequited thirst for spiritual fulfillment; an enticement in that the immanent logic of Romanticism led to the "rifts" embedded in utopianism, in either its idealist or materialist assumptions.

To explain as fully as possible the circumstances that led Russian intellectuals to select and reinterpret their ideas—both foreign and native—Florovsky presented a masterful analysis of the clergy as a social group. For, indeed, it was the clergy that was the main provider, first of ideas and then of the proponents, of Russian philosophical, religious, and scientific thought. Its particular upbringing and education, its special social status and economic circumstances—all results of Peter's reforms—explain its special role in Russian life and thought from the 1700s to the 1900s. In tracing the social and educational history of the clergy Florovsky did not make any new discoveries, but he did make available the fruits of earlier scholarship to a wider audience heretofore ignorant of the clergy's role in shaping modern Russian culture. His was not a social history in the contemporary, quantitatively oriented, sense—this would be the accomplishment of Gregory L. Freeze, who was much inspired by Florovsky.

The preceding pages should make clear that Florovsky's *Puti* marked a new departure in the history of Russia's culture and intellectual evolution. One may say that, consciously or not, approvingly or critically, all subsequent work in Russian intellectual history had to take the *Puti* as a point of departure; it explains the importance and originality of Western contributions to the field, in contrast to the hidebound methodological conservatism of Soviet writings to this day. Florovsky's impact was in no small measure due to the fact, that after 1945, he was able to have a wider influence. Yet it should be stressed that much of his influence was also rooted in the transformation of the Russian cultural and intellectual scene wrought by the Silver Age, and on which he built while living in the Russia Abroad of the twenties and thirties. His émigré status enabled him to develop his talents to the fullest and to absorb Western methodological trends, all the while pursuing another intellectual concern, patristics and philosophy, both of which contributed to the originality of *Puti*.[32]

George Fedotov's contribution was also in the realm of religious life, but not so much in intellectual as existential cultural aspects. Born in 1886, his studies were first interrupted by prison and exile for belonging to a socialist student group. Upon his return from abroad, Fedotov received serious historical training in the seminars of N. Kareev at St. Petersburg University. His specialty was the French Middle Ages, specifically the hagiographic sources of the Merovingian and Carolingian periods. These sources attracted him because, through them, he hoped to penetrate to the realities of religious norms and experiences for a better understanding of the life and spirit of these ages. Actively involved in political activism and ecclesiastic concerns in the early years of the Bolshevik regime, he was forced to emigrate in 1925. He settled in Paris, where he remained until the German occupation, and was active as journalist and as teacher at the St. Serge Theological Institute (he taught hagiographic literature). He was also deeply involved in church and social organizations aimed at easing the lot of the poor. He was attracted to the principles and program of Christian socialism. Fedotov's idiosyncratic and often unpopular opinions on ecumenism and current events (for example, his preference for Dolores Ibarruri over Franco, mentioned earlier) got him into difficulties with ecclesiastic authorities and the émigré community.

In 1941 he escaped to the United States and was appointed to the St. Vladimir Theological Seminary where he taught, without giving up active journalism and scholarship, until his death in 1951.

Here I shall deal only with Fedotov's contributions to Russian historiography. In the twenties and thirties, following upon several articles on French medieval history that appeared in Russia and abroad, Fedotov published a number of studies on Russian religious history that marked a new approach to the field.[33] They served as preparation for a broadly conceived study of Russian religiosity, for which he had gathered material in France and England before 1939. The first volume of his *Russian Religious Mind* (preceded by a valuable anthology of Russian spirituality) appeared in 1946, but the second volume was unfinished at the time of his death. It was published many years later, in 1966, as a set of fragments and notes, edited by J. Meyendorff. *The Russian Religious Mind* is Fedotov's most original contribution to Russian historiography, but I believe that a few words need to be said about his earlier works, for they are the key to the innovations found in his last great book.

Inspired by new trends in French and German historiography of the Middle Ages, which used sources other than chronicles and charters, and in response to his own deep commitment, Fedotov turned to studying religious life, its concepts and its practices, in the early centuries of Christianity in Roman Gaul and the Frankish kingdoms that succeeded it. What fascinated him most was the interplay between pre-Christian notions and values (whether religious pagan or institutional "barbarian") on the one hand, and the church as an institution and the secular authorities of Merovingian and Carolingian kings, on the other. His pursuit entailed reading well-known texts and documents, the lives of saints, with a fresh eye, paying attention to what was left unsaid, and trying to understand the actual words in their true, historical "context." While still in Russia, and in the first years of his exile in Paris, Fedotov published several articles dealing with this set of questions, using the careers of St. Martin of Tours and the first Merovingian kings and bishops as his illustrative material.

His findings shed a novel light on the relationship between church and kingship. He pointed out that it was not simply a case of the Merovingian rulers subjecting the church to their whims. It was rather that the ideals and practices of the church and of its main representatives—which also appealed to the faithful—created a distance between king and clergy, and served to isolate the clergy from the rulers' misdeeds, in order to proclaim and preserve true Christian values. For example, Fedotov noted that many of the miracles reported in Merovingian (and early Carolingian) hagiography dealt with the "liberation" of prisoners, slaves, and so on. At the demand, or upon the direct intervention of a saintly person, prison doors or walls would be shattered or prisoners' chains would fall off. And if the ruler did not take the hint immediately, the saint forced him to do so by producing other miraculous occurrences. The conclusion, argued Fedotov, was obvious and especially relevant in a period of revolution, civil war, and the early years of the Soviet regime. The true Christian ideal of personal freedom does not recognize the claims and power of the secular establishment.

In the first decade of his émigré life in Paris, Fedotov applied the same method and insights to his studies of Russian sainthood. Again his source was the lives of saints. No doubt inspired by the work of abbé Brémond (not cited at the time, but referred to in *The Russian Religious Mind*) he analyzed the hagiographic literature to grasp the nature of Russian religious values and, by extension, the ideals of Russian social life that they expressed. In his book *Sviatye drevnei Rusi* (Saints of old Russia) Fedotov followed this literature from the eleventh into the eighteenth centuries. He established a typology of Russian saintliness—beginning with Saints Boris and Gleb. He was struck by the fact that the earliest, and some of the most respected, saints did not display strictly religious qualities: they were neither witnesses to the faith, nor miracle workers, nor martyrs for the sake of Christianity. Instead, they were meek victims of the brutal acts of the secular, political, authorities. They did not resist these cruel deeds and perished; it is on account of their passive obedience in the face of evil that they are canonized and worshiped, and perform miracles after death. Some other saints—the lay princes—are extolled for having gone to battle against nonbelievers for the sake of the Russian (Rus') land. Finally, most of the other subjects of hagiographic works were elevated to sainthood or blessedness mainly because they lived a righteous life, and helped their poor and weak fellows. With rare exceptions, Russian hagiography does not extol purely Christian martyrs, teachers, or example-setting ascetics. (That we are dealing here with Byzantine topoi does not invalidate Fedotov's interpretation.)

This ideal of the true religious *life*, and the physical submission to evil but its moral nonrecognition, were displayed by Metropolitan Philip of Moscow when he publicly condemned Ivan IV's persecutions, but did nothing to resist them or to call for the tsar's overthrow. For this, Ivan IV deprived him of his see and starved him to death—this martyrdom earned the metropolitan canonization soon thereafter. Fedotov published a biographical sketch of St. Philip of Moscow in 1928; it is a fine example of his understanding of Russian saintly values, but it is obviously also a commentary on the contemporary scene that forced so many to suffer passively and in silence for their refusal to countenance the tyranny of dictators.

In his *Russian Religious Mind*—especially the first volume, since the second is but a fragment—Fedotov carried this approach and interpretation a step further. In the completed volume, the story is carried only to the sixteenth century—the anthology mentioned earlier may be seen as a complementary source book that brings illustrations from the imperial period as well. *The Russian Religious Mind* is a valuable, though unintended, complement and foil to Florovsky's *Puti*. In good populist tradition based on his involvement in the revolutionary movement before 1917, Fedotov focused on the "people," and their religious mores and values before and after conversion to Chris-

tianity. Approaching the chronicles and hagiographic sources in the imaginative way he had used for his work on Merovingian France and for establishing the typology of Russian saints, Fedotov enlarged his conceptual framework by turning to anthropological and ethnographic findings, both Russian
and Western European. Accordingly, he spoke of the history of the "religious
mind" of the Russian people, in modern terms, their religious beliefs, attitudes, and practices, and the changes they underwent over periods of time.
In short, this is what Clifford Geertz defines as the "thick study" of religious
culture. Indeed, Fedotov was a precursor of the anthropology of religion in
a historical context. Although I have found no evidence for it either in his
published work or in his papers, he may have been familiar with the work
being done at the Musée de l'homme in Paris (where Claude Lévy-Strauss
was making his debut), since quite a few Russian émigrés of the younger
generation (e.g., Fel'sen, E. Schreider) were active there in the late 1930s.

The Russian Religious Mind is well known and readily available and need
not be summarized at length. It suffices to point out two of its assertions. First,
the survival of pagan practices and superstitions kept on coloring Russian
Orthodox life long after conversion to Christianity. The religion of the Russian peasant was heavily laden with pagan elements, especially those relating
to the mineral, animal, and vegetable worlds. This is not a startling discovery.
But Fedotov points out how, over the centuries, these pagan elements were
assimilated to Christian beliefs and practices, so that far from being in opposition to each other, there was convergence and eventual blending. Whether
the pagan or Orthodox Christian element predominated depended on the
period, the region, and especially on the facet of life and on the issues involved. (We are in presence here of a syncretism or synthesis, not a "double
faith" (*dvoeverie*). This has been confirmed by recent Soviet anthropological
studies of Old Believers.)

The second point made by Fedotov was a logical extension of his observations on the lives of Saints Boris and Gleb as the prototype of saintliness in
early Rus': Russian piety aims at imitating Christ's self-abasement to serve
fellow humans and guide them toward salvation. Self-abasement, a willingness to take on the humblest form and shoulder the meanest tasks to serve
another—not to mortify oneself—this is the essential, which Fedotov calls the
kenotic aspect of Russian religiosity. This "other-directedness" of the religious
aspiration, its social dimension, so to speak, is—according to Fedotov—Russian
Orthodoxy's greatest contribution to European ethical and spiritual progress.
Naturally, such an interpretation was closely related to Fedotov's own Christian socialist values, hopes, and expectations.

So far as I am aware, Fedotov does not seem to have had an impact on
the study of Russian religiosity and culture. But his is an approach that
should be particularly fruitful for the history of the Old Belief and of its
adherents, a must for all those interested in Russian (or European) religious
history. It fits in well with the methodology and findings of such recent works

as E. Leroy-Ladurie's *Montaillou* and Carlo Ginzburg's *The Cheese and the Worms.*

We are now in a better position to offer some general observations on the issues raised at the beginning of this chapter. What was the emigration's attitude to Russia's past and how did the scholarly émigré community respond to it? As a group, the emigration was ambivalent about its country's past. The burden of experiencing such dramatic historical events had totally "soured" history for the émigrés. They implicitly rejected, and showed little enthusiasm for, Russia's history, as it had been presented in prerevolutionary historiography. To the extent that the émigré scholars carried over the methods, assumptions, and major interpretations that had held sway in happier times, they elicited little interest and received scant support from the émigré communities.

The difficulties of carrying on original work and the limited possibilities for publication discouraged émigré historians from striking out along new paths. This helps explain the great success among the émigré public of the historical novel, a genre that combined nostalgic descriptions, absorbing plots, enviable characters, and skepticism about one's ability to foresee and understand, let alone control, events. It accounts for the popularity of Mark Aldanov—a past master of the genre. Aldanov's novels, despite their stylistic and technical brilliance, have not stood the test of time, although a revival of his popularity is occurring among the third wave emigration and more recently in Soviet Russia for probably the same reasons.

A major factor of the ineffectualness, as well as sterility, of émigré historians at the time was their inability to find a responsive echo in the host countries. In the 1920s and 1930s, whatever curiosity existed about Russia was about the "Soviet experiment." It did not extend to a desire to understand better the past experiences of the country where the experiment was taking place. Those who were enthusiastic about it shared the antihistorical mood of the early Bolshevik years. They were to be disappointed and shocked when Stalin reintroduced respect for the Russian past. Those foreigners who were anti-Bolshevik had little use for the country; they were resentful that Russia had withdrawn from the First World War, reneged on its foreign debt, and supported all kinds of modernistic and nihilist trends in politics, the arts, and literature. They could approve of those liberal émigré historians who wrote of Russia's backwardness in relation to Western Europe, and leave it at that.

To be sure, a few academic circles or institutions (mainly in Germany) were concerned with Russia. But they were unreceptive to new approaches and showed no interest in new interpretations. Theirs were all too frequently narrow utilitarian concerns—of a political, military, or economic kind—and they stood to benefit from factual information about contemporary Russia. They did not feel the need to understand the country's past.

For their part, the émigrés endeavored to concentrate on aspects of Russia's past that would be soothing to them in their difficult circumstances and might offer some prospect as building blocks for the future. This double purpose was served on the one hand by an almost reverential interest in modern Russian literature as symbolized by Pushkin, and, on the other hand, by a renewed commitment to their religious past. As we have seen, the latter resulted in the most notable and innovative contributions of émigré scholarship, for it was an area that could not be studied in the Soviet Union. The seminal works of Florovsky and Fedotov, illuminating Russia's religious traditions, proved to be of lasting value both for Western and Russian (including Soviet) interpretations.

What can we say about the Russian intelligentsia's attitude to the past of their country on the basis of their émigré experience? It seems to me that émigré historiography shows that basically the Russian intelligentsia saw history in mainly "instrumental" terms, as a tool for the ongoing critique and struggle against autocracy, which in the twenties and thirties was automatically redirected against the Bolshevik regime. There was little interest in the past for its own sake, as something meaningful on its own. True, the émigrés did experience nostalgia for the more recent past; witness the popularity of memoirs and historical fiction. But they turned to literature for inspiration and exemplary lessons. And as it had been true of the prerevolutionary intelligentsia, Russian literature of the 1800s, beginning with the Golden Age of Pushkin and concluding with the titantic opuses of Tolstoi and Dostoevsky, was their wellspring of moral and spiritual support and intellectual nourishment.

The Silver Age, it is true, added a significant element: a lively concern for spirituality, philosophy, and religion. However, it also consolidated the rift between those educated as professionals, who were moving away from political engagement, and who were receptive to new trends, and those who were politically committed, who maintained the traditions of the positivist, materialist, and ideologically instrumentalist notions of the nineteenth century. The rift was carried over into emigration—as illustrated by the discussions about the relative role of aesthetic and sociopolitical values, or by the emergence of new tastes and norms on the part of those who had matured in Russia Abroad.

Paradoxically, both traditionalism and innovation were to be of seminal influence in the revival of scholarly interest in things Russian in the West in the decades following the Second World War. This was largely the consequence of the integration into the American (and to a lesser degree English and French) academic world of émigrés who came to the United States in the early 1940s. Only then did Russian scholars find themselves in a position comparable to that of the German-Austrian Jewish émigrés of the 1930s. By the 1940s, the Russians had been absorbed into academe or the professions and could participate and contribute, à part entière, to the war effort and subsequent scholarly developments.

8

Conclusion: By the Waters of Babylon

In this book I have tried to account for the makeup and creative life of a society in exile. But was the case of Russia Abroad one single, specific instance of a number of similar cases, or was it a unique phenomenon? In a very real, but general sense, all of known history—including that of the Western world—has been the history of the interaction between different societies, and the interpenetration of several cultures; an interpenetration that involved the presence of a "foreign, visiting" element in a host milieu. The foreign element might be either a peaceful immigrant or a conqueror. Let us look, therefore, at some other instances of the presence of an alien "tribe" in a resident culture; it may help to pinpoint the singularity or the typicality of Russia Abroad.

One of our oldest written sources, the Bible, tells us about a whole people, an entire society, living, or forced to live, in an alien land. According to the biblical tradition, the Hebrews experienced forced exile in an alien land three times—in Egypt, in Babylon, and in the diaspora after the destruction of the Second Temple. All we know about these exiles is that they preserved their ways in foreign environments—particularly their religion—always hoping for a return, a return which was vouchsafed twice; and three times if we consider modern Israel such a return. During the period that is considered to have been the end stage of the classical world of antiquity, that is, the first centuries of our era, many alien groups lived scattered throughout the Roman Empire. Their presence gave rise to the extraordinarily bracing cultural and philosophical climate of the age: a syncretic, "universal" culture took shape, and, in turn, as we know, it was the source that nurtured medieval civilization, both East and West. In all these cases, however, our evidence permits us only the general assertion that the physical intermingling of alien and host groups resulted in a new cultural synthesis, without our being able to document the actual ways of the process. Most likely, similar developments took place in other parts of the world, as the history of the Far East shows. These precedents, remote in time and space, may not be of much relevance to our case, especially since our knowledge of them is so sketchy. We may be on firmer ground in the modern period, for which our sources are both fuller and more reliable.

The great religious crisis and split in Western Christendom, produced by the Protestant Reformation, brought about the forced departure, for religious motives, of a number of groups of people. In most cases their membership was small, and they did not bring to the new places of their settlement a culture powerful and distinctive enough to create something new. However, one "society in exile" not only maintained for a while a life and identity of its own, but also had a significant cultural impact on its new environment. This was the so-called Great Refuge, the escape, exile, and resettlement of the French Huguenots, following upon the revocation of th Edict of Nantes by Louis XIV in 1685.

The Grand Refuge was also a society in exile in the sense that its members represented most of the social groups and classes that constituted the Protestant minority in France. But unlike the Russian émigrés, the Huguenots never entertained hopes of returning to France. The dynamic and successful Huguenots in exile continued to hold to their occupations and traditions; this was particularly true of the intellectual elite. We need only recall their contribution to the economic development of many a German state, especially Brandenburg-Prussia. Equally seminal was the intellectual output of the *refugiés,* most notably in Holland, where they could easily publish their works. The Huguenot refugees rank among the most significant and active transmitters of the philosophical ideas rooted in the French rationalism and moralism of the seventeenth century. These ideas served as most active ferment for the future Enlightenment; this in addition to their role in disseminating methods of biblical criticism and the concept of toleration. But unlike their Russian successors, the French *refugiés* were eagerly admitted to, and accepted by, the countries of their asylum; it facilitated their rapid integration into the elites of the host countries. At first, special provisions were made to extend to them the benefit and protection of the legal tradition to which they had been accustomed in France. Soon these special provisions fell into desuetude, although not without leaving an impact on the legal and institutional practices of the host country. The process of their integration was completed within one generation or so, even though the descendants of the original refugees continued to speak French—which in any case was the language of the educated throughout the eighteenth and nineteenth centuries. They also continued to be interested in French literature and culture, which they helped to make better known among their new compatriots.

French citizens who left during the revolution of 1789 were quite another matter. They were a relatively small group, and socially they were almost totally made up of members of the Second Estate (the nobility). Many of them started returning during the Consulate, and many more reintegrated with their native society in the course of the Empire, leaving only a hard core of unyielding "reactionaries" to come back in the van of Louis XVIII after

Napoleon's defeat. These factors differentiate their situation from that of the Grand Refuge.

More than a century and a quarter after the Grand Refuge, Western Europe experienced the Great Polish Emigration. Following the repression of the uprising of 1830 by the armies of Nicholas I, several thousand Polish fighters for national freedom were compelled to flee and settle abroad. They found refuge mainly in France and England, and they set up political and cultural centers in Paris and London. Socially, the group was more homogeneous than either the Huguenots of the past, or the Russians of the future: most of the Polish exiles were members of the *szlachta* (nobility). Unlike the Huguenots, they did not have valuable economic skills, so that they had difficulty in finding occupations consonant with their education, upbringing, and past experience. But like the refugees from Louis XIV's *dragonnades*, they were a lively and creative cultural elite, and therein lay their importance for both their homeland and Europe. It is enough to mention the names of A. Mickiewicz, J. Słowacki, J. Lelewel, and A. Czartoryski to suggest the stature of the cultural creativity of the Great Polish Emigration. Living in exile, these men not only wrote the classics of Polish national literature, but they also helped create their nation's historiographical and political traditions. By casting the fate and role of Poland in the image of the sacrificial Christ, the leaders of the Great Emigration sustained their people's hope and faith in the resurrection of an independent Poland, and kept Polish independence on the agenda of European diplomacy and politics. Furthermore, they contributed to the cultural development of Europe as well. Thanks to them the historical fate of Poland entered into the consciousness of an influential segment of Europe's cultural leadership, while they also acquainted the West with the past, culture, and conditions of the Slavic world. The lectures Mickiewicz gave at the Collège de France on the literature and culture of the Slavs were the first successful instance in Western Europe of what, today, we call Slavic studies. Quite unintentionally, but not without historical irony, the Great Polish Emigration was to serve as a model to their erstwhile Russian oppressors when the latter came to share the experience of exile. Many a Russian émigré was well aware of this model and tried to live up to it, as did, for example, the poet V. Khodasevich.

In most other respects, however, the two "great" emigrations were quite dissimilar. The Poles were by far less numerous and, as we have noted, socially more homogeneous. As their exile lasted, many Poles were integrated into the cultural and social elites of the lands of asylum—for they often spoke the same language and shared the same values. This was particularly true in France, where they also partook of the same practices and traditions of Roman Catholicism. The nineteenth century, it is true, was more liberal and tolerant than the twentieth, even in Russia. Some of the Polish émigrés returned to their homeland, either temporarily or permanently, albeit under some police supervision and under a cloud of political suspicion. Communications between the Great Emigration and the homeland were never interrupted, and the exiles' writings circulated in all three parts of partitioned Poland. Other émigrés, politically more committed, did remain abroad, but as individual political exiles and not as members of a "society in exile." Their ranks were swollen by the refugees of 1863, so that at the time of the outbreak of the Great War in 1914, there was still an active Polish political emigration outside the borders of the three partitioning powers—they were to play a major role in the revival of an independent Poland in 1918.

The twentieth century, alas, has witnessed more waves of refugees and émigrés than any other in modern history; and these waves, breaking first in Europe and the Near East, eventually came to roll over all parts of the globe. Here I wish to repeat, and to stress, that I am not considering the flow of immigrant settlers, driven by dwindling economic opportunities or outright starvation at home, who wanted to start a new life in other lands under better material circumstances. This pattern, partly repeated now in Asia, has been well studied for most of the immigrant groups and most of the lands of their settlement—mark well, not of refuge—such as the United States, Canada, Australia, New Zealand, Latin America. In this book we have been concerned only with one instance of genuine emigration, refugees in the precise meaning of the word, who were compelled to flee because of government policies— racial, political, and religious. Many such dislocations during and in the aftermath of World War I, despite their horrors, proved to be relatively temporary. Once the fighting had stopped, and the borders were drawn, many of these refugees and evacuees either returned to their old homes, or were readily integrated into the societies of their ethnic-religious fellows. This was the case of Poles, Greeks, Turks, and Czechs, but not of the Armenians whose fate and status had to be taken up by the League of Nations, alongside with that of the Russians. But since the Armenians had had no independent country of their own in the immediate past, and to which they yearned to return, their situation resembled more that of the Jewish diaspora than that of the kind of emigration the Russians represented. (A number of Armenians emigrated after the occupation of the short-lived Armenian Republic (1918–1921) by the Red Army. Most of them were also Russian-speaking and had close ties with Russian culture and Russia Abroad.)

Unfortunately, the twentieth century saw many countries undergo revolutionary political changes that forced many citizens into exile. By and large they were political exiles in the tradition of nineteenth-century radicals and revolutionaries. They left to escape prison or worse, but they were relatively isolated individuals, whose aim in leaving was to continue their political activities from the haven of a foreign land. They did not constitute a mass phenomenon; although they might appear to be splinter "societies in exile" in the major Western capitals, such as Paris, London, and for a while Vienna and Berlin, they were rather a political faction or "sect" that deemed itself an alternative political center for the homeland. This was the case of some Balts and Poles, many more Romanians and Hungarians, as well as Italians and activists from the Balkans. As a result of World War II, most who had survived could return to their homeland and try to play an active role there again.

Although they shared some of the characteristics of the political exiles just mentioned, the Spaniards who fled across the French border in 1938 in the wake of Franco's victory over the Republic, came much closer to the Russian emigration of the early 1920s. In both cases the cause and circumstances of exile were similar—defeat in civil war. The Spanish refugees also represented a fair cross-section of Spanish society, and they left home in the hope of returning in the near future, after the "inevitable" end of the Franco dictatorship. Whether they would eventually have constituted a "Spain Abroad" is impossible to say. The outbreak of the Second World War precluded such a development, at any rate in France, where most of the refugees had first found asylum. After the war, Franco's regime, which never had been as harsh or closed off from the rest of the world as the USSR, relaxed somewhat; it became possible for most refugees to return to Spain, and many apparently did. As for the members of the political and cultural elites who had exiled themselves, they were welcomed in several South American countries, notably Mexico. Mexico opened its doors to the intellectual exiles and took effective steps to use the Spaniards' talents in promoting the cultural and creative life of Mexico. A university was created for the scholars and scientists in exile, and in due course it became a regular part of the University of Mexico. The Mexican government enabled the exiles to launch a high-level literary and scholarly journal and facilitated publication of their works. Naturally, the great difference between the Spaniards in Mexico (and elsewhere in Latin America) and the Russians in their centers of exile, was the fact that in Mexico the same language was spoken, and that Latin American high culture coincided with Spanish culture (except for Brazil, of course). From all accounts most émigrés from Spain were rapidly integrated into Mexican life, even though some eventually returned to Spain when Franco's dictatorship was liberalized.[1]

One last emigration of the 1930s has to be considered, for it is most frequently cited (especially in the United States) as sharing many traits with the Russian. This is the German-Austrian (primarily Jewish) emigration following Hitler's ascent to power in 1933 and the Anschluss of Austria in 1938. Included in this emigration were the socialist, liberal, most of them Jewish, refugees from Czechoslovakia (after 1938), Hungary, and Romania (in the second half of the 1930s, primarily) who were mostly German by culture.

First let us note its similarities with the Russian emigration, and then mention the differences, so as to make a valid comparison. Like the Russians, the German-Austrian Jews who were forced to go abroad represented practically all strata of their home society, although the professions were also overrepresented. The cultural elite (as well as the political activists, many of whom were not Jewish) left in the hope of returning soon, for they did not believe that Hitler would stay in power for long. They also tried to carry on their previous life style in the centers where they found refuge—Paris first, then in the United States, especially in New York and Los Angeles. The

German Jewish cultural elite, like the Russian, considered its task to be the preservation of the traditional culture of Germany that was now brutalized and perverted by the Nazis, and to continue their creative efforts for the sake of a future free Germany (or Austria). And as we know from the careers of the intellectuals who were forced into exile, they did indeed carry on their work—in literature, the arts, science, and scholarship. Like the Russians, they set up institutions—publishing houses, journals, universities, research institutes—to accomplish this purpose. This, however, is where the similarities end, except that in both cases the émigrés contributed to the intellectual life of the countries of their refuge. We will return to this last point shortly; but let us first note the differences.

From the very outset, the major difference was in the condition of emigration. With the exception of relatively few, mainly those who had been politically prominent and who had literally to run for their lives the moment Hitler came to power, the German Jewish refugees left in a relatively "regular," manner, that is, the left legally and peacefully, albeit reluctantly. The Nazi government encouraged departures, although at a price. (Following the Kristallnacht of 9 November 1938 was a short-lived attempt at mass expulsion of Jews from Poland back to that country.)

For these people, the process of emigration stretched over several years, families were not forcefully separated, and the émigrés were permitted to take along part of their belongings and assets. It enabled many of them to start a new life without having to depend totally on foreign charities. Quite a few managed to take out a fair amount of their property. For example, a stationery store was opened near the Lycée Michelet in Vanves (Seine) by a German refugee with money he had brought out via Switzerland, and a prominent art historian succeeded in shipping to the United States most of his collection and furniture. Of course, the main factor was that Europe was still at peace—the situation changed radically after 1939–1940. Until then, however, the exiles had the benefit of a network of Jewish philanthropies, mainly in the United States, which immediately organized assistance and helped them to travel across the ocean or to countries willing to receive them.

Since we are talking about a group that was overwhelmingly Jewish—even if not very committed to its religious or cultural traditions—we should note that the savage anti-Semitism of the Nazis had quite a different character than the political practices of the Bolsheviks. The Nazis declared that the Jews were, and always had been, an alien element amidst the Aryan Germans; and the majority of the population accepted this view. The fact that Jews were expelled not only from the country of their birth, but cast out of the nation they had considered to be their own was a traumatic experience. (Of course, I am not speaking here of the so-called Ostjuden (from Poland) who had migrated to Germany (or Austria) in the twentieth century, but only of those who were considered (and considered themselves) solidly rooted "Germans of the Mosaic faith.") Most of the German and Austrian Jews, whatever their feelings as Germans or Austrians, felt rejected, and lost any desire to return. They rapidly ceased being refugees and became, in overwhelming majority, genuine immigrants in those countries that would receive them.

Because of prevailing sociopolitical circumstances, and the imminent danger of war, most tried to put the ocean between themselves and Nazi Germany. Most emigrated to the United States, Canada, and South America. Once they arived in the countries of settlement, and since they felt that their ties to the German nation had been severed, they were eager to become assimilated into the new land and people. And in this regard the countries that received them were also more hospitable than the European states where the Russians found asylum. Nor were the cultural differences as great, since the English-speaking world in particular had long standing and close affinities with German ways and culture. Scholars, scientists, and technicians found employment, and easily joined academic or other institutions in the United States, Canada, or South America; doctors and engineers found new positions with relative ease. I certainly do not want to belittle the hardships, sometimes traumatic difficulties, in adjustment for many, especially those of the older generation. But it is important to stress that integration was possible, and deemed desirable by both hosts and émigrés. This was a far cry from the situation and attitudes we have noted in the case of the denizens of Russia Abroad.

It is difficult to gauge the differences due to the respective dates and chronology of the two emigrations. The German-Austrian Jewish emigration took place after the various international refugee organizations and the host nations could have learned from the Russian experience. More important was the fact that the German Jews emigrated just before—in some cases even during—the Second World War. They were immediately caught up in a situation in which their knowledge or expertise could be of assistance to the major powers in combat, the United States and Great Britain, a combat whose major goal was the end of the Nazi regime. (This is not to deny the shabby treatment inflicted on many during the Fifth Column hysteria that followed the outbreak of war, when German refugees were classified as "enemy aliens.")

The period of forced exile for the German-Austrian émigrés was relatively short; after 1947–1948, it was possible for them to return either permanently or to visit the homeland. Most did not return, however. Thomas Mann, for example, preferred to establish his postwar residence in Switzerland. Most refugees did not rejoin the institutions with which they had been affiliated before emigration, although some professors returned to Germany or Austria to lecture. Some political personalities, particularly younger leaders of the Social Democratic party (E. Reuter, W. Brandt, E. Ollenhauer) returned to resume successful careers in West Germany. (A few German émigrés who survived Stalin's purges were installed by the Red Army in the administration of what became East Germany.)

For all these reasons, no genuine "Germany Abroad" came into being. The existence of Russia Abroad is thus a unique phenomenon of the twentieth century. Its lively and creative cultural existence had an impact on the nations of asylum, and now, its cultural achievements are finally becoming known in the USSR. These two aspects make Russia Abroad even more remarkable.

There is no point in merely listing the contributions made by Russian émigrés—writers, scholars, artists, scientists, musicians, and so on: many examples have already been given. I would like, however, to identify a few broad patterns or themes that serve to give some coherence to the phenomenon. The nature and extent of the émigré contributions to their host's intellectual scene depended on whether the Russians remained isolated or could find ways of connecting with the society of asylum and its institutions. This was particularly difficult for those whose chief instrument was language. Writers—and to a large extent scholars in the humanities—were separated from the surrounding cultural world inasmuch as they continued to use Russian in their work. Consequently, the impact of novelists and poets was slight; even when translated they did not affect the local literature. When the writer adopted the foreign language as his or her own vehicle, a direct bond with the local, national literature could be established. But this usually could be the case only for younger authors who had come to maturity in exile: J. Kessel, H. Troyat, Z. Shakhovskaia, Z. Oldenburg, and of course V. Nabokov. Further, the impact of local literatures on the writings of émigré authors was barely noticeable. True, Proust's influence can be detected on occasion—as well as some surrealist elements—but this did not transform Russian literature abroad. In other fields that did not require language as the medium, integration, or at any rate close ties, with the host milieu was established more easily and effectively.

We have frequently observed the importance of the Silver Age in the creative impulses of the Russian émigrés. In their eyes, this heritage was simply an organic part of the "classical" legacy left by the poets and novelists of the nineteenth century, as were the sociopolitical and philosophical trends of that same century. In turn, this legacy drew also strength and inspiration from the pre-Petrine, medieval heritage of Rus', a heritage that had been revived in the Silver Age and was particularly influential for some trends in the arts and in the religious renaissance before 1914. For the foreign world that "hosted" Russia Abroad, however, that legacy of Russian culture held little interest or attraction, except perhaps the novels of Dostoevsky and Tolstoi.

But the Silver Age, with its modernistic traits in music, ballet, painting, and religious philosophy, as well as in its apocalyptic, fin de siècle mood, had an immediate appeal. To the extent that the artists and intellectuals of Russia Abroad continued and disseminated the values of the Silver Age, they found a receptive audience in the host societies. Language barriers aside, the writings of such realists as Bunin had little appeal—even after receiving the Nobel Prize he was little translated or read. In spite of the language barrier, however, the poets, much more modern in tone and sensibility, found a more responsive audience; thus Tsvetaeva and Rilke discovered affinities that no doubt influenced each. But these were occasional episodes, and it is fair to say that émigré literature remained largely unknown to the outside world before 1939. Its impact, albeit indirect, came much later, in the United States and in the Soviet Union, when the modernism of the Silver Age and of the 1920s was rediscovered.

If literature did not radiate outside Russia Abroad this was not the case of painting, sculpture, and music. Here again, those émigré artists whose work was rooted in and continued the modernistic trends initiated by the Silver Age found acceptance. As for artists of the older schools, including even the *Mir iskusstva,* they were treated with respect, given commissions for illustrations and sets or scores, but they did not have much to say to the West of the 1920s and 1930s. Clearly, it was the modernistic features, especially those that could also be related to the innovative trends of Soviet culture in the early 1920s, that elicited the curiosity of the West. This was the case of the creations of Chagall, Kandinsky, Burliuk, Pougni, Stravinsky, Arkhipenko. A specifically Russian element, largely but not exclusively popularized by the émigrés, found its way into contemporary international modernism. As a modernist, artistic avant garde, Russia Abroad belonged to the West. And it is in this aspect that Russia Abroad is now "returning" to a more open homeland, eager to fill the "blanks" of Stalin's time. We have also seen that a similar dynamics was operative in the case of scholarship and science. As direct heir of the achievements in the Silver Age, Russia Abroad contributed to the progress of these fields in the West in the twenties and thirties. And it is exercising a delayed, but notable influence on the Soviet cultural scene today.

Since the recognition that the innovative and creative ferment of the 1920s—in which both Russias participated—had been forcefully interrupted by the imposition of the Stalinist controls, the question of its *prolongement* may be asked. The Silver Age (and the early 1920s) did find a continuation, in Russia Abroad. This phenomenon is now being acknowledged in the Soviet homeland, the names of émigré writers and artists can be mentioned, their works incorporated into the mainstream of the history of Russian literature and culture. The works of Bunin, A. Remizov, and others have been reprinted and are creating an interest in what went on in Russia Abroad, a curiosity that can be satisfied with greater access to émigré publications. The same goes for the arts, as the Costakis collection (and its exhibition) shows, the unofficial collecting of avant-garde Russian art has resumed, and has become more accessible to an interested public. The revival of knowledge was greater in the case of those émigrés who had actually returned to Soviet Russia, as, for example, Marina Tsvetaeva. Her work is now easily accessible and studied (although not yet published in full), and her impact on contemporary poetry is constantly growing.

Still more interesting, although still imperfectly known, is the revival of interest in idealist philosophy and religious thought in recent years in the Soviet Union. The works of Berdiaev—both prerevolutionary and those written in exile—have circulated *sub rosa,* making a powerful impression on select circles of the younger generation. The greater tolerance shown the Russian church, and its more recent cooptation by the Soviet government, as well as by the dissidents, have called attention to the religious thinkers of the early twentieth century. The works and life of Father P. Florensky are the symbol of this revival. It has led to the rediscovery, by certain groups of academics and believing intellectuals, of the writings of G. Florovsky, G. Fedotov, and the activities of St. Serge's in Paris.

It has become quite clear, both in the West and in Soviet Russia, that the émigrés did carry on the work and traditions of their elders and forerunners of the late 1800s and early 1900s. They have been the true extension of the creative spurt of the Silver Age and of the early experimental years of the Soviet regime. Their work preserved features of Russia's cultural history and tradition that had been banned in the years of Stalin, and which are surfacing again to bring new life and variety into official socialist realist formulas. To-day's stress on national elements in Russia's past, and pride in their cultural contributions, have given particular significance to the accomplishments of Russia Abroad in this respect: histories of the church and of religious thought, singling out the religious and spiritual aspects in the life and work of such classical writers as Pushkin, Dostoevsky, Gogol, and Blok—all these scholarly concerns of Russia Abroad are now returning to the USSR. The emigration is now acknowledged to have fulfilled its dual purpose in leaving the Soviet-dominated homeland and in setting up Russia Abroad: to preserve the traditions and values that were not acceptable to the Bolshevik regime and to carry on the creative work begun in the Silver Age.

Still more important, to my mind, is another role that Russia Abroad is called to play now in the Soviet homeland. It serves as an intermediary, transmitting the West's cultural achievements in the 1920s and 1930s back to the USSR. Until recently, because of their isolation, the émigrés had hardly been in a position to convey this Western cultural achievement to their compatriots in Soviet Russia. Now this has become possible to a much larger—and presumably still growing—degree. Even though they did not fully integrate into the Western societies in whose midst they found refuge, and even though they were not as receptive as might have been desirable to the cultural developments in host countries, émigré writers, intellectuals (scholars in particular) inevitably did register what was going on around them, and informing Russia Abroad of these influences in their many publications. Moreover, in the process of defining and proclaiming their Russianness, willy-nilly, the émigrés had to comment on those features and characteristics of the contemporary Western scene that distinguished them from their hosts. It is this information, contained in the journals, newspapers, and books published in Russia Abroad, that is now a source of information for those who manage to gain an access to them in the Soviet Union or abroad. And it is an information that is of vital importance in filling in the "blank spots" created by Soviet Russia's isolation from the outside world in the 1930s and 1940s.

In truth, the intellectuals of Russia Abroad have perpetuated the tradition of the Russian intelligentsia: they offer a moral (political) critique of conditions at home, and serve as channels for the importation and integration of Western knowledge and values. The old intelligentsia's tragedy had consisted in being cut off from the people—and they tried hard to bridge the gap by "discovering," in fact creating, the nation to whom they addressed themselves. In filling this gulf, largely by eliminating the former elites, the Soviet regime had fulfilled one of the missions the intelligentsia had taken upon itself. But it was done at the expense of the intelligentsia's true raison d'être, namely to take an actively critical stance with respect to the prevailing morality and sociopolitical system. It is this salient feature of the intelligentsia's traditional role that was assumed by the intellectuals in Russia Abroad. To the extent that their work becomes known in their homeland, this aspect of their mission will have been accomplished too. Like their ancestors in the nineteenth century, they labored under the handicap of not having direct access to those for whom they presumably were toiling—the Russian people. Will this circumstance also become a factor of ambiguity and ineffectiveness in the immediate future? We hope not, but one cannot be overly confident when one recalls the isolated condition of Russia Abroad. True, this isolation permitted creative efforts in a kind of "sheltered," hothouse atmosphere; yet at the same time it could not but impart a touch of abstractness and unreality to much of their cultural effort. Quite naturally, this was particularly so in the political sphere, but it was also true to a significant degree of the philosophical and literary realms.

From a wider perspective still, the history of Russia Abroad may help clarify the place and role of a culturally creative minority in exile. On the face of it, the conditions for creativity were anything but propitious; yet creative life went forward. The very difficulties, if they did not lead to sterile preservation or mechanical repetition of previous ways, proved to be a challenge and conducive to creative response. Of course, in too many cases, the difficult conditions were too burdensome and proved destructive. Coming into contact, however superficially, with a foreign world made it possible to acquire new perspectives and introduce new features into the Russian cultural tradition. This contact served to strengthen the ties to Western culture, which had inspired Russian culture ever since Muscovy turned its face to "Europe" in the second half of the seventeenth century.

Nor should we ever forget, or underestimate, the fact that the émigrés were totally free to create in whatever way they chose. For the first time in Russian history the intellectual, the writer, and the artist enjoyed absolute freedom, unhampered by censorship. Neither government nor public opinion interfered with their creativity. Such conditions had not been attained even in the heydays of the newly gained freedom in the late months of 1905, or the early weeks of 1917. The host governments and societies did not impose restrictions—except on those manifestations that threatened public order and their diplomatic interests. Such cases were extremely rare, for in their isolation the émigrés could not affect areas of public policy. Nor did the Russians abroad have to pay attention to a foreign public opinion. This heady freedom of expression at times resulted in somewhat exaggerated formulations, but its primary result was open discussion of ideas and artistic expressions.

The creation of culture in Russia Abroad is now a closed chapter, for Russia Abroad is no more. Will its culture be reintegrated into the mainstream in the homeland? We believe that the signs of recent years suggest an affirmative answer. And we have the previous experience of France and Poland to sustain us in this optimism. The cultural scene of France, after the turmoil of the revolution, under Napoleon and during the Restoration, was largely the creation of such émigrés as Chateaubriand, Mme. de Stael, B. Constant, J. de Maistre. It was the émigrés who introduced Romanticism, and advanced knowledge of the literature, thought, and cultures of England, the Germanies, and Italy. The Great Polish Emigration certainly was a major force in the history and development of Polish literature, and in the shaping of a national identity in all three territories of the partitioned country.

As an exemplary instance of an exiled minority's dual role of preserver and contributor to the common fund of a national culture, the history of Russia Abroad and its cultural life have been, and will be, inseparably part of the history of all Russia.

Notes

CHAPTER 1

1. Sir John Hope Simpson, *The Refugee Problem—Report of a Survey* (London, New York, Toronto: Oxford Univ. Press, 1939). Michael R. Marrus, *The Unwanted—European Refugees in the Twentieth Century* (New York, Oxford: Oxford Univ. Press, 1985).

2. Some figures will be provided in Chapter 2.

3. Stalin's policies precluded a mass return to Russia, although several hundred émigrés did go back to Soviet Russia in the immediate aftermath of World War II, in a burst of Soviet patriotism and disgust with life as second-rate inhabitants of France. Theirs was, in most cases, an unenviable fate, to judge by recent memoirs and A. Solzhenitsyn's *Archipelago Gulag*.

4. Sergei L. Voitsekhovskii, *Trest—Vospominaniia i dokumenty* (London: Ontario: Zaria, 1974), and his useful bibliography.

5. Brief accounts of these episodes are in Robert H. Johnston, *New Mecca, New Babylon—Paris and the Russian Exiles, 1920–1945* (Kingston, Montreal: McGill-Queen's Univ. Press, 1988).

6. There is very little information on the Mladorossy: see John J. Stephan, *The Russian Fascists—Tragedy and Farce in Exile, 1925–1945* (New York: Harper & Row, 1978), and the unpublished memoirs of N. P. Vakar at Harvard University. More information exists for the NTS since its leading members were involved with the Vlasov movement during World War II, when Soviet General A. A. Vlasov—taken prisoner by the Germans—tried to organize Russian POWs as an army to fight Stalinist Russia alongside the Germans: see Catherine Andreyev, *Vlasov and the Russian Liberation Movement—Soviet Reality and Emigre Theories* (Cambridge: Cambridge Univ. Press, 1987); A. P. Stolypin, *Na Sluzhbe Rossii* (Frankfurt: Possev Verlag, 1986); B. Prianishnikoff, *Novopokolentsy* (Silver Spring, Md.: Multilingual Typesetting, 1986).

7. Johnston, *New Mecca*; Stephan, *Russian Fascists*; Robert C. Williams, *Culture in Exile—Russian Emigres in Germany, 1881–1941* (Ithaca, London: Cornell Univ. Press, 1972); André Liebich, "The Mensheviks in the Face of Stalinism," in *Ripensare 1956—Socialismo Storia* (n.p.: Annali della Fondazione

Giacomo Brodolini, n.d.), pp. 184–200; Liebich, "Marxism and Totalitarianism: Rudolf Hilferding and the Mensheviks," Kennan Institute for Advanced Russian Studies—Occasional Papers no. 217, 1986; M. Raeff, "Novyi Grad and Germany—A Chapter in the Intellectual History of the Russian Emigration of the 1930s," in I. Auerbach, A. Hillgruber, and G. Schramm, eds., *Felder und Vorfelder russischer Geschichte—Studien zu Ehren von Peter Scheibert* (Freiburg, Breisgau: Rombach, 1985); Raeff, "Le Front Populaire et la presse émigrée russe," in Mélanges Portal, *Revue des Études Slaves,* forthcoming.

8. Cleb Struve, *Russkaia literatura v izgnanii,* 2d ed. (Paris: YMCA Press, 1984); and see E. Etkind, G. Nivat, I. Serman, and V. Strada, eds., *Histoire de la littérature russe—Le XXe siècle: La révolution et les années vingt* (Paris: Fayard, 1988) for a general overview and useful bibliography. See also the suggestive colloquium proceedings: *Odna ili dve russkikh literatury?* (Lausanne: L'Age d'Homme, 1981). N. P. Poltoratskii, ed., *Russkaia literatura v emigratsii—Sbornik statei,* Slavic series no. 1 (Pittsburgh: Univ. of Pittsburgh, 1972).

9. For example, Abraham Ascher, *Pavel Axelrod and the Development of Menshevism* (Cambridge, Mass.: Harvard Univ. Press, 1972); Richard Pipes, *Struve—Liberal on the Right, 1905–1944* (Cambridge, Mass.: Harvard Univ. Press, 1980); Richard Abraham, *Alexander Kerensky: The First Love of the Revolution* (New York: Columbia Univ. Press, 1987).

10. See Johnston, *New Mecca,* Williams, *Culture in Exile,* but also L. Feishman, R. Hughes, and O. Raevskaya-Hughes, eds., *Russkii Berlin, 1921–1923* (Paris: YMCA Press, 1983); Catherine Gousseff and Nicolas Saddier, *L'Emigration russe en France 1920–1930,* Mémoire de Maîtrise d'histoire, Département d'histoire des slaves, University of Paris I, October 1983.

11. Stephan, *Russian Fascists.*

12. Bakhmeteff Archive of Russian and East European History and Culture, Columbia University (hereafter Bakhmeteff Archive), S. G. Svatikov Papers, letters to O. S. Minor, Box 5.

13. Carol A. Leadenham, comp., *Guide to the Collections in the Hoover Institution Archives Relating to Imperial Russia, the Russian Revolutions and Civil War, and the First Emigration* (Stanford, Calif.: Hoover Institution Press, 1986); *Russia in the Twentieth Century—The Catalog of the Bakhmeteff Archive of Russian and East European History and Culture* (Boston: G. K. Hall, 1987); Steven A. Grant and John H. Brown, *The Russian Empire and the Soviet Union—A Guide to Manuscripts and Archival Materials in the United States* (Boston: G. K. Hall, 1981); Janet M. Hartley, *Guide to Documents and Manuscripts in the United Kingdom Relating to Russia and the Soviet Union* (London, New York: Mansell Publishing, 1987). I know of no comparable surveys for France, Germany, or other countries of the Russian diaspora.

14. Tatiana Ossorguine-Bakounine, comp., *L'Emigration russe en Europe—Catalogue collectif des périodiques en langue russe, 1855–1940* (Paris: Institut d'études slaves, 1976 [Bibliothèque russe de l'Institut d'études slaves, XL–1—a second, revised, and complemented edition is in press]); T. L. Gladkova and T. A. Ossorpuine, eds., *L'Emigration russe—Revue et recueils, 1920–1980—Index général des articles* (Paris: Institut d'études slaves, 1988 [Bibliothèque russe de l'Institut d'études slaves, LXXXI]); Ludmila Z. Foster, *Bibliography of Russian Emigre Literature, 1918–1968* (Boston: G. K. Hall, 1970). These works super-

sede Michael Schatoff, comp., *Half a Century of Russian Serials, 1917–1968,* 4 vols. (New York: Russian Book Chamber Abroad, 1970–1972). In addition, the Institut d'études slaves in Paris (Bibliothèque russe—série: écrivains russes en France) has published bibliographies of the works of major Russian émigré writers who have lived in France; more than fifteen volumes have appeared to date. An additional source is Mark Kulikowski, "A Neglected Source: The Bibliography of Russian Emigré Publications since 1917," *Solanus* (International Journal for Russian and East European Bibliographic, Library and Publishing Studies), new series, 3 (1989): 89–102.

CHAPTER 2

1. Z. Schakovsky, *Lumières et ombres* (Paris: Presses de la cité, 1964).

2. See the memoirs of B. Prianishnikoff, *Novopokolentsky* (Silver Spring, Md.: Multilingual Typesetting, 1986), among others.

3. Roman Gul', *Ia unes Rossiiu—Apologiia emigratsii,* vol. 1: *"Rossiia v Germanii"* (New York: Most, 1981).

4. S. G. Isakov, ed., "Bunin v Rige, Iz vospominanii zhurnalista—A. K. Perov," Trudy po russkoi i slavianskoi filologii, XXIV, Literaturovedenie, *Uchenye zapiski tartusskogo gos. universiteta,* fasc. 358 Tartu, 1975, pp. 355–71. For this reference, and a copy of the article, I am indebted to the kindness of L. Fleishman of Stanford University. The papers of A. Amfiteatrov, at the Lilly Library of the University of Indiana at Bloomington, contain numerous examples of his dealings with publishers and colleagues in Warsaw and elsewhere. The Riga daily, *Segodnia,* chronicled carefully and fully all such visits of émigré literary and public personalities.

5. Sir John Hope Simpson, *The Refugee Problem—Report of a Survey* (London, New York, Toronto: Oxford Univ. Press, 1939), pp. 81–82; see pp. 78–80 for detailed figures on refugees in Poland and pp. 68–74 for a description and a breakdown of the numbers of refugees passing through the Black Sea and Istanbul. See also Tables 1 and 2 (pp. 202–3, this volume), from same source (Tables 63 [adapted] and 64).

6. Gul', *Ia unes Rossiiu;* S. Timoshenko, *Vospominaniia* (Paris: Association of Alumni of St. Petersburg Polytechnic Institute, 1963).

7. Simpson, *Refugee Problem,* p. 85.

8. Joseph Kessel, *Nuits de princes* (Paris: Juillard, 1928); Gaito Gazdanov, *Vecher u Kler* (Paris: Povolotsky, 1930).

9. Simpson, *Refugee Problem,* p. 85.

10. Ibid., chapter 9 ("Private Organizations Assisting Refugees"); also summary information in M. R. Marrus, *The Unwanted—European Refugees in the Twentieth Century* (New York, Oxford: Oxford Univ. Press, 1985).

11. University Archives, University of Illinois at Urbana-Champaign, Donald A. Lowrie Papers (Record Series 15/35/53), Box 2 (letters to his mother, January–September 1921).

12. Michel Heller, "Premier Avertissement: Un coup de fouet (l'histoire de l'expulsion des personnalités culturelles hors de l'Union soviétique en 1922)," *Cahiers du monde russe et soviétique* 20:2 (April–June 1979): 131–72.

Table 1. *Distribution of Unassimilated Russian Refugees in Europe and the Near East at Certain Dates* (Figures in brackets are independent estimates.)

Country	1 Jan. 1922 Based on Estimates [. . .]	1 Jan. 1930 Estimates of Sub-committee of Private Organizations for Refugees	1936–37 Nansen Office Estimates
Austria	3,000–4,000	2,958	2,500
Belgium	3,823	abt. 7,000	8,000
Bulgaria	30,000–32,000	21,830	15,700
Cyprus	600–700	40	11
Czechoslovakia	5,000–6,000	15,184	9,000
Danzig	(1,000)	600	747
Denmark	(800)	300	600
Egypt	1,000–1,500	(500)	(350)
Estonia	14,000–16,000	11,200	5,283
Finland	19,000–20,000	10,000	7,932
France	67,000–75,000	150,000–200,000	100,000–120,000
Germany	230,000–250,000	90,000	45,000
Great Britain	8,000–10,000	4,000	(2,000)
Greece	3,000–3,200	abt. 2,000	2,205
Hungary	3,000–4,000	5,045	4,000
Italy	8,000–10,000	2,500	(1,300)
Latvia	16,000–17,000	15,646	12,800
Lithuania	(4,000)	5,000–8,000	5,000
Poland	150,000–200,000	80,000–90,000	80,000–100,000
Romania	35,000–40,000	12,000–15,000	11,000
Sweden and Norway	1,000–1,500	1,000	2,500
Switzerland	2,000–3,000	2,266	(1,000)
Turkey	30,000–35,000	1,400	1,211
Yugoslavia	33,500	29,500	27,000–28,000
Total un-naturalized Russian refugees in Europe and Near East	(mean) 718,000 (668,000–772,000)	(mean) 503,000 (470,000–536,000)	(mean) 355,000 (345,000–386,000)

13. See, e.g., letters of A. S. Jaščenko to I. Gessen confirming receipt of 1,000-mark loan from Treasurer B. I. Elkin, 21 July 1921, and 4 May 1922, which state that he received 3,000 marks in all. A. S. Jaščenko Nachlass, no. 149 (Box I) in Staatsbibliothek, Berlin, Preussischer Kulturbesitz.

14. Prianishnikoff, *Novopokolentsky;* Hoover Institution, Archives, A. S. Paléologue Papers, Box 023, Letter of Directorate, Russian Colony in Belgrade, 16 February 1925 (Hereafter Paléologue Papers).

Table 2.   Distribution of Unassimilated Russian Refugees: Geographical Grouping

Groups of Countries	1922 Numbers	1930 Numbers	1937 Numbers
Turkey	35,000	1,400	1,200
Balkan Countries			
Greece	3,000	2,000	2,200
Romania	35,000	13,000	11,000
Yugoslavia	34,000	30,000	27,500
Bulgaria	31,000	22,000	15,700
	138,000	68,400	57,600
Poland and Baltic Countries			
Estonia	15,000	11,000	5,300
Finland	20,000	10,000	8,000
Latvia	16,000	16,000	13,000
Lithuania	4,000	5,000	5,000
Danzig			
Poland	175,000	85,000	80,000
	230,000	127,000	111,000
Central Europe			
Austria	4,000	3,000	2,500
Hungary	3,000	5,000	4,000
Czechoslovakia	5,000	15,000	9,000
Germany	250,000	90,000	45,000
	252,000	113,000	60,500
France	70,000	175,000	110,000
Other European Countries			
Belgium	4,000	7,000	8,000
Great Britain	9,000	4,000	(2,000)
Italy	9,000	2,500	(1,300)
Scandinavia	2,000	1,500	3,000
Switzerland	3,000	2,300	(1,000)
Others	1,000	2,700	(1,700)
	28,000	20,000	17,000
Far East	145,000	127,000	94,000
Total	863,000	630,000	450,000

15. Paléologue Papers, Box 024, Memorandum 21 May 1925; overall credits were cut to 3.5 million dinars. Ibid., Box 029: in 1931 there was a drastic cut in the budget for Russians because Yugoslavia lost 800 million dinars of German reparations annually as a result of the Hoover Moratorium that reduced the German debt.

16. Summary data on the zemgor are in Simpson, *Refugee Problem,* pp. 181–83, and its *Informatsionnyi list* (*Information Bulletin*). On drives for Russian

children abroad see the journal *Den' russkogo rebenka* (San Francisco, ed. N. V. Borzov) nos. 1–8 (1934–1941).

17. *Golos emigranta* (*Die Stimme des Emigranten,* Berlin) nos. 9, 10 (20 December and 22 January 1922) gives lists of refugee organizations in Berlin, Prague, Paris, Warsaw, and Belgrade. V. A. Obolenskii and B. M. Sarach, eds., *Russkii al'manakh-Spravochnik* (Paris, 1931), pp. 241–57, lists thirteen such organizations in France.

18. Obolenskii and Sarach, *Russkii al'manakh*. The catalog of the Bakhmeteff Archive contains a representative sample of such organizations. *Soiuz russkikh shoferov* (Union of Russian Automobile Drivers), Papers, contains copies of representations made on behalf of members involved in accidents and traffic violations to avoid penalties and withdrawal of licenses.

19. Zinaida Zhemchuzhnaia, *Puti izgnaniia—Ural, Kuban', Moskva, Kharbin, Tian'tsin—Vospominaniia* (Tenafly, N.J.: Ermitazh, 1987); Diaries of Ivan I. Serebrennikov, Hoover Archives. See the charming, semifictional autobiographical sketch, Nina Fedorova, *Sem'ia* (New York: Chekhov Publishing House, 1952).

20. Paléologue Papers, Box 17, file 32, part 2, "Report on the Settlement of Russian Refugees in the Kingdom of Serbs, Croats, Slovenes," 20 February 1922, pp. 6ff. In early 1920, 8,000 refugees set up 57 colonies; after the evacuation of Crimea, the number of colonies reached 323. The rules of administration were worked out in July 1920. The Statute of Court of Honor (to settle disputes within colonies) was approved by Serbian authorities in September 1920, and was renewed and amended in 1921.

21. About this academic core there settled Socialist Revolutionary newspapers and journals, and several writers, for example, Vas. Nemirovich-Danchenko and E. Chirikov, associated with the publishing house F. Topič. B. Khellman, "Cheshskoe izdatel'stvo 'F. Topič' i russkie pisateli," *Novyi Zhurnal* 171 (1988): 269–87.

22. Some examples are the tsarist appointees V. Shtrandman in Belgrade and S. Botkin in Madrid; the Provisional Government sent B. Bakhmetev to Washington, D.C., and V. Maklakov to Paris. Since Maklakov did not present his letters of accreditation to the president of the Republic at the moment of Lenin's seizure of power, he had a special status, but he was the de facto representative of Russian interests until French recognition of the Soviet government in 1924.

23. Hoover Archives, Serge Botkine Collection, Box 7, file 58 ("Istoricheskaia spravka ob organizatsii In den Zelten").

24. Johnston, *New Mecca;* M. Raeff, "Le Front Populaire et la presse émigrée russe," in Mélanges Portal, *Revue des études slaves,* forthcoming.

25. Most Russians who stayed had to flee again in 1945 (e.g., S. G. Pushkarev), or were arrested (e.g., N. E. Andreyev) by the Soviet authorities, or were deported (e.g., P. Savitskii) to the Soviet Union. S. G. Pushkarev, "Praga 1921–1945—Begstvo iz Pragi," *Novyi zhurnal* 147 (1982): 91–99. See also his reminiscences of "Russian Prague" in *Novyi zhurnal* 149 (1982) and 151 (1983). P. N. Savitskii Letters, G. Vernadsky Papers, Box 8, Bakhmeteff Archive.

26. In 1933 the Russian minority constituted about 10 percent of the total population (225,000); it was the largest minority. See *Russkie v Latvii, sbornik "Dnia russkoi kul'tury"* (Riga, 1933). The Riga daily, *Segodnia,* reflects graphically the local situation.

27. (M. Vishniak), "Iz bessarabskikh vpechatlenii," *Sovremennye zapiski* 30 (1926): 409–38. See also Mark Vishniak, *Gody emigratsii 1919–1969—Parizh— Niu Iork (Vospominaniia)* (Stanford, Calif.: Hoover Institution Press, 1970), pp. 96–97. Mark Vishniak's report is perhaps a bit overdramatized.

28. Kessel, *Nuits de princes;* Hoover Archives, Ekaterina Murav'eva Papers, letters to B. B. Mehring, Box 5.

29. For example, S. Paléologue advised A. I. Kuliabko (chairman of the Russian colony in Sremski Karlovci), 16 January 1928, to accept Yugoslav naturalization, and to consider it a form of "dual citizenship" (this refers to the old imperial rule that foreign citizenship could be taken with government approval). Paléologue Papers, Box 026.

30. The Menshevik émigré group organized a cooperative radio assembly shop in Paris in 1933–1934. It did not do well, in spite of subsidies from prosperous well-wishers. The sketches of Teffi and the verses of Don Aminado in the Russian dailies in Paris also provide examples of personal business contacts.

31. The historian A. A. Kizevetter criticized this separatist attitude of the émigrés in a letter to V. A. Maklakov, 1 December 1923: "It seems to me that until there is an opportunity to do a useful job in Russia, the emigration could find a field for activity abroad if it did not fence itself off from the surrounding local life. Are not the Russians abroad making a mistake by lulling themselves with the illusion of a rapid return to Russia? They live abroad as on a station, confining themselves to their own circle, not making contacts with the life that surrounds them." Hoover Archives, B. A. Maklakoff Papers, Box 17. In more general terms, Manes Sperber has also spoken of this isolation of exiles, which he ascribes to a loss of a sense of the present:

> Der Exilierte der flüchtigsten und dennoch belangreichsten der drei Zeiten: der *Gegenwart,* feindlich ist. Nur in der Vergangenheit findet er die eigene Rechtfertigung und Grund, auf eine Zukunft zu hoffen, welche alles gutmachen, die Usurpatoren stürzen, die Verbannten aber in der wiedergefundenen Heimat erheben soll. Dieser gewollte und dennoch täglich aufs neue erlittene *Gegenwartsverlust* hindert ihn, im Asylland Fuss zu fassen. Er wünscht es ja garnicht, denn er ist unterwegs, für ihn ist alles provisorisch, jedes Jetzt wird ihm ein flüchtiges Inzwischen. (M. Sperber, *Bis Man mir die Scherben auf die Augen Legt* [Vienna: Europa Verlag, 1977], p. 104).

32. Hoover Archives, Aleksei A. von Lampe Papers, Box 4, contains a copious correspondence on this subject triggered by General Wrangel's Order No. 82 that veterans should not join political parties or engage in partisan political activities, as demanded by Grand Duke Nikolai Nikolaevich (formally the supreme commander of the White Armies and representative of the Romanov House).

33. See note 29 above. This attitude is reminiscent of the enlightened Jewish stance of "Jew at home and Russian in the street" in the nineteenth century.

Additional Select Bibliography

The most useful guide to émigré cultural personalities:
P. E. Kovalevskii, *Zarubezhnaia Rossiia—Istoriia i kul'turno prosvetitel'naia rabota*

russkogo zarubezh'it za polveka 1920–1970, 2 vols. Paris: Librarie des cinq continents, 1971–1973.
Other sources:
VI. Maevskii. *Russkie v Iugoslavii—Vzaimootnosheniia Rossii i Serbii.* New York: Istoricheskii Kruzhok, 1966.
S. Postnikov, ed. *Russkie v Prage, 1918–1928.* Prague, 1928.
Gennadii Ozeretskovskii. *Rossia malaia—Vol. I: Russkii blistatel'nyi Parizh do voiny. Paris*, 1973.
Ivan K. Okuntsov, *Russkaia emigratsiia v severnoi i iuzhnoi Amerike.* Buenos Aires: Seiatel', 1967.

CHAPTER 3

1. This paragraph owes much to the paper prepared by Mark Johnson for the seminar on political emigrations in the twentieth century at Columbia University in 1986. V. V. Zen'kovskii, ed., *Deti emigratsii—Sbornik statei.* Prague: Pedagogicheskoe biuro po delam srednei i nizshei shkoly zagranitsei, 1925.

2. In the words of A. Petrov, faculty member of the Russian school in Istanbul, in 1924:

> We cannot think only of providing the pupil with some body of knowledge; once and for all we have to give up the old, passive [type of] school. This automatically will bring to the fore the task of upbringing: we have an obligation of bringing up the children, everything else will come easily; one can't think of the intellect only when the whole soul is aching. The school has to be set up in such manner that the lessons in the classroom, the recreation periods, the life of the boarding student, all aim at influencing the whole soul, while at the same time healing, bringing up, and teaching the child or adolescent. Our school must, above all, become a family where the life of the teacher is indissolubly tied to the life of the child, where there will not be two camps of "we" and "they," but where all will be welded into one. Furthermore, in our day the school has to think of developing will and character, and to fight the debilitating softness that has dramatically shown itself in the Russian intelligentsia in the years of our trials.
>
> Lastly, and perhaps most important of all: guided by the newest trends in education and psychology, our school has to be strictly national; on us rests the heavy task of preserving, and in some cases inspiring, in the children the sacred fire of love for the lost homeland, of acquainting them with the greatness of their native history, with the beauty of their native poetry and literature—in a word, of giving them a knowledge and understanding of their native land. (*Russkaia shkola za rubezhom* 9 [1924]: 96)

3. For more detailed breakdown, see Zen'kovskii, *Deti emigratsii*, pp. 249–50, and Sir John Hope Simpson, *The Refugee Problem—Report of a Survey* (London, New York, Toronto: Oxford Univ. Press, 1939), p. 101 (Table 16).

4. The new dating was accepted more readily, as the émigrés had to live in a foreign milieu that reckoned by the Gregorian calendar. For example, the Berlin daily *Rul'* (Rudder) gave both Julian and Gregorian dates until 1925, from then on it only carried the Gregorian one.

5. *Russkii kolokol* (Belgrade) 1–9 (1928–1930); A. M. Chernyi and V. V. Zen'kovskii, eds., *Russkaia zemlia—Al'manakh dlia iunoshestva* (Paris: Religiozno-Pedagogicheskii Kabinet and YMCA Press, 1928); *Valdimirskii sbornik v pamiat' 950-letiia kreshcheniia Rusi 988–1938* (Belgrade, 1938).

6. The well-known children's poet Sasha Chernyi wrote on 15 March 1924 to the writer A. Amfiteatrov from Rome (where his wife was tutoring the children of Leonid Andreev):

> In Paris I'll try to organize a Russian children's journal, be it a most most modest one. . . . Everybody has somehow forgotten the children— yet thousands of them, scattered in all corners of Europe, are forgetting their native tongue; and except for a chance purchase in a second-hand bookstore of an old anthology, they often have nothing [to read]. Will anything come of this, I do not know. Literary talent there is aplenty . . . but as for a publisher . . . (Amfiteatrov Archive, Lilly Library, Indiana University)

7. The journal *Russkaia shkola za rubezhom* (Prague, ed. S. I. Gessen) 1–34 (1923–1929) carried information on these developments and reports on Russian schools in all countries of the diaspora. Of particular interest were the accounts of the Russian Pedagogical Congress in Prague in 1923 (reported in nos. 2–3 [1923]: 1–30), and the Second Congress, 5–12 July 1925, also in Prague (reported in nos. 15–16 [1925]: 209–25).

8. Franz Basler, *Die deutsch-russische Schule in Berlin 1931–1945—Geschichte und Auftrag* (Berlin: Veröffentlichungen der Abteilung für Slavische Sprachen und Literaturen des Osteuropa Instituts an der Freien Universität Berlin, Band 54, 1983). For summary information on émigré schools see P. Kovalevsky, *Zarubezhnaia rossiia*, 2 vols. (Paris: Librairie des cinq continents, 1971–1973), 1:39–65.

9. *Informatsionnyi biulleten' pedagogicheskogo Biuro*, 1926–1927, Prague; *Vestnik pedagogicheskogo biuro*, 1927–1931, Prague. *Biulleten' pedagogicheskogo biuro po delam srednei i nizshei shokoly zagranitsei* (Prague) 1–10 (1923–1927).

10. Bakhmeteff Archive, V. V. Zen'kovskii Memoirs; Sophie Koulomzin, *Many Worlds: A Russian Life* (Crestwood, N.Y.: St. Vladimir's Seminary Press, 1980).

11. V. V. Rudnev, *Sud'by emigrantskoi shkoly* (Prague, 1929), p. 7, gives the following figures for the 1928–1929 school year: twenty-nine kindergartens with 820 pupils (62 boarders); fifty-two primary schools with 1,452 pupils (378 boarders); and thirty-seven secondary schools with 5,401 pupils (about 3,450 boarders). Furthermore, in Slavic countries with about 75,000 émigrés, there were 4,900 children in Russian schools (3,250 boarders), while in non-Slavic countries with more than 325,000 émigrés only 2,600 pupils attended Russian schools (650 boarders), p. 10. These figures illustrate the pull of local schools in non-Slavic, West European countries.

12. See petition for fellowships for the two Oldenburg sisters (Zoé was to become a well-known French writer) to attend the lycée in Paris. Bakhmeteff archive; "Soiuz russkikh pisatefei i zhurnalistov," Box 1.

13. The Russian teacher Fedor Rostovtseff reported that in 1932 the following French lycées offered Russian subjects on an extracurricular basis: six in Paris (Jeanson de Sailly, Buffon, Fénelon, Hoche, Molière, Michelet), four in Nice, and one in Versailles, with a total of 231 pupils attending and twenty-two in-

structors. The official subsidy was 57,000 francs (compared to 38,000 francs, the yearly salary of a regular professor in the lycée). Hoover Archives, Fedor Rostovtseff Papers, Box 2.

14. Koulomzin, *Many Worlds;* See also the schedule of events at the headquarters, January-March 1933, Paul B. Anderson Papers, 1913–1982, University of Illinois at Urbana-Champaign, University Archives, Record Series 15/35/54, Box 23 (hereafter Anderson Papers).

15. *Trudy russkikh uchenykh zagranitsei* 1 (Berlin, 1922): 272–80; "Obzory deitel'nosti Akademicheskoi Gruppy"; Anderson Papers, Box 27, N. Berdiaev to Anderson, 21 February 1928.

16. The following aims were spelled out by the Russian Academic Group: (1) accurate census of Russian scholars abroad and their situation; (2) organization in each country of a local society; (3) ascertain possible positions in each country that could be filled by Russians; (4) recommend Russian scholars to these positions; (5) collection and distribution of contributions in aid of scholars and scholarly work; and (6) provision of books, journals, and educational-scholarly institutions. *Trudy russkikh uchenykh zagranitsei* 1 (1922): 275. For a more general statement, see ibid., p. 272.

17. L. Hamilton Rhinelander, "Exiled Russian Scholars in Prague: The Kondakov Seminar and Institute," *Canadian Slavonic Papers* 16:3 (1974): 331–52. Rhinelander has kindly provided me with a copy of a typescript, "Material Supplied by Dr. N. E. Andreyev, formerly Student, Fellow, and Acting Director of the Kondakov Institute," Cambridge, September 1968.

18. *Uchenye zapiski, osnovannyia russkoi uchebnoi kollegiei v Prage, 1924; Zapiski russk. istoricheskogo obshchestva v Prage, 1927–1930.*

19. Anderson Papers, Box 3; a report of 1 January 1936 gives a total of 9,850 students (an increase of 52 over the preceding month), with 24,392 subjects taken and 5,704 completed. See also "Report on the Organization of the Russian Superior Technical Institute, by the Co-Director, Paul B. Anderson, Febr. 15, 1932," in Anderson Papers, Box 10.

20. Richard Pipes, *Struve—Liberal on the Right, 1905–1944* (Cambridge, Mass.: Harvard Univ. Press, 1980), pp. 395–96; T. Pachmuss, *Intellect and Ideas in Action—Selected Correspondence of Z. Hippius* (Munich: W. Fink, 1972), pp. 219–28.

21. *Izvestiia iuridicheskogo fakul'teta v Kharbine* (Kharbin) 1–12 (1925–1938).

22. *Russkaia obshchestvennaia biblioteka imeni I. S. Turgeneva—sotrudniki—druz'ia—pochitateli—sbornik statei* (Paris: Bibliothèque russe de l'Institut d'études slaves, tome 78, 1987).

23. George Fischer, "The Russian Archive in Prague," *American Slavic and East European Review* 8 (1949): 289–95; Bakhmeteff Archive, Svatikov Papers, Box 5 (Letters to O. S. Minor); and S. Postnikov, ed., *Russkie v Prage, 1918–1928* (Prague, 1928), pp. 41–50.

24. Russkii zagranichnyi istoricheskii arkhiv v Prage, *Bibliografiia russkoi revoliutsii i grazhdanskoi voiny (1917–1921)—iz kataloga R. Z. I. arkhiva,* ed. S. P. Postnikov (Prague, 1938).

25. In addition to Fischer, "Russian Archive," see the memoirs of S. G. Pushkarev, "Praga 1921–1945—Begstvo iz Pragi," *Novyi zhurnal* 147 (1982): 91–99. An unpublished catalogue of the surviving materials of the Prague Archive and Li-

brary has been prepared by Mrs. M. Reiman who kindly showed me her card file at the University of Tübingen.

26. *Student,* Prague, 1921–1922; *Studencheskie gody,* Prague, 1922–1925; *Golos studenta—sbornik,* Prague, 1923.

CHAPTER 4

1. Interview in New York City with the late Dr. A. S. Kagan, cofounder and owner of Petropolis.

2. For example, G. Florovskii, *Puti russkogo bogosloviia,* bears a YMCA imprint (1938); it was printed in Belgrade where the stock was burned during World War II.

3. See Anderson Papers, Box 9, concerning the Ob'edinenie parizhskikh russkikh izdatelei i knigoprodovtsov (Association of Parisian Russian publishers and Book Dealers). Box 3 contains the minutes of the meeting, 1 November 1935, of the Tovarishchestvo ob'edinennykh izdatelei (Company of United Publishing).

4. I. A. Shomrakova, "Zarubezhnye sviazi Gosizdata," *Fedorovskie chteniia—1979* (Moscow, 1982), pp. 113–20; Interview with Dr. A. S. Kagan; L. Fleishman, R. Hughes, O. Raevskaya-Hughes, eds., *Russkii Berlin, 1921–1923* (Paris: YMCA Press, 1983); *Russkaia kniga zagranitsei* (Moscow) 1 (1924).

5. *Russkaia kniga* (*ezhemesiachnyi kritiko-bibliograficheskii zhurnal*), (A. S. Iashchenko, ed., Berlin) 1–9 (1921), succeeded by *Novaia russkaia kniga* (Berlin) 1–12 (1922) and 1–6 (1923). Also *Slavianskaia kniga—Mesiachnik slavianskoi bibliografii* (F. S. Mansvetov, ed., Prague, 1925–1926); and *Svobodnaia Rossiia* (Prague and Berlin, 1924–1926). Trudy Komiteta russkoi knigi, No. 1: *Russkaia zarubezh naia kniga,* S. P. Postnikov, ed. (Prague, 1924).

6. M. Heller, "Premier Avertissement: Un coup de fouet," *Cahiers du monde russe et soviétique* 20:2 (April–June 1979): 131–72. German authorities were most cooperative and helpful in granting visas and arranging transportation; Interview with Dr. A. S. Kagan.

7. Thomas R. Beyer, Jr., "The House of the Arts and the Writers' Club, Berlin, 1921–1923," in T. Beyer, G. Kratz, X. Werner, *Russische Autoren und Verlage nach dem ersten Weltkriege* (Berlin: Arno Spitz, 1987), pp. 9–38. In Appendix I, House of the Arts meetings and lectures are listed; Appendix II gives the lectures and meetings at the Writers Club.

8. Beyer, Kratz, and Werner, *Russische Autoren und Verlage.* An investigation similar to the one undertaken for Berlin for Russian émigré publishing in Paris, Prague, Riga, and Belgrade may yield interesting surprises.

9. *Izdanie I. P. Ladyzhnikova—Katalog* (Berlin: I. P. Ladyzhnikov, 1924); *Knigoizdatel'stvo soiuza molodykh liudei—YMCA Press—katalog 1921–1956* (Paris: Editeurs réunis, n.d.).

10. A. V. Amfiteatrov Papers, Lilly Library, Indiana University, Bloomington (hereafter Amfiteatrov Papers), P. P. Balakshin to Amfiteatrov, 1 May 1934, informs of the organization in San Francisco of a Russian Writers' Guild of California to protect copyright. In a letter of 6 May 1935, he admits that nothing came of his efforts. In same archive, a letter of Teffi from St. Nectaire (France), n.d., to Amfiteatrov mentions that she was used to "theft" of stories for translation and reproduction by Bolsheviks, Serbians, Bulgarians.

11. Full bibliographical data and discussion of YMCA publications are in Chapter 6 on church and religion. The YMCA Press catalogue cited in note 9 above lists the following categories of publications: (1) Theology, Philosophy, Sociology, Apologetics, Hagiography (the largest category, pp. 11–49); (2) Liturgics, Catechisms, Religious Education (pp. 50–55); (3) Belles lettres, Classics, Literary studies, Memoirs, Children's books; (4) Journals (*Novyi grad, Put', Pravoslavnaia mysl'*); and (5) Schoolbooks (including technical pamphlets).

12. Vl. Semichev to S. A. Tsion, 15 July 1921, Hoover Archives, Nicolaevsky Collection, 13–12.

13. Georgii Ivanov, "Bez chitatelia," *Chisla* 5 (1931): 148–52, reprinted in V. Kreid, ed., *Tretii rim—khudozhestvennaia proza: Stat'i* (Tenafly, N.J.: Ermitage, 1987), pp. 239–43.

14. P. Miliukov, *Ocherki po istorii russkoi kul'tury*, vol. 1, "*Iubileinoe izdanie*" (Paris: Sovremennyia zapiski, 1937), p. vii.

15. *Materialy dlia bibliografii russkikh nauchnykh trudov za rubezhom*, fasc. 1 (1920–1930), fasc. 2, part 1 (1930–1940) (Belgrade: [izd.] Russkogo nauchnogo Instituta v Belgrade, 1931–1941), reprinted The Hague, Paris: Mouton—Slavistic Printings and Reprintings, vol. 236, 1970).

16. See Hoover Archives, Gleb Struve Collection, Box 31, letters of Grigorii Landau (co-editor of *Rul'*), from 21 January and 19 February 1930, explaining what kind of materials he would like to have translated from English by G. Struve.

17. T. Ossorguine-Bakounine, comp., *L'Emigration russe en Europe* (Paris: Institut d'études slaves, 1976). Of course, police files and personal papers might shed more light on individual publications.

18. *Posledniia novosti—Ezhednevnaia gazeta* (M. L. Gol'dshtein, and then P. N. Miliukov, eds., Paris) 1–7015 (27 April 1920 to 11 May 1940); *Vozrozhdenie: Organ russkoi natsional'noi mysli* (P. B. Struve, and then Iu. F. Semenov, eds., Paris) 1–4239 3 June 1925 to 7 June 1940; *Segodnia: Nezavisimaia demokraticheskaia gazeta* (M. S. Mil'rud, ed., Riga, 17 August 1919 to 21 June 1940(?); *Novoe vremia: Ezhednevnaia gazeta* (M. A. Suvorin, ed., Belgrade, 1921–?).

19. Iu. F. Semenov, "Kratkaia istoriia zarubezhnoi Rossii 1919–1940," p. 53 in Nicolaevsky Collection, series 10, Box 4, 19–14.

20. Ibid.; M. Raeff, "Le Front Populaire et la presse émigrée russe," in *Mélanges Portal, Revue des études slaves*, forthcoming.

21. *Vstrechi: Ezhemesiachnyi zhurnal* (Paris) 1–6 (January–June 1934); *Vereteno: Literaturno-khudozhestvennyi al'manakh* (Berlin, 1922); *Zveno* (Berlin, 1922, and Paris, 1923–1928), (subtitles varied).

22. *Sotsialisticheskii vestnik, tsentral'nyi organ rossiiskoi sotsial-demokraticheskoi rabochei partii* (founded by Iu. Martov) 1–784 (1 February 1921–November–December 1963). Cf. A. Liebich, "The Mensheviks in the Face of Stalinism," in *Ripensare 1956—Socialismo Storia* (n.p.: Annali della Fondazione Giacomo Brodolini, n.d.); A. Ascher, *Pavel Axelrod and the Development of Menshevism* (Cambridge, Mass.: Harvard Univ. Press, 1972); Leopold H. Haimson, ed., *The Mensheviks: From the Revolution of 1917 to the Second World War* (Chicago: Univ. of Chicago Press, 1974).

23. "Ot redaktsii," *Sovremennyia zapiski: Ezhemesiachnyi obshchestvenno-politicheskii zhurnal* (Paris) 1 (1920).

24. M. V. Vishniak, "*Sovremennye zapiski*"—*Vospominaniia redaktora* (Bloom-

ington: Indiana University Publications, Slavic and East European Series, vol. 7, 1957), p. 116. Vishniak does not give the year when this salary cut took place.

25. *Illiustrirovannaia rossiia: Ezhenedel'nyi* [later *Dvukhnedel'nyi*] *literaturno-illiustrirovannyi zhurnal* (Paris, 1924–1939). *Dlia vas: Ezhenedel'nyi illiustriro-vannyi zhurnal* (Riga) (24 December 1933–27 June 1940).

26. *Novyi grad* 10 (1935): 132–38 and 11 (1936): 136–60. See also G. Adamovich, "Table Talk," *Novyi zhurnal* 64 (June 1961): 114–15; V. Ia-novskii, *Polia eliseiskie* (New York: Serebriannyi vek, 1983), English translation, V. Yanovsky, *Elysian fields—A Book of Memory* (De Kalb: Northern Illinois Univ. Press, 1987); *Krug—Al'manakh* (Berlin, Paris, 1938–1939).

27. "Bratstvo russkoi pravdy" (*pravda* means both justice and truth in Russian). Cf. Amfiteatrov Papers, letters from Vl. Burtsev; Nicolaevsky Collection, no. 228.

28. Roman Gul', "Ia unes Rossiiu," *Novyi zhurnal* 152 (1983): 41–64; Nico-laevsky Collection, no. 213 ("Lotoš" Istoriia obrazovaniia i deitel'nosti 1933–1949— Paris, 1950).

29. Beyer, "The House of the Arts"; see also V. S. Varshavskii, *Nezamechennoe pokolenie* (New York: Chekhov Publishing House, 1956); Ianovskii, *Polia elisei-skie*; Gul', "Ia unes Rossiiu."

30. *Churaevka: Literaturnaia gazeta kruzhka iskusstv, nauki i literatury chura-evka* (Kharbin, 1932–1934).

31. For France we have a chronicle for the years 1920–1930: Michèle Beyssac, *La Vie culturelle de l'émigration russe en France—Chronique 1920–1930)* (Paris: Faculté des lettres et sciences humaines de l'Université de Clermont-Ferrand, 2e série, fasc. 32, 1971).

32. According to some, the Zemgor leader Prince P. Dolgorukov was the ini-tiator, but the appeal was issued in the name of the following organizations: Prav-lenie soiuza russkikh akademicheskikh organizatsii zagranitsei (Board of the Union of Russian Academic Organizations Abroad), Pedagogicheskoe biuro po delam srednei i nizshei shkoly zagranitsei (Pedagogical Bureau for the Affairs of Second-ary and Primary Schools Abroad), Ob'edinenie russkikh uchitel'skikh organizatsii zagranitsei (Association of Russian Teachers' Organizations Abroad), Ob'edinenie russkikh studencheskikh organizatsii (Association of Russian Student Organiza-tions Abroad). Datelined Prague, March 1925, the appeal read in part:

TO RUSSIAN PEOPLE ABROAD

Several millions of Russians are forced to live beyond the borders of today's Russia. They are scattered in practically all countries of the earth. Even where they are numerous they have no ties and no cul-tural concerns to unite them. The majority are so absorbed by the need of [earning their] daily bread that they do not pay adequate attention to the needs of the spirit. If this situation lasts for any length of time not a few Russians will be threatened with losing their patriotic sense. Such a loss has become already noticeable among a significant segment of the young who do not attend Russian schools and who have left Russia at an early age. Direct memories of their country are fading, and in some cases they have been lost altogether. Many are abusing their native tongue, and there are even some who have forgotten it completely. In the future this phenomenon may acquire a mass character—and [affect] not only the children. How will these people then fulfill the hopes of the over-whelming majority of the Russians abroad, i.e., return to Russia and la-

bor at its re-creation? . . . The undersigned organizations abroad have
decided to appeal to local Russian associations, societies, and groups to
organize yearly a "Day of Russian Culture" as a desirable [and appropri-
ate] means for uniting all Russians. We propose for this day to select
8 June, new style (26 May old style)—the birthday of Pushkin who,
more than anyone, has left the imprint of his genius on the language of
the Russian people.

Such a celebration, . . . will contribute to raise the spirit of all
Russians abroad in their difficult circumstances.

It is to be desired that the yearly Day of Russian Culture become a
[regular] custom and that it be celebrated in as many localities as possible, even in the present year. It is imperative to associate with this enterprise broad circles from all layers and all ages of the Russian population [abroad]. Local organizations should combine [their efforts].

Obviously, the organization of such an enterprise cannot and should
not receive instructions from one center. The celebrations may take the
most varied forms and have varied programs. This will be best worked
out locally in accordance with local conditions. . . . (Paléologue Papers, Box 023, f. 368)

33. Memorandum of M. V. Biskupskii to United Meeting of Parish Councils
of Russian Church in Belgrade and Committee for Organization of Celebration of
St. Vladimir, November 1930, and Bulletin no. 11 of Union of Russian Educators in the Kingdom of Serbs, Croats, and Sloveness, 28 February 1931, in Paléologue Papers, Box 029.

CHAPTER 5

1. Marina Tsvetaeva, "Moi Pushkin," in *Izbrannaia proza v dvukh tomakh
1917–1937*, vol. 2 (New York: Russica, 1979), 2:249–304, 356–59; this was
published as a separate book, *Moi Pushkin* (Moscow, 1967), with references to
original places of publication.

2. S. Frank's articles on Pushkin's religiosity and political ideas are conveniently collected in S. L. Frank, *Etiudy o Pushkine* 3d ed. (Paris: YMCA Press,
1987); P. B. Struve, *Dukh i slovo—Sbornik statei* (Paris: YMCA Press, 1981);
G. Fedotov, "Pevets imperii i svobody," *Sovremennyia zapiski* 63 (1937): 178–97.

3. D. Merezhkovskii, *L. Tolstoi i Dostoevskii* 2 vols. (St. Petersburg: M. V.
Pirozhkov, 1903). A. Liuter [Luther], "Dostoevskii v Germanii," *Literathrnyi
al'manakh "Grani,"* vol. 2 (Berlin: 1923), pp. 127–60.

4. N. Berdiaev, *Mirosozertsanie Dostoevskogo* (Prague, Paris: YMCA Press,
1923, 1968); there are several translations into many languages, see *Bibliographie
des oeuvres de Nicolas Berdiaev établie par Tamara Klépinine* (Paris: Institut
d'études slaves, 1978). G. Florovskii, *Puti russkogo bogosloviia* (Paris: YMCA
Press, 1938). K. Mochulskii, *Dostoevskii—Zhizn' i tvorchestvo* (Paris: YMCA
Press, 1947). The "forefather" of this Dostoevsky reinterpretation, besides Merezhkovsky, was S. Bulgakov's "Ivan Karamazov kak filosofskii tip," in his *Ot marksizma
k idealizmu—Sbornik statei* (1896–1903) (Frankfurt: Possev Verlag, 1968), pp.
83–112.

5. V. A. Maklakov, "Lev Tolstoi (Uchenie i zhizn')," *Sovremennyia zapiski*
36 (1928): 220–63, and "Tolstoi kak mirovoe iavlenie," ibid., 38 (1929): 224–

45. See also the chapter entitled "Maklakov i Tolstoi," in G. Adamovich, *Vasilii Alekseevich Maklakov—Politik, iurist, chelovek* (Paris, 1959), pp. 80–99.

6. N. M. Zernov and M. V. Zernov, *Za rubezhom* (*Belgrad—Parizh—Oksford, 1921–1972*) (Paris: YMCA Press, 1973), part II, section 2.

7. V. N. Ipat'ev, *Zhizn' odnogo khimika, tom II: 1917–1930* (New York, 1945); S. Timoshenko, *Vospominaniia* (Paris, 1963).

8. Amfiteatrov Papers, M. A. Aldanov to Amfiteatrov, February 1933, states that 3,000 francs were sent to him by the Bunin Committee. Bunin expected to have 70,000 to 100,000 francs to distribute, believing that he would get 150,000 francs in royalties in addition to the Nobel Prize money, but this did not happen. Bunin allotted 40,000 to 50,000 out of the 600,000 francs of the prize money. See also letters of Aldanov to Amfiteatrov of 27 November 1933 and 9 January 1934 (the latter states that an additional 50,000 francs were distributed by Bunin to seven famous writers, among whom was Amfiteatrov). Bunin was most shabbily treated by German border officials and guards on his way to Stockholm to receive the prize. It made him an outspoken hater of Nazism. During the war he refused to return to German-occupied Paris, in spite of N. Berberova's assurance of the good behavior of German troops and her belief that Bunin's presence there would benefit the Russians. Bunin also gave refuge to the Jewish littérateur A. Bakhrakh in his house near Grasse during the German occupation of the so-called Free Zone.

9. As observed in a talk by V. Aksenov at Columbia University.

10. Soviet poets were reviewed by such critics as M. Slonim, K. Mochulskii, and D. Mirskii (Sviatopolk-Mirskii) in the major "thick journals," in particular *Volia rossii* and *Sovremennyia zapiski*. See also the bibliographical guide, Emmanuil Shtein, *Poeziia russkogo rasseiania 1920–1977* (Ashford, Conn.: Lad'ia, 1978).

11. Za vse, za vse spasibo, Za voinu . . ." was first published in *Novyi korabl'* (Paris) 4 (1928). It was republished in G. Adamovich, *Na zapade* (Paris: Dom Knigi, 1939), p. 50, and in his postwar selection, *Edinstvo* (New York: Russkaia, 1967), p. 21, with a better layout of the last lines. The publishing house Dom Knigi put out a series of "Russkie poety," which published (or planned to publish) the works of poets living in France—each edition had a print run of 200 copies (of which 20 were not for sale). Among those published were G. Adamovich, A. Ginger, B. Poplavskii, S. Pregel', N. Staniukovich, N. Tsetlin, Amari (M. Tsetlin), Iu. Terapiano, V. Smolenskii, A. Golovina, Viach. Ivanov, Z. Hippius, and L. Kel'berin.

Here is Adamovich's poem in a literal, prose version: "Thank you for everything, everything: for war, revolution, and exile, for the indifferent, bright country where today we 'drag out a miserable existence.' There is no lot sweeter than to lose everything; there is no fate more joyful than to become a wanderer. And you were never nearer to the heavens than here—tired of boredom, tired of breathing, without strength, without money, without love—in Paris. . . ."

12. G. Struve, *Russkaia literatura v izgnanii*, 2d ed. (Paris: YMCA Press, 1984); and the collections and autobiographical volumes of G. Ivanov, "Bez Chitatelia," *Chisla* 5 (1931): 148–52, reprinted in V. Kreid, ed., *Tretii Rim* (Tenafly, N.J.: Ermitage, 1987); V. Yanovsky, *Elysian Fields* (De Kalb: Northern Illinois Univ. Press, 1987); V. Varshavskii, *Nezamechennoe pokolenie* (New York: Chekhov Publishing House, 1956). See also D. Aminado, *Poezd na tret'em puti*

(New York: Chekhov Publishing House, 1954); N. Otsup, *Sovremenniki* (Paris, 1961); V. Khodasevich, *Literaturnye stat'i i vospominaniia* (New York: Chekhov Publishing House, 1954); N. Berberova, *Kursiv moi—Avtobiografiia*, 2d ed., vol. 1 (New York: Russica, 1983); I. Odoevtseva, *Na beregakh Seny* (Paris: La presse libre, 1983).

13. V. Veidle, "O frantsuzskoi literature," *Sovremennyia zapiski* 39 (1929): 491–502.

CHAPTER 6

1. Gregory L. Freeze, "Handmaiden of the State: The Church in Imperial Russia Reconsidered," *Journal of Ecclesiastical History* 36 (January 1985): 82–102.

2. For obvious reasons I shall not enter into strictly theological issues, for example, the teachings of S. Bulgakov on the Holy Wisdom of God (sophiology).

3. The letter of John D. Rockefeller, Jr.'s assistant, W. S. Richardson, sets forth the terms and schedule of payments. Richardson to Dr. John R. Mott, 19 March 1926, in Anderson Papers, Box 8.

4. For details on the first-year admissions—and budget—see "Khronika Bogoslovskogo Instituta," in *Pravoslavnaia mysl'* 1 (1928): 226–31. For a three-year report, see "Otchet o deitel'nosti Pravoslavnogo Bogoslovskogo Instituta za trekhletie 1927–1930 godov," ibid. 2 (1930): 200–209.

5. "Memorandum concerning Russian Contributions to the Orthodox Theological Academy Paris," by Paul B. Anderson, 11 May 1928, in Anderson Papers, Box 8, and Edgar MacNaughton to A. V. Morozoff and F. T. Pianoff, 19 August 1932, ibid., Box 3.

6. Lev A. Zander, ed., *List of the Writings of Professors of the Russian Theological Institute in Paris*, vols. 1–4 (Paris, 1925–1954). Handy histories of the St. Serge Institute are to be found in Alexis Kniazeff, *L'Institut St Serge—De l'académie d'autrefois au rayonnement d'aujourd'hui* (Paris: Beauchesne, 1974 [Le Point Théologique no. 14]), and in Donald A. Lowrie, *Saint Sergius in Paris—The Orthodox Theological Institute* (New York: McMillan, 1954). Nicolas Zernov, comp., *Russian Emigre authors: A Biographical Index and Bibliography of their Works on Theology, Religious Philosophy, Church History and Orthodox Culture, 1921–1973* (Boston: G. K. Hall, 1973). A. D. Schmemann, "Russian Theology 1920–1965: A Bibliographical Lecture," Seventh Annual Lecture, Union Theological Seminary in Richmond, Virginia, 1969.

7. A second edition of the *Puti russkogo bogosloviia* was published in Paris by YMCA Press in 1981 (with a preface by Father John Meyendorff). A bibliography of the published works of G. Florovsky has been compiled by Thomas Bird, to be published in the first volume of a three-volume Festschrift edited by Andrew Blane, *Russia and Orthodoxy*, which may still be forthcoming.

8. A bibliography of G. Fedotov's publications was compiled by his widow, *Bibliografiia trudov G. P. Fedotova 1886–1951* (Paris: n.p., n.d.). G. P. Fedotov, *Sviatye drevnei rusi*, 3d ed. (Paris: YMCA Press, 1985). John Meyendorff, ed., G. P. Fedotov, *Russian Religious Mind*, 2 vols. (Cambridge, Mass.: Harvard Univ. Press, 1946, 1966).

9. See *Knigoizdatel'stvo i knizhnyi sklad vozstanovlennoi istoricheskoi po-*

chaevskoi tserkovnoi tipografii pr. Iova vo Vladimirskoi na karpatskoi Rusi v Chekhoslovakii—Katalog 1924–1936 (Ladomizovu: 1936).

10. Prot. Sergei Gakkel', *Mat' Mariia (1891–1945)* (Paris: YMCA Press, 1980). The Soviets recently awarded Mother Maria a posthumous military decoration. See Radio Free Europe-Radio Liberty Research release, 26 June 1985, "Awards for Russian Emigrés in French Resistance Movement," by Julia Wishnevsky.

11. On intellectual background and involvement of laymen in the religious life of Russia Abroad, see Bishop Kassian, "Rodoslovie Dukha (Pamiati Konstantina Vasil'evicha Mochul'skogo)" *Pravoslavnaia mysl'* 7 (1949): 7–16.

12. A useful listing of conferences found in A. P. Obolenskii, comp., *Ukazatel' avtorov, predmetov, retsenzii k zhurnalu put'* (New York: Transactions of the Association of Russian-American Scholars in the U.S.A., 1986), pp. 37–38. The main conferences of the movement were those at Bervilliers, 1926; Clermont en Argonne, 1926, 1927; and Argeron, 1925.

13. See Paul B. Anderson to Dr. John R. Mott, 29 December 1934, with attached budget summaries, Anderson Papers, Box 10. Interesting glimpses on the inside workings of the relationship of YMCA to various Russian émigré religious enterprises can be found in the Minutes of the Meeting of the Council of the Russian Student Christian Movement Abroad, 3–6 February 1928, Anderson Papers, Box 6.

14. Secretary of Movement, Deacon Dr. L. N. Liperovskii, to Metropolitan Antonii, 20 May 1926, Metropolitan Antonii to Paul B. Anderson, 28 November [11 December] 1926, Anderson Papers, Box 3.

15. See note 12, above. The meetings were at St. Albans, 1927; High Leigh 1929, 1930, 1931; Newcastle and Cambridge, 1930; and Oxford, 1937.

16. "The Russian Student Christian Movement Abroad has as its prime goal to unite the believing youth in the service of the Orthodox Church and to bring the nonbelievers to the faith in Christ. It endeavors to help its members in developing a Christian philosophy and has as its task to prepare defenders of church and faith capable of carrying on a struggle with contemporary atheism and materialism."

17. See note 11, above. On the Priiutino Brotherhood, see the interesting memoirs of G. V. Vernadskii in *Novyi zhurnal* 93, 95, 96, 97 (1968–1969).

18. Anne Heurgon-Despardins, ed., *Paul Desjardins et les décades de Pontigny (études, témoignages et documents inédits)* (Paris: Presses Universitaires de France, 1964).

19. "Soirées franco-russes," *Cahiers de la quinzaine* 20:9 (20 September 1929, 26 November 1929, 18 December 1929, 28 January 1930). St. Fumet and G. Fedotov, "Le Renouveau spirituel en France et en Russie," *Cahiers de la quinzaine* 22d series, 1er cahier (1932).

20. "Minutes of a Conference . . . regarding the Project of Publishing a Russian Religious Periodical: Held in Paris October 6, 1924," "Minutes of the Meeting on the New Russian Religious Journal, Held in Paris on December 4, 1924," and Paul B. Anderson to E. T. Colton, 9 December 1924, Anderson Papers, Box 6.

21. John B. Dunlop, *The New Russian Revolutionaries* (Belmont, Mass.: Nordland, 1976).

22. See Obolenskii, *Put'*, index.

23. These ideas of Berdiaev's were reflected in his well-known book, *The Russian Idea* (New York: Mcmillan, 1947). He was also much criticized for his posture in 1945 when he went to the Soviet embassy to obtain a Soviet passport.

24. *Smena vekh* (Change of Landmarks or Signposts), a collaborative volume—followed by *O smena vekh* (Concerning the Change of Landmarks)—were published by Logos in Prague in 1921. They expressed the idea that the Bolshevik revolution had triumphed; that it was good for Russia, since it had restored its state power; and that the émigrés should accept this situation and return to their homeland and work for its progress within the Soviet system. Some of the advocates of a "Change of Landmarks" were close to Eurasianism, and many Eurasians felt an affinity for *Smena vekh*. The reputation of the Eurasian movement was undermined when it was discovered that its members (among them S. Efron, the husband of Marina Tsvetaeva) had been involved in the assassination of I. Reiss (a former Soviet diplomat) in Switzerland.

25. *The Way*'s book reviews are conveniently listed in the Obolenskii's bibliography for *PUT'*. The major meetings were at Stockholm, 1925; Lausanne, 1927; Edinburgh, 1937; and Amsterdam, 1939.

26. As a letter from I. Fondaminskii to Paul B. Anderson makes clear, the YMCA subsidy took the form of a guaranteed purchase of a number of copies (350–500) at regular price. This correspondence suggests that the print run of the journal was 800 copies. Letter, 19 December 1933, Anderson Papers, Box 3. See M. Raeff, "Le Mouvement de la cité nouvelle," *Cahiers du monde russe et Soviétique*, 29 (No. 3–4) (1988), pp. 543–52.

27. In issue 14, dated 15 October 1936, of the journal *Novaia rossiia* (edited by A. F. Kerensky in Paris), Fedotov published an article entitled "Pasionaria" in which he stated that, forced to make a choice, he preferred La Pasionaria (Dolores Ibarruri, a prominent Spanish Communist leader) to Franco. The argument was similar to that of Georges Bernanos in his *Les Grands Cimetières sous la lune* (Paris: Plan, 1938), and it produced a similar storm in émigré public opinion. The effort to have Fedotov dismissed from the St. Serge Institute, spearheaded by Iu. Semenov in *Vozrozhdenie*, failed when Metropolitan Evlogii supported academic freedom, although he mildly admonished Fedotov (on this episode see the voluminous correspondence in Bakhmeteff Archive, G. P. Fedotov Papers).

28. See M. Raeff, "Novyi Grad and Germany," in I. Auerbach, A. Hillgruber, and G. Schramm, eds., *Felder und Vorfelder russischer Geschichte* (Freiburg, Breisgau: Rombach, 1985).

29. Fedotov's prewar cogitations on Soviet Russia are most readily found in his book *I est' i budet* (*razmyshleniia o Rossii i revoliutsii*) (Paris: Novyi Grad, 1932), and in the collection of his articles from *Novaia rossiia* in G. P. Fedotov, *Zashchita Rossii—Stat'i 1936–1940 iz "Novoi rossii,"* vol. 4 of his *Polnoe sobranie statei* (Paris: YMCA Press, 1988).

Additional Select Bibliography

The unpublished memoirs of V. V. Zen'kovskii on his participation in the "govment" of the Russian Student Christian Movement, as well as on his directorship of the Religious Paedagogic Biuro, are to be found in Bakh-meteff Archive, V. V. Zen'kovskii Papers. For a comprehensive chronicle of the Russian Orthodox Church abroad, see Gernot Seide, *Geschichte der russischen orthodoxen Kirche im Ausland von der Gründung bis in die Gegenwart* (Wiesbaden: Otto Harrassowitz, 1983 [Veröffentlichungen des Osteuropa Institutes, München, Band 51]).

Nikolai P. Poltoratzky, ed., *Russian Religious-Philosophical Thought of the 20th Century (A Collection of Articles in Russian)* (Pittsburg: Univ. of Pittsburg, Slavic Series no. 2, 1975).

Mitropopit Evlogii, *Put' moei zhizni—vospominaniia mitropolita Evlogiia*, izlozhennyia po ego rasskazam T. Manukhinoi (Paris: YMCA Press, 1947).

Helen Iswolsky, *Light before Dusk—A Russian Catholic in France 1923–1941* (New York: Longmans, Green, 1942).

Ethan Theodore Colton, *Forty Years with Russians* (New York: Association Press, 1940).

Nicholas Zernov, *Russian Religious Renaissance of the Twentieth Century* (New York: Harper & Row, 1963).

Otto Böss, *Die Lehre der Eurasier—Ein Beitrag zur Russischen Ideengeschichte des 20. Jarhunderts* (Wiesbaden: Otto Harrassowitz, 1961 [Veröffentlichungen des Osteuropa Institutes, München, Band 15]).

Nicholas V. Riasanovsky, "The Emergence of Eurasianism," *California Slavic Studies* 4 (1967): 39–72.

CHAPTER 7

1. People of the "Great Emigrations" that preceded the Romantic period and the rise of modern nationalism, for example, the Huguenots, did not share this need and problem. Their exile was motivated by religious beliefs, and their frame of reference remained totally religious: the suffering of exile had to be borne as a witness to God's will and for the sake of salvation, not because of some human, historical, secular process. In addition, their sense of "nationality" lacked a historical dimension. Finally, the refugees from Louis XIV's persecution, for example, moved into an international community that readily integrated them. *Immi*gration to America, even when triggered by religious or political persecution, was different in essence from an *emigration* of the kind we are concerned with here. We know too little about the scale and nature of "mass" exile or emigration in the still remoter past, from Byzantium or in antiquity, for example, to make any meaningful comparison.

2. I shall not deal with those scholars who took the history of other countries and periods as their professional province, for example, M. Rostovtsev, the historian of antiquity, or A. Vasiliev, the Byzantinist.

3. On this expulsion, see M. Heller, "Premier avertissement: Un coup de fouet (L'histoire de l'expulsion des personnalités culturelles hors de l'Union soviétique en 1922")," *Cahiers du monde russe et soviétique* 20:2 (April–June 1979): 131–72.

4. Iu. Got'e, *Times of Trouble*, transl. and ed. by T. Emmons (Princeton, N.J.: Princeton Univ. Press, 1988).

5. *S'ezdy russkikh akademicheskikh organizatsii za granitsei* (Prague, 1923), pp. iii, 3, 5–6.

6. S. Pushkarev, "Russkie v Prage," *Novyi zhurnal* 149 (1982): 150–63. S. Postnikov, ed. *Russkie v Prage 1918–1928* (Prague, 1928).

7. Paul B. Anderson Papers, University Archives, Univ. of Illinois at Urbana-Champaign, Box 10, Edgar McNaughton to Ethan T. Colton, 16 December 1931.

8. Closely related to this form of scholarship were the festschriften in honor of émigré or foreign colleagues. The two most important volumes dedicated to émigré scholars were *Sbornik statei, posviashchennykh Pavlu Nikolaevichu Miliukovu 1859–1929* (Prague, 1929), and *Sbornik statei posviashchennykh Petru Berngardovichu Struve ko dniu tridtsatipiatiletiia ego nauchno-publissisticheskoi deiatel'nosti 1890 30 ianvaria 1925* (Prague, 1925). An early overview of all this scholarly historical production can be found in Antoine Florovskij, "La littérature russe en émigration—Compte rendu 1927–1929," *Bulletin d'information des sciences historiques en Europe orientale* 3, fasc. 1–2, Varsovie, 1930, pp. 25–79, and for the years 1921–1926, ibid., 1, 1928, pp. 83–121. See also Wolff Leppmann, "Die russische Geschichtswissenschaft in der Emigration," *Zeitschrift für osteuropäische Geschichte* 1:2 (1931): 215–48.

9. Viacheslav Ivanov i M. O. Gershenzon, *Perepiska iz dvukh uglov* (Peterburg: Alkonost, 1921), (English translation by G. Vakar, in *Russian Intellectual History—An Anthology*, M. Raeff, ed. (New York: Harcourt Brace, Jovanovich, 1978).

10. On the German, and generally European, academic immigration to the United States, see D. Fleming and B. Bailyn, eds., *The Intellectual Migration: Europe and America 1930–1960*, vol. 2 of *Perspectives in American History* (Cambridge, Mass.: Harvard Univ. Press, 1968); Lewis A. Coser, *Refugee Scholars in America—Their Impact and Their Experiences* (New Haven, Conn.: Yale Univ. Press, 1984); Laura Fermi, *Illustrious Immigrants—The Intellectual Migration from Europe 1930–41*, 2d ed. (Chicago: Univ. of Chicago Press, 1971); and the "soured views" of Anthony Heilbut, *Exiled in Paradise—German Refugees and Intellectuals in America from the 1930s to the Present* (Boston: Beacon Press, 1983).

11. This was the case of M. M. Shtrange who joined a Communist resistance group during the war and became an agent of the Soviet intelligence establishment in France before returning to Soviet Russia where he gained professional recognition at the Institute of History of the Academy of Sciences as a historian of the French revolution and of its impact on Russia. A. F. Damanskaia, manuscript memoirs, Bakhmeteff Archives.

12. The "history-memoir" of General A. Denikin, *Ocherki russkoi smuty*, 5 vols. (Paris, 1921–1926) also belongs to this category. P. Miliukov, *Istoriia vtoroi russkoi revoliutsii*, 3 vols. (Sofia: Rossiisko-Bolgarskoe Knigoizatel'stvo, 1921–1924), and *Rossiia na perelome*, 2 vols. (Paris, 1927).

13. Postnikov, *Russkie v Prage*; Ia. Slavik, ed., and S. Postnikov, comp., *Bibliografiia russkoi revoliutsii i grazhdanskoi voiny—iz kataloga biblioteki russkogo zagranichnogo arkhiva v Prage* (Prague: Rusky, Zahranični Historicky Archiv v Prage, 1938). Carol A. Leadenham, comp., *Guide to the Collections in the Hoover Institution Archives Relating to Imperial Russia, the Russian Revolu-*

tion and Civil War, and the First Emigration (Stanford, Calif.: Hoover Institution, 1986).

14. W. H. Chamberlin, *The Russian Revolution 1917–1921* (Princeton, N.J.: Princeton Univ. Press, 1987).

15. The historians also contributed memoirs on their own lives and careers, for example, A. A. Kizevetter, *Na rubezhe dvukh stoletii* (Prague: Orbis, 1929), and N. Miliukov, *Vospominaniia, 1859–1917*, 2 vols. (New York: Chekhov Publishing, 1955).

16. *Arkhiv russkoi revoliutsii* 1–22 (I. Gessen, ed., Berlin, 1921–1937); *Istorik i sovremennik* 1–5 (I. Petrushevskii, ed., Berlin, 1922–1924); *Na chuzhoi storone* 1–13 (S. Mel'gunov, ed., Berlin, Prague, 1923–1925). The first title was a kind of parallel to the Soviet publication *Krasnyi arkhiv*, whereas the latter was the continuation of the prerevolutionary *Byloe*.

17. A. Amfiteatrov, "V. O. Kliuchevskii kak khudozhnik slova," *Literaturnyi al'manakh Grani* 2 vols. (Berlin: Grani, 1922–1923), 1:173–79.

18. Paul Milioukov, C. Seignobos, and L. Eisenmann, *Histoire de Russie*, 3 vols. (Paris: Librairie Ernest Leroux, 1932–1935), translated by Charles Lam Markmann, *History of Russia* (New York: Funk & Wagnalls, 1968–1969).

19. O. Böss, *Die Lehre der Eurasier* (Wiesbaden, 1961); Nicholas V. Raisanovsky, "The Emergence of Eurasianism," *California Slavic Studies* 4 (1967): 39–72. P. Savitskii developed a theory of spatial movements of civilization depending on the mean yearly temperatures.

20. The New Economic Policy raised the hopes for taming the Bolshevik regime and for greater "legitimacy" of the revolution. But the policies adopted in 1928 left only the "statist" and imperial character of Soviet Russia as a positive element.

21. As E. Gellner put it, "If citizenship, effective membership, 'belonging' but also less sentimentally, effective enjoyment of rights, depends on culture, it follows that loyalties will also be expressed in terms of it. . . . Nationalism hasn't created the situation in which culture defines groups and provides the criterion in which membership and loyalty can be expressed. It is, on the contrary, a consequence of this situation obtaining independently." Ernest Gellner, *Thought and Change* (Chicago: Univ. of Chicago Press, 1964), p. 157.

22. *Vladimirskii sbornik*, Belgrade, 1938, Hoover Institution Archives, S. N. Paléologue Papers.

23. The process itself was viewed more critically in line with A. Presniakov's interpretation in his *Obrazovanie velikorusskogo gosudarstva—Ocherki po istorii XIII–XV stoletii* (St. Petersburg, 1918).

24. Report on discussion in *Poslednie novosti* (Paris) no. 5100, 10 April 1935, p. 3, signed by N.P.V. (Vakar?), and the article by D. Odinets, *Sovremennye zapiski* 59 ("Moskovskoe tsarstvo") (1935): 297–317.

25. A. V. Miakotin, *Ocherki sotsial'noi istorii Ukrainy v XVII–XVIII vekakh*, 3 vols. (Prague: Vataga-Plamia, 1924–1926); A. Florovsky's articles are scattered in *Uchenye zapiski uchevnoi kollegii v Prage* and *Nauchnye trudy russkogo narodnogo universiteta v Prage*.

26. S. Pushkarev's studies were republished in a revised edition, *Krest'ianskaia pozemel'no-peredel'naia obshchina v Rossii* (Newtonville, Mass.: Oriental Research Partners, 1976); V. B. El'iashevich, *Istoriia prava pozemel'noi sobstven-*

nosti v Rossiia, 2 vols. (Paris, 1948–1951); P. B. Struve, *Sotsial'naia i ekonomi-cheskaia istoriia Rossii* (Paris, 1952). Struve also wrote the chapter on Russian serfdom in the first volume, first edition, of The *Cambridge Economic History of Europe* (Cambridge: Cambridge Univ. Press, 1941).

27. S. Svatikov, *Rossiia i Don 1549–1917* (Belgrade, 1924); Boris Nolde, *La Formation de l'empire russe—Etudes, notes et documents*, 2 vols. (Paris, 1952–1953); V. A. Riasanovskii, *Mongol'skoe pravo* (Kharbin, 1931), his *Obychnoe pravo mongol'skikh plemen* (Kharbin, 1924), and his *Fundamental Principles of Mongol Law* (Tientsin, 1937). His historical survey of Russian culture was written and published after the Second World War in the United States.

28. See M. Heller, "Premier avertissement."

29. For a biography and bibliography of G. Florovsky, see A. Blane, ed., *Russia and Orthodoxy*, vol. 1, forthcoming.

30. M. S. Shatz and J. E. Zimmerman, trans. and eds., *Signposts: A Collection of Articles on the Russian Intelligentsia* (Irvine, Calif.: Charles Schlacks Publisher, 1986), and W. F. Woehrlin, trans. and ed., *Out of the Depths (De profundis): A Collection of Articles on the Russian Revolution* (Irvine, Calif.: Charles Schlacks Publisher, 1986).

31. Florovsky, *Puti russkogo bogosloviia* (Belgrade, 1938 [2d ed., Paris: YMCA Press, 1981]), p. 274.

32. Igor Smolitsch's and A. Kartashev's contributions after 1945 were much more traditional, though quite useful in acquainting the West with Russian ecclesiastic history. Igor Smolitsch, *Geschichte der russischen Kirche 1700–1917*, vol. 1 (Leiden: Brill, 1964 [Studien zur Geschichte Osteuropas]). The second volume is forthcoming. A. V. Kartashev, *Ocherki po istorii russkoi tserkvi*, 2 vols. (Paris: YMCA Press, 1959).

33. For a bibliography of Fedotov (unfortunately not quite complete), *Bibliografiia trudov G. P. Fedotova 1886–1951* (Paris: n.p., n.d.). A biographical sketch appears in a collection of his essays, *Litso Rossii* (Paris: YMCA Press, 1967), pp. i–xxxiv.

CHAPTER 8

1. I owe most of this paragraph's information to a paper prepared by Elliot Isaac for a seminar on political emigrations in twentieth-century Europe at Columbia University in 1986. I am most grateful for his input.

Name Index

Note: Not all dates and full names could be established or verified for reliability

Subject Index

Emigré population
  demographic characteristics of, 24–27
  size of, 23–24
Emigré schools
  coeducation, 53
  concessions to foreign environment in,
    51–52
  curriculum in, 49
  financing of, 56–57
  number of, 49, 57
  pedagogic approach in, 49–50, 52,
    53–54, 55–56
  at primary level, 56
  religious instruction and, 131
  Russian orthography and, 50
  at secondary level, 56–57
  teaching of history in, 50–51
  technological education in, 51–52
Employment opportunities
  in Baltic republics, 40
  for émigré doctors, 108
  for émigré jurists, 106
  in Nazi Germany, 37
  in professions in France, 37–38
  settlement patterns and, 32–33
  in Yugoslavia, 39–40
Engineering, émigré contributions in,
  108–9
England. *See* United Kingdom
English language, 81
Estonia. *See* Baltic republics
Ethnicity, 26–27
Eurasianism, 84, 107, 149, 166–68,
  216n24
European countries. *See* Countries of
  asylum; *specific countries*
European intellectuals
  émigré contact with, 140–44
  Put' and, 149–50
  Russian history and, 161–62, 185
Exile, as term, 3
Exile, ordeal of, 118–19. *See also*
  Hardships
Exit, places of, 17–23

Family, loss of, 44
Far East. *See also* Kharbin
  political developments in, 6
  refugees in, 22–23, 24, 32
  student circle in, 92–93
Fiction, émigré, 60, 111–12
Finland, 22
For You (Dlia vas), 90
France. *See also* Paris
  émigré church in, 125
  employment opportunities in, 33
  government refugee assistance in, 28–29
  intellectual world in, 24, 140–41
  Office russe in, 35–36

Popular Front in, 152–53
refugee policies in, 37–39
"societies in exile" from, 188–89
Fraternity of Russian Justice, 92
Free Russia (Svobodnaia Rossiia), 76
Free Spiritual and Philosophical Academy
  in Berlin, 60
Free Spiritual and Philosophical Society
  in Berlin, 126, 140. *See also Put'*
French Huguenots, as society in exile,
  188–89
French Revolution, refugees from, 188–89

Gallipoli veterans, 31
Georgia. *See* Black Sea, as area of exit
German-Austrian Jews, compared with
  Russia Abroad, 191–94
Germany. *See also* Berlin; Nazism
  émigré scholarship and, 60
  government aid in, 29
  intellectual trends in, 141–42
  perceptions of the past in history of,
    157
  political developments in, 6
  refugee policies in, 37
  refugees in, 21–22
  Trust Office in, 36
Grand Refuge, of French Huguenots,
  188–89
Great Depression, 31, 38, 150, 151, 152
Great Polish Emigration, 157, 189–90
Greece, 20
Green movement, 142
Griadushchaia Rossiia (Dawning Russia),
  87
Groups
  military character of, 18
  settlement by, 31–32

Hagiography, 183, 184
Hardships, 18–19, 25, 81
Higher education, 58–61, 64–65
Historians, German, 161–62
Historians, émigré
  conditions facing, 157–62, 185
  definition of Russia as political unit
    and, 168–69
  Eurasianism and, 166–68
  positivist orientation of, 164–66, 167,
    168
  in Prague, 158
  receptivity to historical knowledge and,
    160–63, 166
  revisionism and, 175–76
  sponsorship of, 107–8
  study of Russian history in West and,
    174, 185
  themes of, 170–74
  work of Fedotov and, 181–85